LEARNING EVERYWHERE ON CAMPUS

D1569565

Although student affairs practitioners play a key role in student learning, few are familiar with learning theories, the design of experiential education, or pedagogical theory. This edited collection describes programs in which student affairs professionals work independently or in collaboration with academic faculty and community partners to create more intentional and consistent approaches that enhance student learning. Examples, models, and case studies throughout the chapters make the theories and ideas specific and practical. Exploring educational opportunities in and outside the classroom, such as peer education, leadership development, life and career planning, civic engagement, service-learning, and study abroad, this book provides both theories and pedagogical frameworks for organizing and integrating the entire institution to promote and support learning. Drawing on multiple perspectives, *Learning Everywhere on Campus* shares the interventions and strategies necessary to help students learn new information, acquire skills, and understand the value of this knowledge in constructing their sense of purpose and self in the world.

Jane Fried is a consultant to colleges and universities in faculty development and student affairs, and Professor Emerita at Central Connecticut State University, USA.

Ruth Harper is American Indian Graduate Cohort Coordinator and Professor Emerita at South Dakota State University, USA.

LEARNING EVERYWHERE ON CAMPUS

Teaching Strategies for Student Affairs Professionals

Edited by
Jane Fried and Ruth Harper

Routledge
Taylor & Francis Group

NEW YORK AND LONDON

First published 2018
by Routledge
711 Third Avenue, New York, NY 10017

and by Routledge
2 Park Square, Milton Park, Abingdon, Oxon, OX14 4RN

Routledge is an imprint of the Taylor & Francis Group, an informa business

Library of Congress Cataloging-in-Publication Data
A catalog record has been requested

ISBN: 978-1-138-63672-9 (hbk)
ISBN: 978-0-415-78926-4 (pbk)
ISBN: 978-1-315-20580-9 (ebk)

Typeset in Bembo
by diacriTech, Chennai

Jane Fried wishes to dedicate this book to her doctoral advisor, Burns B. Crookston, and to his doctoral advisor, Esther Lloyd-Jones, for their great vision in teaching the student affairs profession to focus on educating the whole student. She also wishes to thank Donna Fairfield for teaching her that experiential education is both teaching and learning and that these methods help to guide students on their own transformative paths to meaningful lives.

Ruth Harper dedicates her efforts in this book to her master's degree advisor, Laurine (Betty) E. Fitzgerald, who convinced her that student affairs was her calling, and to her first father-in-law, Dudley Bailey, who convinced her she was a capable human being. She is grateful for the kindness and friendship of so many former students, who shared the wonder of the teaching and learning process with her and now contribute to the profession. And her deepest thanks goes to her family, whose interest and involvement in this and every other project make the journey as pleasant and profound as the destination.

CONTENTS

FOREWORD

By Larry D. Roper

The first and most enduring message I received upon my entry into the student affairs profession was the idea that student affairs professionals are educators. At various points along my graduate and professional journeys I have been challenged by non-student affairs colleagues and those within the student affairs profession to provide evidence to support that claim. On one level the confrontations seemed to be aimed at compelling me to provide evidence of an actual curriculum to support that contention, while on another plane the questioning seemed to seek evidence of the disciplinary foundation from which student affairs professionals work. Regardless of the rationale for the challenge, I have felt a career-long pull to live into the professional orientation I received, a belief that those of us in the student affairs field, as well as those in other co-curricular arenas, are educators. In my outlook, I include non-student affairs professionals in the educator category because of the fluid nature of what constitutes student affairs on various campuses and based on the fact that they generally work with students in contexts similar to those of student affairs professionals.

Throughout my career and the diverse institutional affiliations I have had along the way, the approach to manifesting the teaching role of student affairs has varied greatly and the expectation for rigor has been uneven. Through every interview process I have ever experienced, I could count on being asked by members of the student affairs staff to describe the philosophy of student development to which I subscribed; however, I cannot ever recall being asked about my teaching philosophy. If we in fact are educators, should I not have been asked about my pedagogy? Repeatedly, during my time as a student affairs professional, I encountered for others and personally asserted the contention that those who work in the co-curricular domain are educators. At the same time, I was personally uneasy that our approaches did not add power and substance to that claim.

Several years ago, in an effort to facilitate a more intentional approach to co-curriculum development efforts at my institution, I worked with a colleague to develop a position to provide leadership and support for curriculum design in the student affairs organization on my campus. The new position was titled Assistant Director for Co-curricular Learning. The focus of the position was to work directly with student affairs leaders to bring the same rigor to the design of student affairs learning initiatives that is expected of those delivering the university's academic curriculum. In an effort to connect the curriculum standards of student affairs to institutional standards, I worked with other campus colleagues to have the position be housed in our university's Center for Teaching and Learning. When working to develop the position, I looked around the country for models to replicate, but was frustrated in my efforts. Student affairs needs more rigor in its educational approaches and more discipline in the design of student affairs curriculum. This book represents a major thrust in that direction.

The authors of *Learning Everywhere on Campus: Teaching Strategies for Student Affairs Professionals* provide an innovative and provocative resource to the student affairs profession, other co-curricular educators, and educational communities served by those professionals. With the publication of this book, Fried and Harper not only reinforce the assertion that student affairs professionals are educators, they also raise the stakes of that statement by proffering that in order to be an educator one must understand pedagogy, be disciplined in the practice of pedagogy, and must apply pedagogy in the various domains of one's work.

What follows in this book is a well-constructed examination of the many contexts in which student affairs professionals work and the diverse settings through which opportunities to perform as co-curricular educators are presented. Through vignettes and examples, the authors provide guidance for how student affairs professionals, no matter one's role, can apply more intentional design to learning experiences and, in the process, elevate the success of their work. While the strength of *Learning Everywhere on Campus: Teaching Strategies for Student Affairs Professionals* is in the applied learning theories and instructional design strategies it provides, it brings added value through the new framing it offers for student affairs professionals; this publication provides more explicit and precise language about the nature of student affairs work in various educational arenas. Those who read this book will be challenged to think about designing learning experiences in ways that they may have not done previously; for example, differentiating between designing training programs and constructing effective curricula or having an educational philosophy and committing to a pedagogical approach.

This publication will not only provoke thought, it will transform behavior; it will provide co-curricular educators with concrete, applied approaches to improve the individual and collaborative aspects of their work. Readers will be provided with frames to better navigate their environments to identify opportunities to apply pedagogical designs, as well as tools to enhance the effectiveness of teaching in the various settings where those opportunities arise.

As you read this book, appreciate the contribution the authors have made to the practice of student affairs. The contents of this publication will enrich our efforts, provoke us to reconsider our language, bring more thoughtfulness to our approaches to teaching and learning, and allow us to more fully live into the core aspect of our roles—we are educators. Appreciate the gift of *Learning Everywhere on Campus*.

Larry D. Roper
Professor, School of Language, Culture and Society
Oregon State University

PREFACE

Learning Everywhere on Campus: Teaching Strategies for Student Affairs Professionals

Jane Fried

Learning really does happen everywhere—on campus, off campus, and throughout the lives of almost every person on the planet. Why is it important to create a book that highlights the ubiquity of learning? The simple answer is that, under the special circumstances of university culture, learning is viewed as a process almost exclusively restricted to the classroom and led by faculty members. Learning is considered a subset of all the activities that students engage in, limited by time, location, and the ability to demonstrate that learning has occurred. In one sense, all humans learn their way through life, most of the time in places and situations where no classroom is obvious and no teacher seems to be present. One way to describe learning is that it is a process that occurs when people have new experiences, reflect on the experiences, and derive some verbal description of the meaning, value, and possibly skills associated with those experiences. For example, a typical comment might be "I learned never to do that again," whatever "that" might be, e.g., driving drunk, pulling an all-nighter, telling a person that some new article of clothing makes them look fat. On a more positive note, "I learned that when you smile at people they are generally nicer to you and give you what you are asking for." Who can deny that these situations involve learning? So, despite the traditional, constricted understanding of teaching and learning, it is evident that learning can happen without teachers, and teachers often "teach" without a lot of learning going on (Fried, 2016).

Following this line of thinking about learning from experience, it is no surprise that student affairs professionals often talk about student learning because students have so many learning experiences in the various domains of campus that student affairs professionals manage. If learning happens because of the work of student affairs professionals, through either intentionally designed training or by engaging students in "teachable moments," why aren't student affairs staff members generally seen as legitimate educators? The teaching/learning process on college campuses is seen through that traditional lens and becomes visible (and valued) only in the presence of a teacher/professor situated in a classroom or laboratory. Other activities related to learning are almost invisible in the university context. Consider how students learn to drink responsibly; develop intimate relationships and practice safe, respectful sexual behavior; compromise with roommates whose living habits are different from their own; organize and lead student clubs; or differ civilly with people who are of different ethnic origins, sexual orientations, faith traditions, or political perspectives. Clearly, a great deal of important learning occurs while students are in college, and much of it does not involve traditional teaching methods.

Increasingly, student affairs professionals are being called upon to teach. Students in a master's-level student affairs professional preparation program were recently asked to describe whether and how they teach in their various job and graduate assistant roles. Within the relatively small group, students were co-teaching first-year seminars (FYSEM); training peer mentors, residence assistants, and orientation leaders; leading workshops on financial aid, time management, and similar topics; supervising undergraduate interns both on and off campus; working in the university's writing lab; advising a student organization; running a book group at the American Indian Center; creating and managing social networking sites for students in a particular major or residence hall—and more. Yet few had any background in instructional design, classroom management (virtual or face-to-face), assessment of learning, or other skills associated with effective teaching. Still, these young professionals were unambiguously and enthusiastically engaged in coordinating and leading student learning.

Some of their activities are easily identified as teaching and some are not. However, if students learn in these contexts, we can infer that there has been an intentional provocation of learning, typically created by student affairs professionals. Examples of student affairs professionals taking advantage of teachable moments and capitalizing on group processes for problem solving appear in the chapter on group meetings. I (Jane Fried) am beginning to believe that learning, broadly defined, should be the predominant focus of higher education. After learning goals are established, we can decide how students will engage with learning experiences. When that is accomplished, we can begin to talk about who is in charge of the experiences. For the moment, we are generally concentrating on the pedagogy of student affairs, but this is likely not the end of the conversation.

The Pedagogy of Student Affairs: Making Learning Visible

What are the pedagogies of student affairs? Service-learning is an excellent example. As Jacoby writes elsewhere in this volume:

> Service-learning is education that is grounded in experience as a basis for learning and on the centrality of critical reflection intentionally designed

to enable learning to occur. Service-learning educators select service experiences, as they would select texts or other learning activities, that they believe will be most effective in enabling students to learn and apply knowledge and develop skills.

Service-learning is grounded in the work of John Dewey, who believed that all learning is contextual, and that it occurs when students engage in significant experience, reflect on the meaning of the experience, and typically discuss it with others (Dewey, 1938). Service-learning is one of the most well-articulated pedagogies used in student affairs (even though it is not typically restricted to student affairs activities), because of its roots in the Deweyan tradition and the scholarship that has developed to describe its purposes, content, and process (Jacoby, 1996, 2015). Service-learning can be considered one of the bridge pedagogies between student affairs and academic affairs because it often involves collaboration as well as learning in many contexts.

The profession of student affairs has always presented itself as having significant educational responsibilities on campuses in the United States (Crookston, 1975). Unfortunately, most master's and doctoral training programs do not include the study of learning theories, epistemology, the neurology of learning, or the design of experiential education or pedagogy. The notion that educational leaders should organize their approach to management around the question, "Will this activity, policy, or decision help students learn something that this institution values?" is barely discussed (S. Borrego, personal communication, January 22, 2017). It is time to begin to think about learning as a process that may or may not include traditional teaching, and to consider the institutional context as a large part of the framework in which learning occurs. Indeed, the context, both on campus and with community partners, is a fundamental educational resource for learning. Beyond conventional ideas about teaching and learning, the outcomes of many educational experiences organized by student affairs professionals are often transformative for students. Since these experiences and reflections occur in the complex environments of campus life, students are often pushed to reconsider previous frames of reference and expand their understanding of their own complex worlds. This transformation becomes necessary when students who are unfamiliar with each other's worldviews try to work together.

Most Western educators see the world through binaries of separation between subject and object, thinking and feeling, teaching and learning (Fried, 2016). Eastern cultures are much more contextual in their framing of the learning process and of processes in general (Chavez & Longerbeam, 2016). Buddhists have a saying that causes and conditions create all situations. These situations arise and fall away as causes and conditions change. Student affairs professionals are expert in creating the causes and conditions for learning or in taking advantage of those conditions when they appear. Throughout this book are numerous examples of student affairs professionals helping students learn valuable life lessons, but rarely are these encounters called teaching.

The Purpose of this Book

The purpose of this text is to provide frameworks for the kinds of educational activities in which student affairs professionals are engaged, either within their designated professional roles or in collaboration with academic faculty or community partners. Working within these frameworks, derived from an array of disciplines, student affairs educators can create more intentional and consistent pedagogical approaches to use when carrying out their educational activities with students. These may include peer education, leadership development, life and career planning, skills for academic success, civic engagement and service learning, multicultural competency and study abroad, as well as classroom extension programs/lessons/modules to be used in and across academic content areas. A key purpose of all these interventions and strategies is the stimulation of meta-cognition, that is, helping students learn new information and skills and, further, to understand the value of this knowledge in constructing their sense of purpose and self in the world.

This is an edited volume that contains chapters by authors who are at various stages in their own careers. Some of the chapters are written or co-written by new professionals and are aimed at helping new professionals understand how to frame, describe, and conduct educational activities, as well as research related to those activities. Chapters are contributed by top-ranking executives, including two presidents, a provost, and a vice president for student affairs, from the perspective of organizing the entire institution to support integrated, transformative learning. Some chapters are theoretical, providing the cultural and scientific frameworks that inform our work and make it effective. Finally, several chapters provide technical insights into methodologies that give readers tools to conduct and create the kind of learning experiences that are described. Each chapter is written in the unique voice of its author or authors and very little effort has been given to forcing all the authors into a similar style. Because of this approach, it is not necessary to read the book in order. Readers are encouraged to start with the chapters that would be most interesting and then move around as information in one chapter suggests a desire to read another.

Leadership and Institutional Context

In this section, two presidents, a vice-president, and a provost describe how they are transforming their campuses to create opportunities for integrated learning. *George McClellan, an experienced Vice President for Student Affairs*, describes processes for bringing the educational work of student affairs to the attention of the academic staff and integrating learning across institutions. This chapter sets the stage for the rest of the book by addressing teaching and learning from the personal, divisional, departmental, and institutional levels. *Elsa Núñez, President of Eastern Connecticut State University*, discusses the process by which she engaged all members of the campus community in rethinking college purposes and processes. ECSU, a liberal arts institution, now has opportunities for integrated, transformative learning in many courses, often in collaboration with student affairs professionals. *Melissa Morriss-Olsen and Kristine Barnett, Provost and Assistant Provost/Dean of the Division of Student Engagement and Liberal Studies*, respectively, reorganized the curriculum and structure of Baypath University to meet the needs of a changing student population. First-generation students at this institution needed professional education and training along with leadership preparation for new roles in their communities. Authors of this chapter share how they used the notion of an "institutional thumbprint" to present the core values on which all of the learning experiences are now organized. *Michael Laliberte, new president at SUNY Delhi*, spent the first six months of his presidency listening to all members of his campus community and then created three new departments designed to integrate learning, culture, and student success.

Frameworks that Shape Teaching and Learning

This section contains five chapters that describe worldviews and theoretical frameworks that influence our approaches to the teaching/learning process. *Jane Fried* reviews the cultural assumptions that shape the dominant individualistic Western instructional methods. These pedagogies often disadvantage students who see the world through collectivist lenses. She suggests a more integrated approach to educators so that they can learn to build on the strengths of all students. *Stephanie Waterman (Onondaga, Turtle)* and *Seán Carson Kinsella (nêhiyaw/ otipemisiwak/Nakawé/Irish)* speak from their Indigenous perspectives, giving readers an opportunity to experience (in a very small way) the border crossings that are necessary for people of the First Nations to succeed in North American universities. They apply their insights to teaching graduate courses in student affairs as well as undergraduate classes in Indigenous Studies. Next, *Barbara Jacoby* presents an extensive description of the theory of service-learning in the broader context of experiential education. She then offers a detailed discussion of methods for creating service-learning programs based on effective implementation of this theory. In the chapter on pedagogy, *Fried* defines the term, which is not often used in student affairs discourse. This chapter helps readers learn about pedagogy and the design of learning experiences in order to improve and systematize their educational work. *Daniel Murphy and Ruth Harper* share a detailed process for organizing educational activities with the learning outcomes in mind from the outset. Using the backward design process developed for K-12 teachers allows assessment to become more systematic and accurate.

Learning Contexts and Locations

The purpose of this section is to give the reader examples of complex programs that support student learning across cultures. *John Howe* draws on his significant sojourns as a global traveler and experienced educator to address issues regarding the learning that occurs when students visit and live in other cultures. He emphasizes the need for students to process their experiences through meaningful reflection and ongoing dialogue, and also points out opportunities for cross-cultural experiences without travel. *Constanza Cabello*, a native of Chile and a member of an immigrant family, writes about her approach to helping students learn about diverse cultures through her work at an intercultural center. She applies a social justice lens to educational programs so that students who were born into privilege can begin to understand systemic oppression. Translating the time-honored work of Arthur Chickering into the era of technology, *Greg Heiberger and Ruth Harper* relate the seven elements of good practice in undergraduate education to technology-based interactions with students. Their chapter shows how a first-year seminar was transformed into a highly interactive learning program incorporating scientific teaching and social media. *Aynsley Diamond* focuses on the unique education and support that returning veterans need to succeed academically. She underscores the assets that veterans bring to campus because of their involvement in experiential learning, leadership, and goal achievement.

Learning Processes and Student Affairs Pedagogy

The final segment of this book shares research and practices that transform and deepen learning. *Margaret Miller and Ruth Harper* illustrate how student affairs professionals can utilize popular culture (e.g., films, television, and contemporary fiction) to teach in memorable, impactful ways. They recommend three critical lenses—reception criticism, structuralism, and identity criticism—to help students grapple with difference and social justice topics. *Jane Fried* describes the role that group participation and human interaction play in learning. She draws on her own experience and the work of some of her former students in creating learning experiences in groups and capitalizing on them in dyadic conversations. *Chelsea Sorensen and Ruth Harper* discuss achievement differences between students who have a growth mindset versus those who use a mastery-based goal orientation. They apply the results of extensive research to the process of academic advising and helping students choose to value learning over test scores. Next, *Jane Fried* explains how the use of contemplative practices allows students to both gain new insights and retain what they have learned. She also presents a brief review of the neurological processes that support this type of learning. In the final chapter on learning through the supervisory relationship, *Ruth Harper and Katelyn Romsa* adapt a counseling supervision model to student affairs settings. This framework, unfamiliar to most student affairs professionals, offers supervisors role options and stresses the importance of the developmental level of the supervisee.

Professional Audiences

This book is something of a smorgasbord of authors and professional perspectives intended to introduce student affairs professionals to the important topic of pedagogy. It should be of interest to practitioners at all levels of the profession, as well as graduate students. If we are all educators, and we believe that teaching and learning are foundational to the practice of student affairs, then we all must begin to focus on the elements and contexts of the learning process. Assessing learning outcomes is important but not enough. We must begin with the assessment of learning needs, understand and relate to the learning goals embedded in our institutional missions, design experiences that lead to valued learning outcomes, develop methods for assessing learning and present it all to our various stakeholders, beginning with students. We must be able to talk about how and why the teaching we do, in its varied contexts, has value to our students and our institutions.

As Esther Lloyd-Jones originally told us, student affairs professionals educate the *whole* student (1954). She didn't say that faculty members educate students and we do something else. She made it very clear that education includes understanding ideas, applying ideas, and working in groups to achieve the social changes that these ideas suggest. Lloyd-Jones was heir to the ideas of educational philosopher Dewey (1938) as cited by Jacoby in this volume. The pedagogy of student affairs is experiential, critical education. Its breadth encompasses nothing less than helping students create meaning in their lives. What could possibly be more important?

References

Chavez, A., & Longerbeam, S. (2016). *Teaching across cultural strengths*. Sterling, VA: Stylus.

Crookston, B. (1975). Milieu management. *NASPA Journal, 13*(1), 45–55.

Dewey, J. (1938). *Experience and education*. New York, NY: Collier.

Fried, J. (2016). *Of education, fishbowls, and rabbit holes: Rethinking teaching and liberal education for an interconnected world*. Sterling, VA: Stylus.

Jacoby, B. (1996). *Service-learning in higher education: Concepts and practices*. San Francisco, CA: Jossey-Bass.

Jacoby, B. (2015). *Service-learning essentials: Questions, answers, and lessons learned*. San Francisco, CA: Jossey-Bass.

Lloyd-Jones, E., & Smith, M. (1954). *Student personnel work as deeper teaching*. New York, NY: Harper.

ACKNOWLEDGEMENTS

Ruth Harper would like to acknowledge the editorial assistance of Larry Rogers, Margaret Miller, Chelsea Sorensen, and Wiyaka His Horse Is Thunder in the preparation of this manuscript. Thank you for being delightful to work with, bringing an eye for detail, and knowing the right ways to do things.

SECTION I
Leadership and Institutional Context

1

WHEN PEOPLE ASK ME WHAT I DO

Perspectives on Learning from an SSAO

George S. McClellan

It is as common an experience as can be. Two or more people meet for the first time. They exchange greetings, introduce themselves, and set about the process of learning more about one another. Early in the conversation someone asks, "What do you do?" Not surprising, really. Our names, and through them our families, where we live, and how we make our living are the more salient features of our identities and ones about which it is generally socially acceptable for strangers to inquire. For many of us in student affairs, being asked what we do can present a challenge. Students affairs is, after all, a broad umbrella term for a field that includes a host of related yet distinct areas of professional practice. It is also a term with which a fair number of people are unfamiliar because they did not go to college, went but did not knowingly interact with student affairs professionals, or went but attended an institution where student affairs either did not exist as a division or existed but went by another name (for example, student services, student success, or campus life). Even if you are speaking with someone who is familiar with student affairs, you have conveyed only the general arena of your professional endeavor. It is like saying you live on the east coast of the United States. It could mean Gullah country in South Carolina, Southie in Boston, the lobster fishing villages in southern Maine, or a host of other distinctive environs—all vibrant, interesting, and culturally rich; yet each is distinct from the other.

So, what to answer when asked what you do? I have for years replied that I am an educator, and I teach and learn in university communities. It has been my experience that the answer is responsive to the question, relatable for most people, and allows me a base from which to expand on the answer with additional details if there is interest. It also has the added value of conveying to those with whom I am interacting what is important to me and how I see what I do. I am an educator—engaged in both teaching and learning—working primarily, though not exclusively, outside the formal classroom.

Student affairs practitioners play many roles in fulfilling their professional responsibilities. Among these are administrator, advisor, caregiver, change agent, confidant, counselor, consultant, crisis responder, diplomat, disciplinarian, entrepreneur, fundraiser, grant administrator, leader, programmer, and more (Barr, McClellan, & Sandeen, 2014). Embracing all of these roles, I see and understand my work in student affairs first and foremost as a process of teaching and learning. This construction provides me with a framework within which to engage in professional practice as well as a rich body of professional literature to draw upon, an established set of ethics for guidance, a means of articulating and assessing both processes and outcomes related to my work, invaluable and natural links to colleagues in the faculty and academic administrative roles, and a context in which to articulate the connections between my work and that of my student affairs colleagues to the primary enterprise of our institution.

This chapter will address how the view of myself as an educator plays itself out in my professional practice as a senior student affairs officer (SSAO). It will begin at the personal level of self and then move to efforts at the division, individual department or unit, institution, and professional field level. The discussion is shared not to say that this is the one correct way in which to understand and enact service as a senior student affairs professional but rather as one story that I hope encourages readers to reflect on, revise, and reinforce their own understandings and actions in support of the success of the students and institutions they serve.

Self

Approaching student affairs as teaching and learning requires at least two important core characteristics: curiosity and commitment. Doug Woodard, my doctoral advisor, used to say that people in student affairs need to be *students of students*. It seems to me we have to be curious about a number of things. Among them are:

- Students—Who are they? What are their beliefs, values, interests, and motivations? What are their experiences? What are their goals?
- Student success—What does success mean to various stakeholders? What processes, experiences, programs, and environments support student success? How do we support student agency?
- Teaching and learning—How do they work in a variety of postsecondary settings? What facilitates the learning processes? How do we measure what is taking place?
- Self—What are my strengths and beliefs about teaching and learning? Which of my beliefs and experiences shape these strengths and beliefs? How can I continue to expand on my knowledge and skills about teaching and learning?

We also need a commitment to actively pursuing answers and insights in ways that reflect both good scholarly activity and ethical professional practice, as well as to sharing those answers and insights in order to enhance knowledge and practice (Carpenter, 2001).

Dedication to developing knowledge and skills related to teaching and learning is essential. Student affairs professionals who view themselves as educators should also engage in the scholarship of teaching and learning. Magolda and Ribera (2016) describe this area of scholarship as "any effort to gather, analyze, interpret, and disseminate evidence of teaching and learning for individual improvement, institutional improvement, and the advancement of the larger profession in student affairs" (in McClellan & Stringer, p. 164). The concept of scholar-practitioner is relevant here, a reflective practice that cultivates "values, habits of mind, and the ability to balance and integrate 'doing' with 'knowing'" (Kupo, 2014, p. 89).

This approach also requires that one has thoughtfully considered and adopted a philosophy of teaching and learning. I see teaching and learning as a shared process drawing on the knowledge, skills, experiences, and insights of all those involved together in that enterprise. I see myself as guide and facilitator for that process, both inside and beyond the formal classroom.

My service in that role is shaped by the work of Sanford (1962) on college teaching, particularly the importance of challenging and supporting learners. I have incorporated a third element as a central tenet of my teaching philosophy: celebrating. A teaching and learning environment should challenge all in it to stretch themselves and one another to pursue significant growth goals. It must be an environment in which all involved feel supported in the sort of risk-taking that pursuing such growth requires and act on a duty to support one another in their shared journey. The environment should also be celebrative, with recognition of both the journey and the attainment of goals.

I find myself in agreement with the thought that frequently is shared on the Internet and attributed to Alexandra K. Trenfor: "The best teachers are those who show you where to look, but don't tell you what to see." I believe that the best teachers also help you consider the ways in which you might interpret what you see. Part of being a good teacher is introducing learners to multiple ways of making meaning of data or an observed phenomenon through introducing them to theories and models and inviting them to use these resources.

Creating an engaging, inclusive, respectful, and trusting environment is important, and the person responsible for a particular learning space must be a leader in articulating the importance of such an environment and taking the responsibility for everyone involved in doing so. I enjoy fostering active learning and flipped learning spaces as well as challenging learners to use creative and contemporary technologies in their work. I always appreciate what I learned from Robert Menges, a faculty member in my master's program, who shared with his students and readers so many wonderful approaches to effective teaching (Menges & Weimer, 1995). It has also been important for me to be proactive in seeking and remaining open to feedback from colleagues, both staff and faculty, as well as from students, about their observations of me, and situating that feedback within my goals as a teacher and learner. That feedback has been invaluable.

My view of teaching and learning is based in my beliefs about the roles of higher education and my identity as a first-generation learner, student affairs scholar/practitioner, and criticalist. I am drawn to the work of Giroux (2005), who carefully articulates the obligations of being intentional about crossing borders and helping others to do likewise. Higher education can be understood both as a site of social reproduction and social mobility (Pusser, 2010), a mechanism of both stratification and liberation. Encouraging students to explore these dimensions of the challenges of higher education in the context of their own identities is one of the true joys of guiding and facilitating a group.

Finally, self-concept and self-awareness are also critical in this exploration. Knowing who we are and being mindful of how our identities play out in our work and lives is essential to our success in serving and supporting our students and our institutions. It is no less essential to us as teachers and learners.

Division

Senior student affairs officers and other division leaders who prioritize teaching and learning may wish to shape their division's programs and practices in ways consistent with their beliefs. Fostering a shared sense of purpose and creating a framework for practice can be powerful in focusing the work of the division. In the case of using teaching and learning as a framework, it can also help strengthen the link between student affairs programs and services with institutional mission and build collegial and productive bridges to the work of colleagues in academic affairs. So how does one go about shaping a division in this way?

Leaders always need the support of top administration, who may need to be reminded of this aspect of the teaching and learning mission of student affairs. One should not assume that senior leaders outside (or even inside) the division will immediately see the potential benefits to shaping programs and services in this way. Identifying and articulating the links to mission, goals of shareholders (including boards of trustees or regents, applicable state entities, donors and other funding entities, employers, faculty, and most importantly students and their families) will be important in garnering support of senior leadership for implementing the framework.

Once assured of leadership endorsement, the next step is introducing the idea to the division. Start by discussing the idea with key players—unit heads and others—as well as with leadership in the student government. Full engagement by the unit heads will be very important for obvious reasons. Consulting with student leaders is a matter of professional responsibility and respect. This may also be a matter of being sure that fee funding allocated through student government will be available to support the shift in focus for programs and services.

In discussing the framing of the division's work as teaching and learning, the question of learning outcomes ought to be addressed. Explicitly identifying learning outcomes for the division (or your program or role within it) is valuable for any number of reasons. Student affairs must frame its own learning outcomes within the context of the general education learning outcomes that the college or university has adopted. Sometimes it is helpful to invite a group of faculty colleagues to sit with leadership from student affairs to develop learning outcomes (Barr, McClellan, & Sandeen, 2014).

Once adopted, these learning outcomes must be operationalized by incorporating them into the annual reports for units and the division, using them as a component in annual staff evaluations, and requiring that they be addressed as part of any and all resource allocation decisions in the division. One of my proudest moments in the profession was when I learned that the Indiana-Purdue Student Government Association at Indiana University-Purdue University Fort Wayne, at which I was serving as SSAO at the time, had adopted the University's Baccalaureate Framework (faculty-approved learning outcomes also adopted by our Student Affairs Division) for use in consideration of any funding proposals forwarded to them!

Making sure that everyone sees themselves as having a place in the student affairs teaching and learning enterprise will help determine the degree to which the shift in focus is successful and sustained. This means addressing issues of breadth of functions. Many student affairs divisions have within them units that may be seen as primarily focused on service and for which people may struggle at first to find a connection to the new focus on education in the division. Thinking broadly can help. As an example, consider a unit responsible for testing support, such as an academic success center that offers a variety of online testing such as GRE, LSAT, or other exams. It may also serve as a testing site for a number of online departmental exams where faculty wish the testing to be monitored. This unit is incredibly important and successful as a service unit, but how does it engage in teaching and learning? Take a look at those learning outcomes. Do they include reference to development of ethics? Perhaps the unit could be involved in providing information about academic integrity in online learning and testing. Do those outcomes address developing a healthy and balanced lifestyle? The unit could share information about stress management and testing. Remember, too, even if there is not a specific faculty-approved learning outcome addressing it, we in student affairs always have opportunities to engage with students in teaching and learning about problem-solving and personal responsibility.

A leader who wishes to include teaching and learning in the mission will also need to be mindful of the range of developmental levels within the staff. A thoughtful staff development program may contribute a great deal in this regard. Just because people have college degrees, even master's or doctoral degrees, does not necessarily assure that they have had the chance to learn about learning or teaching. And just because people have no degree does not mean they have no relevant experiences that could help them see themselves at work as teachers and learners. Consider a staff development program with a range of offerings including theory, research findings, techniques and strategies, and bringing relatable experiences (for example, what you may know about teaching and learning as a result of raising children) into your workplace. Sharing that the change in focus includes recognizing that all of us are both teaching and learning is important. This includes our relationships with both students and with colleagues. We are all teaching and learning all the time, or we can be if we orient ourselves in that way. Student affairs divisions wishing to move in this direction should create a co-curriculum that is enacted through leadership development events, formal advising activities, disciplinary proceedings, and other structured programs. It should also pervade our phone conversations, email exchanges, and interpersonal interactions as we greet students in our offices, residence halls, or campus commons areas. Teaching and learning ought to be an everywhere, all-the-time endeavor.

Unit or Department

Having shared some thoughts on leading a student affairs division in a shift to focusing on teaching and learning, it is important to note that much of the actual work directly involving students will take place at the department level. Hence, it is also the level of change at which much of the assessment of learning will need to occur. This assessment must be folded into each program and service offered by a unit and then drawn into annual reporting as well as future planning. There are any number of excellent resources on developing learning assessments, and it will be very important for senior student affairs leaders and unit heads to be familiar with the information in these resources and to be sure staff members have the opportunity to develop and demonstrate skills in this area. Data about making a difference in learning—student learning in particular, but also learning for staff, faculty, and others—will be invaluable to informing the change and telling the story.

The unit or department is also the level in the institution at which the strongest and most direct links between the co-curriculum and curriculum can be developed. Student affairs professionals, including SSAOs, need to be aware of where those linkages might be developed and then reach out proactively to faculty colleagues to explore opportunities for collaboration. Who is teaching leadership? Who is teaching communication? Who is teaching ethics? Find these faculty members and help them become faculty friends who partner in interesting and innovative initiatives to connect learning inside and outside the classroom. Unit-level social media, websites, and other forms of communication will also be sessential in spreading word to a variety of constituents about the change in student affairs focus. Here, at the departmental level, is where many people will come to know what the change looks like and what the signs are of progress and rewards for the investment of time, energy, and other resources.

A senior student affairs administrator can do much to help unit heads and staff in this regard. Share information about faculty interests. Help make introductions. Offer support in the way of resources and through helping free up the time necessary to explore options for innovative linkages. Work with senior leadership in academic affairs to have them offer similar support from that side of the house or to be sure there will not be a problem if you offer support directly. (For example, a little bit of travel support for junior faculty can help them and the desired shift in student affairs go a long way.) Be supportive of risk-taking while remaining focused on individual and organizational learning from these risks. Finally, speak with unit heads and staff members every chance you get about your own journey as teacher and learner. Listen to the stories of their journeys. Incorporate lessons learned and celebrate the achievements, privately and publicly, in ways big and small.

Institutions

Senior student affairs officers are often also officers of the institution, positions that involve unique opportunities and challenges. These opportunities include advocating for the framework of teaching and learning in student affairs, which will vary, depending on the mission of the institution.

An SSAO might also advocate by making the educational work of student affairs visible in reward ceremonies and publications. University co-curricular transcripts are another valuable strategy in this regard because they document the importance of co-curricular learning.

Professional Field

Another unique opportunity available to SSAOs is through their engagement with the professional associations, their conferences, educational resources, guidelines, and publications. Although the profession of student affairs has focused on experiential learning for more than 70 years, it is still necessary to write and speak about our educational role in the professional journals (e.g., *Journal of Student Affairs Research and Practice*, *Journal of College Student Development*, etc.). These journals and related publications provide foundational information to the field and can articulate the educational value that student affairs staff, programs, and services provide to college students.

SSAOs lead by example in teaching and learning through their personal presence and activities. Which speakers do you attend? What resources do you post on social media? What do you write for publication or present at conferences? All of these are opportunities to shape student affairs as a field and increase its orientation toward teaching and learning.

Conclusion

While there are some critics who scoff at the idea of student affairs professionals as educators, the idea of student affairs as teaching and learning has its origins in the earliest days of our profession and has been a part of our conversations with colleagues from those days forward (Magolda & Ribera, in McClellan & Stringer, 2016). My final suggestion is that we make decisions about what we do based on what we believe is best for our students and our institutions, and then dedicate ourselves to pursuing that decision fully and faithfully in a spirit of adventure, gratitude, and joy. In my own professional practice, I have chosen to focus my work on teaching and learning, both inside and outside the formal classroom in college settings. I consider this the most valid form of educational and professional practice for student affairs. What is your story? What do you do?

References

Barr, M. J., McClellan, G. S., & Sandeen, A. (2014). *Making change happen in student affairs: Challenges and strategies for professionals*. San Francisco, CA: Jossey-Bass.

Carpenter, S. (2001). Student affairs scholarship (re?)considered: Toward a scholarship of practice. *Journal of College Student Development, 42*(4), 301–318.

Giroux, H. A. (2005). *Border crossings: Cultural workers and the politics of education* (2nd ed.). New York, NY: Routledge.

Kupo, V. L. (2014). Becoming a scholar-practitioner in student affairs. In *New Directions for Student Services* (No. 147, pp. 89–98). San Francisco, CA: Jossey-Bass.

Magolda, P. & Ribera, T. (2016). Teaching and learning beyond the classroom: Responding to the internal and external challenges facing student affairs. In G. S. McClellan & J. Stringer (Eds.), *Handbook for student affairs administration* (4th ed.). San Francisco, CA: Jossey-Bass.

Menges, R. J. & Weimer, M. (Eds.). (1995). *Teaching on solid ground: Using scholarship to improve practice*. San Francisco, CA: Jossey-Bass.

Pusser, B. (2010). Of a mind to labor: Reconceptualizing student work and higher education. In L. W. Perna (Ed.), *Understanding the working college student: New research and its implications for policy and practice*. Sterling, VA: Stylus.

Sanford, N. (1962). *The American college*. New York, NY: Wiley.

2

STUDENT ENGAGEMENT AT A PUBLIC LIBERAL ARTS UNIVERSITY

Elsa M. Núñez

College campuses across America are teeming these days with out-of-classroom opportunities for students. Student clubs, intramurals, leadership programs, service-learning/community service projects, internship programs, and other activities are designed to engage students as they apply the theories and principles learned in class to real-world situations. Such learning opportunities can be found in every corner of campus, and even extend to the communities beyond our campuses' borders. And student affairs professionals are often at the center of creating, carrying out, and evaluating these learning events and processes. How does student engagement take place on my own campus—Eastern Connecticut State University?

Eastern is Connecticut's public liberal arts college. Its motto is "A Liberal Education. Practically Applied." As a residential campus focused on undergraduate education, we are committed to providing students with a well-rounded academic foundation that is grounded in the best principles of a liberal arts education. At the same time, like so many other institutions of higher education today, the faculty and administration keenly recognize the importance of preparing our students for the realities of the twenty-first century. A program of out-of-class experiences that motivates and engages students is an essential element in providing them with the relevant skills they need to compete and prosper in today's global society.

How does Eastern's identity as a public institution with a liberal arts focus inform our approach to student engagement? To understand how the university's public mission and liberal arts curriculum frame academic and campus life at Eastern requires some discussion of the history of the liberal arts and of public education in the United States.

Content and Process: The "Artes Liberales"

Many books have been written to describe the rich history of the liberal arts and liberal education, and I will not attempt to replicate that discussion. However, there are aspects of the liberal arts and liberal education that bear mentioning, for they are at the heart of the educational enterprise at Eastern.

First, let us acknowledge the difference between "the liberal arts" and "liberal education." People sometimes confuse the two terms or assume they refer to the same thing. Nonetheless, these are not equivalent terms. Maurice O'Sullivan, professor of literature at Rollins College, makes a simple, convenient distinction between the two by saying the liberal arts is about "content" and liberal education is about "process," or a "coherent, systematic approach to a body of knowledge" (O'Sullivan, 2009, pp. 24–25). The classic liberal arts have been taught since Greco-Roman times and came to be known in the Middle Ages as the "Trivium" (grammar, logic, and rhetoric) and the "Quadrivium" (music, arithmetic, geometry, and astronomy). Today, those seven disciplines are still taught, albeit in new ways, on college campuses throughout the world. Of course, new disciplines— psychology, electrical engineering, astrophysics, and computer science, for example—have been added to college curricula. Yet even with the exponential growth of knowledge in the world and the evolution of technology, we continue to explore the human condition and the world around us as we have for thousands of years. Language, thought, and the scientific method still serve as the building blocks of intellectual discourse.

When the Association of American Colleges and Universities (AAC&U)—the nation's leading advocate of undergraduate education—talks about the broad intellectual competencies found on today's liberal arts campuses, we can see the influence of the classical liberal arts tradition in today's focus on critical thinking (logic), communication skills (rhetoric and grammar), and various aspects of the physical world (arithmetic, geometry, and astronomy). It has always intrigued me that the ancients saw music as a science—the science of managed sound!—and certainly the performing arts, visual arts, and music remain important subjects taught on college campuses.

At Eastern, our liberal arts core curriculum reflects the traditions of the liberal arts. All of our students take English composition. All students must complete two math courses, as well as two science classes, including a lab course. Every student must also take courses from the arts, humanities, and social sciences. The core of 46 credits represents a broad set of academic disciplines that form the foundation for all majors, as we prepare students for the known world of today and the unknowns of tomorrow. Just as Eastern has taken the "content" of a classical liberal arts education to form the basis for our core curriculum, we have also incorporated the principles found within the concept of a "liberal education." If "liberal arts" refers to core academic content, then "a liberal education" refers to the way in which courses are taught.

More than a decade ago, the faculty at Eastern Connecticut State University developed a new liberal arts core curriculum that sought to encompass the best principles of liberal education. The core was divided into tiers that represented the sequential evolution of learning. Tier One gives students an introduction to theory, research, and college writing. Tier Two courses provide opportunities to apply conceptual frameworks, while Tier Three courses offer culminating "capstone" experiences for seniors. In these classes, students produce signature works that reflect their learning as they articulate the intellectual progress that has taken place during their time at Eastern.

This tiered, sequential approach is also interdisciplinary, not only in terms of team-teaching and other cross-disciplinary approaches to teaching, but also by the nature of the classroom setting. Students from all majors sit together to learn broad intellectual competencies and master core abilities such as critical thinking, ethics, communication, information literacy, historical and cultural perspectives, and computational skills. Over the course of the three-tiered liberal arts core, each student integrates these core competencies into their major, enhancing the knowledge gained in their respective discipline.

A Public Purpose

While we can trace Eastern's liberal arts curriculum back to its historical roots, two more recent developments have served to move Eastern's brand of liberal education into the twenty-first century and inform student engagement on our campus. One development has been the public funding of higher education in the United States, a dramatic shift from the fourteenth century and the "Artes Liberales." At that time, the term was used to broadly describe both the liberal arts taught and the social class that benefited from such an education. "Free" men (few women were allowed to pursue an education in those days) were the elite—wealthy landowners, men of means unencumbered by the daily demands of work. Such an education was distinguished from the vocational training, rudimentary as it may have been 500 years ago, necessary to turn a plow, mine a granite quarry, or mill grain. This training was called the "artes illiberales" and left for laborers. By the Enlightenment, a liberal education was also seen as the type of education that could "free your mind" from stagnant thought and narrow solutions. The role of education in ensuring the freedoms of our new democracy was also on the minds of our Founding Fathers, who understood that education should be publicly supported and available to all citizens, not just the privileged class.

In his book, *Beyond the University, Why Liberal Education Matters*, President Michael Roth of Wesleyan University quotes Thomas Jefferson, who wrote that publicly supported education was necessary "to enable every man to judge for himself what will secure or endanger his freedom," so that learned people would (in Roth's words) have "the capacity of independent judgment" (Roth, 2014, p. 24). Jefferson went to William & Mary; John Adams attended Harvard; James Madison went to what is now Princeton; and Alexander Hamilton attended college at what is now Columbia University. All were products of a liberal education! It was the only education they were familiar with, so it is not hyperbole to say that Jefferson and his peers were advocating for "publicly" supported liberal education, a similar form of the college education we teach today at Eastern. Jefferson, Madison, Adams, and their peers attended private colleges because nothing comparable to our current system of public education existed. Over time, we have developed a system of public higher education in the United States that is the envy of the world. Whether we think of the surge in public university enrollments in the 1950s, spawned by the GI Bill, or the growth of community colleges in the 1960s, we have worked hard to create a system of "public" higher education in America. During this period women, people of color, and other underrepresented populations have moved across the threshold into the halls of higher education. This public mission has given Eastern a focus on educating the residents of Connecticut and serving our local and state communities for more than 125 years.

The New Workplace

The second development that has altered the role of higher education has been the dramatic change in the skills needed in the modern workplace. Robotics have changed manufacturing, and the computer has changed most other industries. Workforces have been flattened, brand-new industries and occupations have emerged, and today's workers are expected to have skill sets previously only required at the higher levels of an organization. As a result, a college degree will increasingly become the minimum educational requirement for jobs in this country. In 2010, the Center for Education and the Workforce at Georgetown University projected that 63 percent of all jobs by 2018 would require at least a two-year degree (Carnevale, Smith, & Strohl, 2010).

Employers of workers requiring a four-year education are also telling us clearly that broad intellectual skills, not narrow specialization, is what they are seeking in new recruits. In separate surveys conducted in 2007, 2008, 2010, 2013, and 2015 by AAC&U, the vast majority of employers say they are less interested in specialized job proficiencies, favoring instead analytical thinking, teamwork, and communication skills—the broad intellectual and social competencies available through a liberal arts education. Not only must today's workers possess these broader intellectual skills, they must be ready and able to adapt to change. Today's technological world—where knowledge doubles every 18 months and entire industries are created in less time—requires workers with the transferable skills they need to be ready for many different jobs in a lifetime. As David Kearns, the late Xerox CEO, noted in 2002, "The only education that prepares us for change is a liberal education. In periods of change, narrow specialization condemns us to inflexibility" (as cited in Simon, Behmand, & Burke, 2015, p. 24). In a dramatic sense, the education limited to the privileged class centuries ago has now been made available to people from all backgrounds, at the same time that the purpose of liberal education has been broadened to serve a highly useful purpose in today's workplace.

"Practically Applied. . . ."

How can we best leverage the broad intellectual skills of a liberal education to address modern life? The obvious answer is to provide students with opportunities to use the academic skills they develop in class to engage the world around them. Such a twenty-first century model of liberal education breathes life into intellectual discourse by providing daily application of theoretical concepts in practical settings. As mentioned, Eastern's tagline is "A Liberal Education. Practically Applied." This reflects a commitment to two separate concepts—that students learn broad intellectual skills grounded in the liberal arts that they can then apply to solving the challenges facing modern society. This model not only reflects the realities of modern life, it also acknowledges that engaging students in active learning experiences is the best way to teach and learn.

A Plan for Student Engagement

Putting this vision into action at Eastern did not happen by chance. I (Núñez) had the good fortune to join Eastern as its sixth president in 2006. Two years prior, the university was accepted into the Council of Public Liberal Arts Colleges (COPLAC), a group of small, public colleges and universities in the United States that exemplify the traditions of residential, liberal arts institutions. As I was becoming president, the university was preparing to launch its next strategic planning process, and the faculty was eager to move to the next phase in our evolution as a public liberal art university. We used an inclusive, campus-wide planning process involving more than 250 faculty and staff to create the 2008–13 Strategic Plan, which was updated in 2013 to continue the progress we have made over the past decade.

Through our Strategic Plan, Eastern has made engaged learning a critical element of a student's educational program. Campus-wide engagement activities, as well as those that extend learning off campus, have been shown to be strong motivation for students to stay in college. Student clubs, leadership programs, intramurals, internships, residential life, community service, and other programming also give students myriad opportunities to apply theoretical learning. Students grow personally as well as they engage their values and ethics in responding to practical challenges. Not only is such experiential learning informed by classroom instruction, it facilitates intellectual exploration, with students learning to articulate the inter-connectivity of the knowledge they gain, and the intersection of values, theory, and practice. Most importantly, national data consistently demonstrates that engaged students—the busiest students!—receive better grades and are retained and graduate at higher rates.

Residential Life

Campus engagement comes in many forms. At the most basic level is on-campus residency, and the data are fairly conclusive that students who live on campus have better retention and graduation rates and higher GPAs than commuters. This is not hard to understand—being near the library, computer labs, and faculty mentors helps a student succeed.

At Eastern, 90 percent of freshmen and 60 percent of all students live on our campus. We are the smallest of Connecticut's four state universities, yet still have the highest percentage of full-time undergraduate students living on campus. Having the majority of students live on campus provides Eastern an opportunity to engage them directly in campus life through an active residential life program. It starts with our Six-Week Challenge, a combination of social events, orientation programs, and one-to-one networking opportunities designed to quickly acclimate first-year students to college life. The program was established through our 2008–13 Strategic Plan in response to national data that showed the risk of dropping out of college was greatest during a student's first six weeks on campus.

Through the leadership of hall directors and resident assistants in our 13 residence halls, other residential life initiatives include career development programs, selecting a major, and cultural events. In addition, the "Warrior Cup" is a friendly competition among the residence halls that builds school spirit while encouraging academic excellence, community service, and campus leadership.

Clubs and Organizations

Another way to engage students is through student organizations and co-curricular clubs. Not all clubs are grounded in an academic discipline. However, those that are can provide a strong connection between a student's academic program and student life activities, ensuring that the skills they learn in both settings inform their personal and professional growth. We have more than 80 student clubs at Eastern, a number that grows each year as students create new clubs to explore shared interests. Eastern data have consistently shown that students who participate in club activities have higher GPAs than our campus average. A related program is the LEAP leadership program, which supports campus leaders and mirrors the tiered approach of Eastern's liberal arts core. Freshmen leaders in LEAP Tier One learn time management, group dynamics, and conflict management. In Tier Two, current student leaders in clubs and other positions participate in networking and public speaking sessions. Senior leaders in Tier Three have the opportunity to mentor freshmen in Tier One, completing the cycle.

Civic Engagement

Community service and civic engagement are also valuable avenues for engaging students on and off campus. Social responsibility is one of Eastern's six core values, and students express this value by providing important services across the community—working in after-school programs, in middle school mentoring programs, at the local food pantry, in social service agencies, and in many other public and nonprofit organizations. Critical to this service commitment is the Center for Community Engagement (CCE), which was established in 2009 as part of our Strategic Plan. Prior to that time, resident students were required to perform eight hours of service in the community each year, yet with little attempt at coordination or reflection. Other volunteer activities occurred in a random, unorganized fashion. Even though Eastern had been serving the local community since its beginnings as a normal school (or teachers' college) in 1889, we weren't matching our students' skills and time with community priorities.

Since the CCE was created, volunteerism has increased, and service performed by students has been aligned with clearly defined community needs. By coordinating our campus's commitment to the local community, the CCE has greatly expanded Eastern's impact on the lives of local residents. At the same time, Eastern's commitment to community service has resulted in national recognition, including President Obama's Higher Education Community Service Honor Roll and Carnegie Foundation Community Engagement Designation.

Our faculty also has created "service learning" courses where students apply skills learned in class to perform specialized community projects. One English class created business plans for local Latino businesses. Another group of students from the psychology, social work, and education programs initiated a mentoring program for local middle school students. Business information systems students set up a website for the local soup kitchen. Mentored by their faculty, graphic design students have performed pro bono design work for a local dairy and Paul Newman's "Hole in the Wall Gang" camp for children with serious illnesses. All of these are examples of how students applied their classroom learning to support community causes. It is no surprise that these are some of our best students.

Environmental Stewardship

Another aspect of Eastern's commitment to local and state communities that offers engagement opportunities for students is our Institute for Sustainable Energy, which serves municipalities (free energy audits), school districts (sustainable curriculum), and fellow college campuses (as co-chair of the Connecticut Alliance on Campus Sustainability with Yale University). The institute works closely with our Environmental Earth Science Department to provide on-campus internships for students in our Sustainable Energy program, and also collaborates with our facilities department on a variety of green campus initiatives. These efforts have resulted in Eastern being named one of the nation's top "green" colleges for the past seven years in a row by The Princeton Review and the U.S. Green Building Council. Through Eastern's "three-legged" approach—ISE's outreach, green campus initiatives, and a sustainable energy major—we are able to appeal to the environmental consciousness of today's Millennials while providing another engagement opportunity to students.

On-Campus Internships

One of the more innovative strategies we have in place at Eastern to enhance student engagement is our on-campus internship program. Such a program is different from developing and encouraging students to take internships off campus. Most universities support off-campus internships. At Eastern, those include placements at ESPN, Aetna, Pfizer, United Technologies, and many other sites in Connecticut and elsewhere. Even though these off-campus internships (for credit) and co-ops (paid internships) are important aspects of applied learning at Eastern, our on-campus internship program provides a unique opportunity for students while strengthening our ties with major state employers. It began in fall 2011 when Eastern partnered with Cigna, the international health care provider headquartered in Bloomfield, Connecticut, to open a "Work Hub" on campus as part of Cigna's Technology Early Career Development Program. The facility gives students an on-campus location to develop practical skills completing real-time work assignments without having to travel off campus.

Since the Work Hub's inception, more than 70 Eastern computer science and business information systems majors have held paid internships in the program, and 54 have continued with Cigna as full-time employees after graduation. Eastern's relationship with Cigna has opened opportunities to work with other major employers in the state. One is The Jackson Laboratory for Genomic Medicine (JAX), a major biomedical research facility based in Farmington, Connecticut. A summer program at JAX to provide Eastern interns with opportunities to conduct bioinformatics and computational biology research has been so successful that plans are underway to bring JAX to Eastern to be part of the on-campus Work Hub. Other additions to the Work Hub include Horizons, a local nonprofit organization and, most recently, the Connecticut Department of Energy and Environmental Protection (DEEP). Students studying geographic information systems in the Environmental Earth Science Department have been tasked with developing a searchable database for all state land holdings (state parks, forests, and other properties) under DEEP jurisdiction.

Beyond the Campus Grounds

Student engagement and experiential learning at Eastern goes far beyond our campus borders, or even our local community in Willimantic, Connecticut. Our students have traveled to Jamaica to build wind turbines for schools; journeyed to Ghana, West Africa, and Nepal to study those countries' public health systems; studied geological formations in Providence State Park in Georgia; explored the coral reefs of Tahiti; built Habitat homes in West Virginia; and interned in

New York City, Washington, D.C, and at Disney World in Orlando, Florida, to name just a few examples of off-campus engagement opportunities for Eastern students.

Educational Access

In discussing the many ways that Eastern Connecticut State University provides engagement opportunities for its students, I need to draw attention to a special part of our public mission— our commitment to expand educational opportunity to populations that have been historically underrepresented. That includes low-income students, minority students, first-generation students, and other groups that deserve the same promise of a college education enjoyed by the affluent and privileged. Ensuring engagement opportunities for underrepresented student populations requires active investments. For instance, we provide scholarships to allow low-income students to study abroad. The on-campus internships described earlier are especially appreciated by students without personal transportation to off-campus internship locations. We encourage and support minority students in pursuing campus leadership roles as resident assistants and student club officers. It is also heart-warming to see how many students from underprivileged back-grounds participate in community service projects, showing generosity with their time and limited resources.

Being an inclusive university only works when everyone values diversity and supports the rich social and cultural fabric found on campus. The Intercultural Center, Women's Center, and Pride Center not only provide support for minority groups, they educate the entire campus on important issues related to race, gender, and sexuality. The events and programs these offices sponsor teach all our students that the world they live in is bigger than they may have realized. Through a welcoming, empowering environment, Eastern teaches its students to respect and celebrate the world's diversity as they learn to be part of a global society.

Conclusion

With their historical focus on serving regional constituencies, public universities like Eastern are well positioned to use their campuses and local communities as laboratories for social change while addressing community needs and other regional concerns. In addition, students can develop their leadership skills through co-curricular clubs, addressing environmental issues, and providing applied learn-ing opportunities through on- and off-campus internships. At Eastern, our stu-dents have the valued-added opportunity to apply the broad-based intellectual skills taught through our liberal arts curriculum—critical thinking, ethics, com-munication skills—as they practice problem-solving strategies they will be able to use throughout their lives.

Student engagement has been found to be highly effective in helping students achieve success and prepare for professional careers and engaged lives as active citizens. Students who live on campus, participate in student clubs, engage in internships and study abroad opportunities, and volunteer for service in the community have higher GPAs, stay in school, and graduate at higher levels.

While the university is held accountable for such institutional measures, our graduates measure their success in personal, lifelong arcs—how effective are they as working professionals? How engaged are they in meeting the civic challenges of their local communities? Are they living active personal lives? Do they engage state, national, and international concerns?

It is my belief that the model we have developed at Eastern, wherein a foundation of liberal arts education grounds student engagement and applied learning, holds great promise for preparing ethical, knowledgeable, and independent thinkers for the world ahead. Our hope is that graduates leave Eastern ready to live productive lives as professionals seeking to contribute to society. We have faith that they are ready to lead fulfilling personal lives as individuals with broad intellectual skills and a global perspective. We want them to be ready to adapt to the social, economic, and technological changes that will continue to be part of modern life. Most importantly—perhaps never more importantly—we want our graduates to live engaged civic lives as members of a democratic citizenry that governs itself, participating in the public dialogue, and investing their time to confront the social, economic, and political challenges that face our nation.

Aristotle once suggested that "It is the mark of an educated mind to be able to entertain a thought without accepting it." Today, being an active citizen is not only an act of consciousness, it is often an act of bravery. Questioning and testing the status quo is not always popular, but it has never been more critical to our survival. George Will, the conservative columnist and also a product of a liberal arts education, said in a 2005 speech at the University of Miami: "The greatest threat to civility, and ultimately civilization, is an excess of certitude. The world is much menaced just now by people who think that the world and their duties in it are clear and simple."

Our lives are clearly not simple, although a common reflexive response to the world's uncertainty is to yearn for easy answers. Unfortunately, the challenges facing us today will not be solved by simple solutions. Nor will they be solved alone by our leaders—only an engaged citizenry, working together, can meet today's global issues.

America is a great experiment in democracy and freedom. It works only when all citizens are invested in self-governance and committed to protecting the freedoms all of us enjoy. I continue to believe that a liberal education, practically applied, is the best way we have to provide Eastern students with the intellectual tools and experiences they need to strengthen our great democracy and contribute to a society that will need their leadership in the coming years.

References

Carnevale, A. P., Smith, N., & Strohl, J. (2010). *Help wanted*. Georgetown University: Center on Education and the Workforce, Georgetown Public Policy Institute.

O'Sullivan, M. (2009). Artes illiberales? The four myths of liberal education. *Change Magazine*. September–October, pp. 24–25.

Roth, M. S. (2014). *Beyond the university: Why liberal education matters*. New Haven, CT: Yale University Press.

Simon, R. B., Behmand, M., & Burke, T. (Eds.). (2015). *Teaching big history*. Oakland, CA: University of California Press.

Will, G. (2005, May 22). The oddness of everything. *Newsweek*, p. 84.

3

BAY PATH UNIVERSITY
Educating Students for Life and Career

Melissa Morriss-Olson and Kristine E. Barnett

When Bay Path University first opened its doors to students, typewriters and calculating machines dominated in the classrooms. Today, the university operates in a world driven by iPads, mobile phones, and laptops. Throughout Bay Path's more than 100-year history, it has been true to its core promise of providing innovative, career-focused educational programs that have evolved in response to the economic, cultural, and technological influences of our time. Founded in 1897 as Bay Path Institute, Bay Path was one of the largest and most respected co-educational business schools in the region. Known for its accelerated 48-week format and strong programs, Bay Path flourished for nearly 20 years until World War II profoundly affected its focus. All young, able-bodied men enlisted for the war effort. Noticing the opportunity to expand the role of women in business, a leading Springfield businessman purchased Bay Path Institute in 1945. Bay Path shifted to all-women, changed its name to Bay Path Secretarial School for Women, and moved to a new campus. In 1949, it became Bay Path Junior College. In 1988, the institution's name was changed to Bay Path College, indicating the commonwealth's approval to grant bachelor's degrees. Bay Path has undergone momentous changes culminating with the name change to Bay Path University in 2014, to more accurately reflect its current curricular mix and institutional complexity. Today, with more than 3,200 students in Bay Path's four divisions (traditional undergraduate, the One Day A Week College, The American Women's College, and the graduate college) across multiple instructional locations and online, Bay Path has broadened its focus, expanded its mission, and moved toward meeting the learning needs of a new, first-generation population.

Mission and Unique Qualities

A Bay Path University education is intended to empower students to become leaders in their careers and communities so that they can use innovative approaches to learning and flourish in a constantly changing world. This experience is designed to be transformational. Our women-only undergraduate programs and our coeducational graduate programs are offered both on campus and online, enhancing flexibility for learners at all stages of life and career. Bay Path students find a supportive and diverse community, close mentoring, and rigorous preparation for success in a complex and globally interdependent society. Students graduate with the applied knowledge, a portable skill set, and confidence to thrive in their professions, identify and realize their dreams, and make a lasting difference in the world.

Bay Path's mission is designed to ensure that women, particularly those who may be disadvantaged by income, racial discrimination, environment, or other circumstance, have access to a college education, as well as the support to succeed academically, and the opportunities to help them leverage their academic achievement into meaningful career directions. The university serves a traditional undergraduate student population that is predominantly low to moderate income, with 51 percent reporting a family annual income of less than $60,000. According to the institution's recent self-study for accreditation, the majority are the first generation in their families to attend college (65 percent of first-year students) and 43 percent are students of color. Often, these students are likely to enter college underprepared academically and unsure of what to expect from the college experience. Many need to strengthen the writing, presentation, and critical thinking skills essential to college success, yet lack confidence to seek out and use the support and resources they need to adjust to college life and succeed academically. And the vast majority have never had opportunities to cultivate leadership skills or to engage in the personal exploration, self-assessment, and experiential learning that has proven to be transformational for college-going students, especially young women.

With the appointment of a new provost in 2010, a new era of educational transformation began. Based on feedback from faculty and students, a critical priority emerged, namely the transformation of the undergraduate experience to more effectively meet the learning needs of Bay Path's unique student population and enhance student engagement and learning in and beyond the classroom. A nine-month process and two highly collaborative efforts, the Council on Undergraduate Education (CUE) and the Academic Restructuring Team (ART), introduced programs and initiatives that cohered the undergraduate program around the institution's mission, embedded the mission throughout the curriculum, and created a common intellectual experience. The transformation continues to this day, with the outcomes of the work of the CUE and ART now deeply integrated into the undergraduate experience.

A critical first step involved the development of Thumbprint Aspirations. Now in its second iteration, the Thumbprint represents the most fundamental meanings associated with the entire Bay Path educational experience. A product of in-depth research, community input, and clear and genuine institutional introspection, the Thumbprint defines attributes and values reflecting the evolving aspirations of the learning experience for the students Bay Path serves:

- **Highly personalized** in which each student's unique strengths, needs, intentions, passions, and potential are intentionally and fully leveraged;
- **Relevant** with a focus on interdisciplinary learning that is **readily adaptable** to contemporary and emerging issues;
- Delivered within a caring environment that encourages **social awareness** and the confidence and conviction necessary to act upon this awareness **for the good of others**;
- Committed **to empowering** students to take ownership of their lives and learning by engaging them in **transformative, purposeful leadership opportunities**;
- Based on an abundance of **experiential opportunities** that foster self-discovery and **career and life preparation**;
- Dedicated to providing **global, multicultural perspectives** that promote an understanding about one's place in the world and enable one to be ready for whatever challenges the future will bring;
- **Portable** through the development of **flexible, adaptable skill sets** essential for lifelong success.

The Thumbprint finds expression at Bay Path in the curriculum, in co-curricular programming, and in the approaches taken to support students in their educational journey. Most centrally, the Thumbprint is the foundation of Bay Path's institutional learning outcomes and connects these distinctive elements with the whole of the educational experience at the undergraduate and graduate levels (Baypath, 2016). The institution has in place a process to ensure that each aspiration is lived out in tangible ways. Through Bay Path's WELL program and restructured Division of Student Engagement and Liberal Studies, the Thumbprint aspirations are perhaps most intentionally realized.

As part of the transformation process, the undergraduate experience was reviewed to consider programs and initiatives that would have maximum academic and student development impact. National Survey of Student Engagement (NSSE, 2009) data and internal analyses made clear that the integration of high-impact educational experiences, particularly a common intellectual experience for students, would promote stronger engagement and retention. The generative discussions about the optimal solution were predicated on the parallel intention to embed the Association of American Colleges and Universities' (AAC&U) high-impact educational experiences into the curriculum. The outcome was the Women as Empowered Learners and Leaders (WELL) program, which comprises the spine of the core curriculum and creates a laddered model of progressive exposure to both leadership and to the knowledge, skills, and abilities needed for personal and professional success. The overarching goals of the WELL Program are to better meet the learning needs of the student population by: 1) providing a common curricular experience and connect undergraduate students in a very tangible way to the mission and vision of Bay Path University; 2) preparing students to be reflective and capable people, scholars, and professionals who can influence and advocate for others; and 3) enabling students to be more purposeful in shaping their Bay Path undergraduate experience to realize personal, educational, and career aspirations.

Framed as a multi-year and multidimensional experience, the WELL program components are illustrated in the chart below. This chart is used for internal conversations and presentations, but until now has not been published outside the institution (Figure 3.1).

Each of the components of the WELL program is detailed here:

1. **The Academic Component.** Four courses, three of which are embedded within the required core curriculum, frame the academic component of the WELL program:

   a. **WELL 100**

      WELL 100 is offered in the first semester and sections are led by faculty drawn from all disciplines who also serve as first-year advisors. This is where students begin to connect their values with what they want to do; we think of it as connecting passion to potential. Students are introduced to the annual university theme through the first-year read. The book serves as a springboard in the WELL 100 class, where students begin to develop their voice and style through discussions

Women as Empowered Learners and Leaders

Academic Component

A series of four credit-bearing (10 credits total) academic courses that serve as the centerpiece of the core curriculum for all undergraduates.

Intentional, Holistic & Integrated Educational and Career Planning

Educational and career development milestones are embedded throughout the Bay Path University experience and students are engaged through the WELL courses in an intentional process of purposeful planning and goal setting.

Team of Advisors

Through WELL, students are supported by a team of advisors who work together to ensure your success.

Leadership Development

Through a series of experiences, students are guided to develop their own definition of leader and provided a variety of opportunities to develop their unique leadership potential.

Common Intellectual Experiences

Many experiences across the year bring our students together to consider important questions and issues.

Digital Portfolio and Badges

Beginning in WELL 100, students will create a digital portfolio through which they will illustrate their best work and document their growth and development as a learner and leader.

Consolidated and Comprehensive Support Services

Through our highly personalized and technology-infused approach to teaching we work with each student to maximize her potential as an empowered learner.

FIGURE 3.1 WELL Program Components

and writing. A peer mentor, an upper-class student who has taken WELL 100, is assigned to each section to help new students navigate the transition to all aspects of college life, an important first step in gaining confidence.

b. **WELL 200**

This elective course specifically addresses an opportunity for growth in personal presentation skills from which students will benefit. This is where students begin to tell their stories—not just in a classroom, but on stage. WELL 200 is taught in Bay Path's Mills Theatre, home for performing arts events. The audience consists of classmates, and students are asked to consider key questions, such as "How do you present yourself?" "What is your body language?" "How do you relate to your listener?" These are skills they will use in interviewing, networking, and presenting themselves professionally. It's an essential part of building confidence.

c. **WELL 310**

WELL 310 is all about getting ready to launch and preparing for career or graduate school. This course helps students take concrete career steps: interviewing, résumé building, creating a LinkedIn profile, and a portable e-portfolio that represents the student's accomplishments and goals. Throughout the course, students receive feedback from career planning professionals as well as professionals in the student's prospective field.

d. **WELL 400**

In WELL 400, students blend all the skills they have learned during the WELL program—leadership, critical thinking, research, writing, analysis, and public presentation—with a community service project. Empathy, respect, and tolerance are the core human values that are stressed. These qualities are what every good leader needs to confidently show the way. Sections are led by faculty from across the disciplines and offer different themes and levels of involvement with a community project. The course culminates with a group presentation that details the research, achievements, and impact of the project with the community partner. Students also complete, reflect upon, and present their e-portfolios.

2. **Team of Advisors**: Each incoming student has her own personal team of advisors consisting of a full-time faculty member who teaches her WELL 100 section, a peer mentor who is also assigned to her WELL 100 section, a career coach who works out of the Sullivan Career and Life Planning Office, and a faculty member in the anticipated major. Together, these individuals provide a "safety net" and are available to assist, teach, and support throughout the student's entire undergraduate experience.

3. **Learning to Lead**: Through experiences that are woven into the classroom and community projects, students are introduced to the concept of self-leadership, or the idea that through self-growth and mentoring, they should become leaders in their own lives who can also strongly advocate for others.

Students are guided to develop their own definition of leadership and helped to define their own personal leadership style. They are exposed to role models through various academic assignments and experiential learning opportunities, such as Bay Path's annual Women's Leadership Conference.

4. **Digital Portfolio and Badging**: Beginning in WELL 100 and culminating in WELL 400, students create digital portfolios that document their growth as learners and leaders. Very much akin to a digital diary, the eportfolio holds the student's research papers, reflections on career exploration experiences such as job shadowing and internships, awards and recognitions, leadership experiences, as well as photos and videos. Additionally, students have the opportunity to earn and post digital badges to document attainment of skills and learning in areas that are directly related to Bay Path's institutional learning outcomes as well as marketable skill and knowledge areas. Upon graduation, the e-portfolio and badges are proof of all that the student has learned and achieved—both in and out of the classroom—while at Bay Path.

5. **Common Intellectual Experiences**: An annual university theme program provides a unifying concept around which a host of events, lectures, class assignments, common readings, student essays, and discussions are offered during the academic year. The university theme addresses an enduring issue or question pertaining to the role of women as learners and leaders, with a new theme each year. The culminating event of this program is the annual Academic Achievement Day, where students present their work. The campus community, nonprofit partners, and family members are invited to attend.

6. **Career Development and Support**: As NSSE results revealed a gap in the number of Bay Path students who discussed career plans with a faculty member or advisor, the university embedded the development of career goals in WELL to provide opportunities for faculty to discuss career planning with students throughout their four years. Career development milestones are set as part of the e-portfolio to help students stay on track. Through WELL course assignments, internships, field placement experiences, job shadowing, career seminars, mock interviews, and other career development experiences, students are helped to identify and fully leverage their unique strengths, needs, intentions, passions, and potential.

7. **Unified Support Services**: Through the state-of-the-art Learning Commons, academic support is available for all students in all courses at all times. Students have access to a wide range of academic writing, learning, and study strategies through assistance of peer tutors, learning coaches, and special sessions. All incoming students are provided with an iPad and faculty in many classes have embedded the use of the iPad as a critical learning tool.

Since the initiation of the WELL program, first- to second-year retention of first-time, full-time students has increased from 74 percent (Fall 2011 Cohort) to 79 percent (Fall 2015 Cohort), suggesting that the redesigned undergraduate experience is indeed creating the conditions for students to be successful and to establish the necessary foundation for persistence.

As the WELL program developed, and an increase in retention was noted, and as the impact of collaborative student support efforts was clarified, Bay Path continued to refine the undergraduate experience to reflect the Thumbprint Aspirations. Because the WELL program combined resources and best practices from academics and student life, the institution considered how to more fully ensure a seamless and comprehensive student learning experience. For this reason, Bay Path elected to merge aspects of academic affairs and all of student life in support of learner-centered, holistic development. A new division emerged from a process wherein several administrators, staff, and faculty listened carefully to Bay Path students through what they shared in their academic work in the WELL program, through circles of influence exercises organized by an external marketing consultant, and through student survey data such as the graduating senior survey and the NSSE. Students described a remarkably unified experience in which all aspects of campus life, whether it be in the classroom, on the athletic field, through a leadership experience, field work, or a social event, combined and contributed to learning and personal development. Thus, Bay Path sought to align resources to better leverage curricular and co-curricular opportunities. Knowing that students who engage in high impact educational practices, including first-year and capstone classes, research projects with faculty, travel, learning community experiences, service-learning, and writing-intensive courses, learn more deeply, persist in greater numbers, and develop lifelong learning habits, Bay Path realigned part of its institutional structure.

Structural Reorganization

Now in its second year, the Division of Student Engagement and Liberal Studies was created by merging the areas where students reported impactful overlap and success: Liberal Studies houses many of the faculty who teach first-year students as well as high enrollment core curriculum courses, including WELL and introductory writing courses. The Liberal Studies area also houses travel opportunities, such as the successful history course/travel experiential partnership called One America, and the Bay Path general education core curriculum, performing arts, and the honors and writing programs. By melding areas and pooling resources, the university aims to prompt deeper and more meaningful collaboration among staff, faculty, and students and encourage students to engage in myriad opportunities.

The creation of a division to bring together student life and key components of academics at Bay Path was intended to support the following benefits:

- Deepen opportunities for student engagement, student success, and holistic development to ensure that learners have transformative, cohesive educational experiences;

- Align student learning outcomes for the undergraduate experience;
- Improve student access to programs and services;
- Align resources, including and especially the talent of faculty and staff;
- Merge the strengths gleaned from best practices in student affairs (e.g., community building, understanding of student development, etc.) with best practices in academic affairs (e.g., assessment, understanding of teaching and learning);
- Improve efficiency and communication among areas.

The positive effects of participation in the WELL program are becoming clearer now that the program is fully implemented. The class of 2015 was the first to graduate having completed all required components of the WELL curriculum. While analyses of the effects of the program will be conducted over a longer time horizon, qualitative information in the form of student comments in WELL 400 represent a synopsis of the transformational nature of the program. One student added these remarks to her eportfolio reflection paper:

> I never really thought about how much I was really going to learn in college. I knew I was going to obtain a degree someday but none of my cognitive reserves were going to the meaning behind it all. I learned about who I am as a person, student, and a leader.

Throughout its evolution, Bay Path has responded to external and internal influences to provide an individualized, quality education. The more recent focus on the undergraduate experience, including the creation of the WELL program and the Division of Student Engagement and Liberal Studies, is in response to and preparation for changes in student needs and objectives as well as calls for evidence of the value of a college degree. With a clear mission and Thumbprint aspirations, Bay Path intends to continue to meet the needs of today's learners and leaders.

References

Bay Path University. (2016). *Bay Path self-study for accreditation.* Longmeadow, MA: Author.

National Survey of Student Engagement (NSSE). (2009). *Bay Path College institutional report.* Bloomington, IN: Indiana University Center for Postsecondary Research and Planning.

4

TRANSFORMING A TECHNICAL COLLEGE INTO AN APPLIED LEARNING INSTITUTION

Michael R. Laliberte

Leaders in higher education, especially those with a background in student affairs, bring an exciting and novel perspective to the changing landscape of colleges and universities. They are in positions to restructure higher education in ways that will enhance student learning, both inside and outside of the classroom. Here is the story of how one vice president of student affairs, who transitioned to a college presidency, is trying to accomplish this task.

Introduction

Like many in our country, I come from humble beginnings. I grew up in a small working-class community in New England, where both of my parents had been raised. First-generation Americans, and first-generation high school graduates, they both worked blue-collar jobs. My mother was a telephone operator, and my father worked in a textile mill. The main aspiration they had for their four children was to "find a path to a better life." This meant that we (especially their three sons) were expected to seek out a union or government job. Although I wanted that path to a better life, I was curious enough to seek out other routes. I saw higher education as one of those routes. So, throwing all caution to the wind, I applied to our state university. I was not really sure what I was doing or, for that matter, why. However, I did know that I always enjoyed learning and that educated people seemed to get better jobs. I wanted more out of my life, and I believed that somehow higher education might offer me that opportunity.

Thanks to the Federal Pell Grant and student loan programs, I was one of the first members of our extended family to enroll in college. However, like so many other first-generation college students, I found that college was not without its obstacles. I quickly learned that I had no idea how to navigate the world of higher education. As a result, my first wake-up call was discovering that I had no residence hall room, because I did not know that you had to submit a housing application in addition to the college application. And to make matters more complicated, the residence halls were full, and the only thing to do was to put my name on a waiting list. To top it all off, I was without a class schedule, because I had left new student orientation early in order to make alternative housing arrangements on or near campus.

Since my family home was so far from the college, and I was without a car, I knew I had to find something either close to campus or on a bus line. I was fortunate to find out that some of the fraternity houses on campus took in non-member borders for a semester or a year (as it helped in recruiting new members). My only frame of reference for fraternities was the movie *Animal House*, and that didn't seem all that bad, so I knocked on doors until I found the first place that was available, signed a contract, and considered myself lucky. Next, I had to figure out how to sign up for classes and which to take. With the help of my newfound friends in the fraternity house, I learned about the university course catalog and fall course schedule—tools that I would need to master in order to be a fully enrolled student. On registration day, I packed up my notes, pencils, and new guidebooks, and marched off to the university gym. Armed with a positive attitude and a purpose, I waited in lines, begged instructors, and cajoled my way throughout process, emerging three hours later with my first official registration card for 15 credits. I didn't know it at the time, but this perseverance and determination would prove valuable during my college years. It would also become a defining leadership quality for my life and career.

Student Affairs/Higher Education

My relationship with higher education and the field of student affairs began in those early undergraduate days. Since I did not want anyone to know that I was the only person on campus who did not understand the college system, I learned as much as possible, and as quickly as I could. I pretended to know what I didn't; I absorbed information like a sponge; and I observed and copied those I saw as successful. Soon, I acted like I was at ease and that I belonged. Still unsure about my place and function within this new world, I refused to let that be known. I eagerly sought out opportunities to learn. I attended meetings. I worked as a student manager in the student union. I joined the fraternity where I was living— and I even went to class. But as my grade point average would reflect, I did not put the same effort and determination into my studies as I did my social and leadership development.

I was captivated by this world of higher education. I even became a new student orientation leader, spending the entire summer welcoming new students to the campus. I joined the student senate, chairing a committee that planned our senior year, senior week, and commencement activities. Little did I know that

I was discovering a profession that, up until this point in my life, I had no idea even existed. I clearly recall a defining moment in this realization, when I sat down with the advisor of one of my groups. She was a *student affairs professional* (but I did not yet know those words), and I asked her how I could get a job like hers. She told me about graduate school programs and traditional pathways to the profession. I knew that was the road I wanted to take. But it took me over eight years to gather the courage and confidence to apply to graduate programs and get back on the path to the profession that I believe was my calling in life.

The Presidency Background

I spent over 25 years as a student affairs professional, moving through various roles, in a variety of departments, at both private and public institutions. I was very fortunate to be mentored by some outstanding individuals and was privileged to be a member of some outstanding teams, doing incredible work with students. I served as a Senior Student Affairs Officer (SSAO) for more than 12 years, first at a medium-sized public institution, and then at a large public institution. These experiences provided me with solid insight regarding my leadership skills and shortcomings, and further strengthened my commitment to students and their success.

I soon learned, however, that not all members of university senior administrations shared my views and values. From my broad experiences, I found that many individuals had limited contact with students and were not aware of students' struggles to find success. And I found even fewer individuals who understood and were concerned about the real-life difficulties that students faced on a daily basis. I often realized that I was the sole voice speaking on the evolving needs of our students, and calling into question our institutional responsibility to provide resources and assistance to them. Don't get me wrong; I did find some incredibly hard-working, committed individuals at every institution at which I was employed. But I was, perhaps naively, surprised that this was not the norm. I realized that if I were to continue my work in higher education, I must be willing to put myself and my values out there and be committed as a leader to providing vision to an organization that shared my passion for student success.

The Process

I began my quest for a presidency about ten years before I actually submitted an application. Like any good student affairs professional, I did my research. I took the time to speak with many people, gathering ideas, looking at postings, observing behaviors, noting actions, and examining campus happenings and responses. I spoke to mentors and colleagues, obtaining their feedback, opinions, and advice. I attended leadership programs and participated in groups for aspiring presidents. I did self-evaluations, worked on professional action plans, and sought out new experiences and opportunities. I tried to be as fully prepared as possible for what I saw as an exciting experience, but I had completely underestimated the heavy demands of the search process.

I discovered that the experience of applying for a college presidency was unlike any other process in my career. For me, it began with quite a bit more introspection than was necessary in my searches for an SSAO position. In my presidential searches, while institutional type and values were important, I also considered location, portfolio, and sitting leader's vision. In order to imagine myself as that leader with a vision, I considered a number of questions: What type of institution do I feel that can truly represent? What types of academic programs are prominent? What is the typical student profile? What institutional values are most important to me? The process of answering these questions helped me with imagining myself as the leader, but it also begged more questions: What type of leader do I want to be? What is my leadership style? How will I be similar to or different from others before me? How will I bring my unique experiences to the presidency, in order to positively impact student success? I came to the realization that if I truly saw myself as a leader, I needed to make sure that I knew myself as a person. I needed to know, understand, and embrace my passions. I also needed to be aware of my shortcomings, triggers, and ambivalences. Exploring these questions gave me a solid foundation on which to map out my future as a college president. They were also helpful in more practical matters, such as applications and interviews. And this process increased the likelihood that I would be selected to lead an institution that clearly matched my strengths, values, commitments, and style. I am proud to say that where I have landed as a president is a student-centered institution, focused on students' personal and professional development and success. I became the president of the State University of New York at Delhi in July 2016. SUNY Delhi was founded in 1913 in Delhi, New York (present population 5,000) as an agricultural school. The college has a student body of just over 3,500, representing virtually every county in New York State. Delhi's students reflect the diversity of the state's population; students of color account for approximately 35 percent; 58 percent are first-generation students; and over 60 percent are Pell Grant eligible. Delhi offers certificate programs, associate degrees, bachelor's degrees, and online degrees, including a master's. Delhi is known for its commitment to providing a student-centered, residential collegiate experience that focuses on academic excellence, innovation, and experiential learning.

The Listening Tour

Introduction

The most important leadership skill that I embraced as I began my new position as college president was listening. I had been advised by many individuals to hone this skill as soon as I was appointed president, even before arriving on campus.

Listening and observing is something that I was conditioned to do throughout my career. As a student affairs professional, I had taken all of the required counseling courses that taught us to be good listeners. As an academic advisor, I learned to listen and focus on what students were saying, as well as be attuned to what they were not saying. As a student government advisor, I often assessed situations based solely on a few spoken words, silences, or body language. I also learned, especially as a campus judicial officer, to pick up on nuances, to seek out more than one source, and to refrain from making a decision until all information was gathered. I learned to sharpen these skills through my interactions with students, faculty, parents, neighbors, alumni, and all of the different constituent groups that we deal with on a regular basis. My student affairs training provided me with a solid set of skills on which to approach my new position.

As the new leader of the institution, I needed to maximize my active listening skills with members of the campus community. This required me to put aside all preconceived notions about the institution, to not take into account all of the "inside information" that helpful individuals who knew the campus were sharing, and most of all to practice biting my tongue and opening my ears. Although many individuals were seeking my input on various issues, I had to feel comfortable with sitting back, listening to them, and then gathering more information before providing a response. I found that this process allowed me to "sleep on it" and examine requests from multiple perspectives. It took me back to my judicial affairs role, as I looked at and for alternatives, sought input, and carefully processed the information that was shared with me. I quickly learned to reincorporate this approach into my daily routine, and it has made quite a difference. And to publicly and formally acknowledge this approach, I initiated a campus listening tour.

The Process

Wanting a very visible and open process (and using some of my student affairs skills), I decided to brand my listening tour like a music concert tour. I had a name, logo, posters, and even t-shirts with the dates and locations on the back. Although these may seem like minor details, I found that the process needed its own identity and focus, rather than just another opportunity to meet with the new campus leader. I set up 28 sessions and advertised two weeks before they started. I held these sessions on different days of the week, at different times of the day, and in different academic buildings and residence halls. I reached out to students, faculty, and staff, but also held listening sessions off campus for the community, alumni, and friends of the institution. Online forums were set up for those who taught or studied using only that platform.

I opened each session by reading the same set of ground rules: be honest and respectful; give examples of what you mean; take turns sharing ideas, comments, or answers; everyone participates; no one dominates; keep your responses brief and to the point; everyone's opinion is valuable; and don't be afraid to repeat ideas.

I further explained the process: I was there to listen and not speak. I did not ask for individuals to introduce themselves, trying to keep comments anonymous. A note-taker also attended each session, to record comments and capture the essence of the conversation, freeing me up to actively listen.

I also held open forums at the start of the new semester in order to share with the community what I had heard, my reactions, major themes, and my vision for moving forward. I used the same questions, in the same order, for each session: What do you see as the major strengths and assets of our institution? What do you believe are the major challenges for our institution? What are your hopes and dreams for our institution five to ten years from now? What, if any, are your concerns about our institution's future? What would you want me to know about our institution that I may not know to ask?

Benefits

This process proved to be an incredibly effective and useful tool. Every session provided insight into individuals' observations and interpretations of the institutional culture. While one might expect that, given the opportunity, people would speak only about the problems and negative experiences that they have had, I found quite the opposite. Feedback was balanced, if not tipped toward the positive. Participants' comments not only helped me to better understand the campus issues, concerns, and problems, but also provided me with an understanding of the actual and perceived history of the institution. I learned quite a bit by just watching how students, faculty, and staff interacted in these sessions. These gatherings gave me a perfect opportunity to observe, through their behavior, how various individuals characterized their roles on campus. They also showed me how others perceived those roles, such as when supervisors were in attendance with members of their staff. All of the information, both spoken and observed, afforded me an incomparable opportunity to better understand not only the culture of the institution, but to observe some of the community's cultural norms by seeing people in their element.

Observations

Initially, when I began this process, my expectations for gathering useful data were rather low. I believed that there would be few issues brought to light, and that they would be repeated in most groups, so I would need to look for other ways to gather information. Well, I was mistaken. The abundant and valuable data that I gathered from interacting with and observing over 500 members of our campus community was unparalleled. I can honestly say that from every single session, I able to gather some new piece of information. Whether it was a small fact about the campus, or insight into how particular policy was enacted, or why a specific procedure was put into place, people were more than willing to share constructive feedback on how they perceived the college. They provided honest and thoughtful examples of their ideas, as well concrete illustrations of what they had experienced. They were given the opportunity to display pride in their community as well as their individual and collective accomplishments. Through both declarative statements and vivid examples, participants demonstrated their deep-seated commitment to our students and their success. As anticipated, they also identified many needs for the campus, from facilities to human resources, but always with the understanding that all could not be resolved overnight. I must admit that I wasn't sure how people would behave if given the opportunity to speak their minds. I am pleased to discover that, if provided with a clear structure and an open ear, people will offer their honest thoughts, ideas, and impressions.

Major Themes

As a result of this process, many concepts, ideas, challenges, and perceptions were shared. Many of the comments were directed to particular situations on our campus, but the major themes that were revealed are relevant to most institutions.

Community

One of the most consistent messages in these forums was related to community. In each and every session, someone brought up the topic and, for the most part, it was presented as both an asset and a deficit. Those who saw community as an asset described the close-knit family feeling of being on campus. Others went on to share that the relationships they have with colleagues and students were one of the reasons they chose higher education as a career path. They also enjoyed the complexity of these relationships, including the various roles that they play in each other's lives. Among the identified deficits were training and resources. Although individuals generally had a clear understanding of the complex nature of our work in higher education, they realized that students (and sometimes colleagues) had needs that were outside of the traditional scope of academia. For example, in meeting with students for academic advising, any topic could arise, including topics not at all related to advising.

For most individuals, the listening sessions were valuable, but they could be unsettling. Some in attendance felt that they did not have the tools to adequately address the needs of students and sometimes colleagues. Generally, they believed that it was part of their responsibility as community members to provide input and support when these needs arose. I was very pleased to hear this commitment to supporting our students, which is part of our student-centered philosophy at SUNY Delhi. And I recognize the lack of resources and the importance of comprehensive training for faculty and staff within our institution. In many ways, I see these relationships that have developed among faculty, staff, and students functioning as a twenty-first century version of the traditional dean of students role.

Students have significant existing relationships with campus administrators through academic advising, financial aid advising, first-year seminars, or any other caring connection on campus. However, we need to transform those relationships to meet student needs. Consequently, it is essential that we support all members of the academic community with the resources and training necessary to successfully manage these relationships.

Following the listening sessions, I announced the development of the Center for the Collective Pursuit of Academic and Social Support (C-PASS), which will have two distinct functions: 1) It will function as a resource for students, linking them with peer mentors who will guide them through the collegiate experience. It will also connect students to academic advising, academic support services, and tutoring, as well as the non-academic areas of campus, such as housing, financial affairs, and health and counseling services. 2) It will provide members of the campus community with professional development opportunities focusing on the developmental and social needs of students. One of the major goals of the C-PASS initiative is to be a bridge between the students' academic and social development needs. Student affairs professionals understand the numerous obstacles that students face (especially first-generation and low income students) as they attempt to successfully navigate the system of higher education. While some of these obstacles are developmental in nature, others are more tangible (e.g., health issues, housing, food, etc.). C-PASS will use an integrated services model to address these needs so students can be successful, both inside and beyond the classroom. Through this collaborative approach, we hope to remove barriers that prevent students from being fully engaged in the learning process.

Excellence

Another consistent theme was excellence—academic excellence, pride in the diverse course offerings, students bragging about the outstanding support they receive from the faculty and staff, the exceptional reputation the institution has in the local community, and how gratified the faculty felt when struggling students mastered their subject. While I was overwhelmed with pride as people talked so positively about our institution, I was somewhat perplexed at the same time. I appreciated the accolades and praise bestowed upon the students, faculty, and staff, but this theme was not apparent in campus daily life. Nor was this sense of excellence captured in any of the campus publications, the campus website, or visible in any way on campus tours. And while appreciative of this quality, most individuals were simultaneously concerned about the institution's ability to maintain the same level of quality into the future. They were afraid that new members of the community would not share their passion, and that the institution's limited resources would not be directed at activities to support this cultural norm.

I assured the community that I was aware of their concern. And that while there are budgetary constraints on every campus, we as a community could prioritize our investments in order to preserve this campus value. I suggested that we establish, in addition to C-PASS, a Center for Excellence in Teaching and Learning (CETL), providing the faculty with the tools they need to create and maintain an outstanding learning environment. CETL will offer faculty teaching consultations and observations; educational technology training and support; programs and events, including workshops, orientations, and institutes. It will promote pedagogy that is inclusive and student-centered. And it will share knowledge about college student development with the faculty. As student affairs professionals, we are trained in student development, understanding the changing needs of the student population, and prepared to "meet students where they are." Most faculty members are not exposed to student development research, which sometimes results in their frustration with students or worse—disengagement. This center will help the faculty better engage with students both inside and outside the classroom and, as a result, enhance the students' overall learning experience.

The concept for C-PASS and CETL stems from feedback from students at one of the listening sessions. These students were frustrated with a faculty member who was using "a new technique," having students watch an online video before class, with the expectation that the students would discuss what they learned in the next class session (sometimes referred to as a flipped classroom). The students were frustrated because they expected the faculty member to deliver a lecture, assign readings, and for them to be tested on the material. They were not prepared for a discussion on the topic. After closer inquiries, I found that while the faculty member was trying to engage students at a different level of learning, the students did not have the tools they needed to feel comfortable with the activity. The identification of both student and faculty needs led to the development of these centers. Cooperatively, they perform a critical role in the development and improvement of student learning at our institution. In order for our students to experience success, we need a faculty that not only possesses outstanding teaching tools, but also fully understands the learning process so they can provide students with the resources and strategies that will lead to success. The linking of these two centers will give a more consistent approach to enhancing and supporting student and faculty development. From a structural perspective, I was able to launch these centers at little new cost to the institution, capitalizing on existing expertise, and refocusing individual resources toward the more comprehensive goal of overall student success.

Diversity

Another issue that consistently arose from these discussions was the concept of diversity. I use the word "concept" because one message repeated throughout these sessions was that a uniform definition of diversity does not exist. Some individuals discussed the diversity of our community, identifying race and ethnicity. Others talked about the diversity of ideas and academic offerings.

And still others focused on the diverse socioeconomic make-up of our community. While there existed a deep appreciation for the benefits of diversity, some struggled with trying to be all-inclusive, but often feeling like they were coming up short. This led to some healthy and challenging discussions. Although this was not the intent of these sessions, it did provide a good starting point for future conversations. Our next steps include both formal and informal opportunities to connect with me and other members of our administrative team to discuss and explore a broad spectrum of topics related to diversity and inclusion.

As follow-up to these sessions, it was important for me to take a leading role in identifying the lack of cohesiveness, as well as the willingness of individuals to be engaged in discussions. As a result, I have created the Division of Diversity, Equity, and Inclusion on our campus. This vice president-led division, while still in the development stage, will be the campus leader for diversity initiatives. These will include services and programs for members of our community from historically marginalized groups, providing campus-wide trainings and resources, and engaging the entire academic community in structured and unstructured "Campus Conversations" regarding issues of diversity. As a campus, we need to be prepared to support students as they develop their identities, ever-ready and always inclusive of their needs.

The creation of this division within the university structure, while perhaps not groundbreaking, is essential to the growth of our community, which, like many in the U.S., has become increasingly diverse over these past few years. The definition of diversity has also broadened, and we have become more accepting of the notion that one's identity can be fluid and can change over time. Consequently, we need to be very intentional in providing opportunities for students to explore their present and emerging identities. This exploration (or at times lack of exploration) could impede a student's ability to be fully engaged in the learning process. By purposefully helping students to discover their own concepts of self and identity, we hope to remove potential barriers that would prevent students from being engaged in curricular or co-curricular learning processes.

Institutional Identity

One of the most concerning themes that came up during the listening tour was about our campus identity. When the institution was founded, it was based on the agriculture and technology model from the late nineteenth and early twentieth centuries. At the time, this model made sense, as the majority of the jobs in the surrounding areas were in these fields. However, as many of the small farms were bought up or closed down, the focus of the institution shifted to emerging fields of manufacturing, applied technologies, animal care, hospitality, and business. Within the state system of higher education, we are still classified uniquely as an applied technology institution. While some individuals understand this terminology, many others are confused by it. It is often equated with technology schools or polytechnics (neither of which describes us). Additionally, the state system of higher education has four categories for its institutions: Research, Comprehensive, Community College, and Tech Sector (we are classified as Tech Sector). This categorization is not only confusing to most people outside of the institution; it is also difficult for most college community members to understand and articulate. Often, I find community members describing us as what we are not: "Well, we are not a community college, but we offer associate degree programs; we are not a comprehensive, but we offer. . . ." This lack of a common yet distinct definition has created uncertainty and confusion for the institution, resulting in a bit of an inferiority complex. This also reflects what I see as an identity crisis in higher education. I find that so many institutions compare themselves to their "aspirational peers," rather than looking at themselves to see who they truly are.

Although this is not a situation that is easily remedied, I have begun the process of helping our community to imagine/reimage our identity. We are an institution that prides itself on its commitment to student success. We adapt and flex to keep up with changing industries and demands. Every program we offer includes a hands-on learning experience. We need to embrace these qualities as strengths, in order create our own identity within the state system and the nation. As an ever-evolving applied-learning community, where student success is our most important value, we must continue to explore how we define ourselves, and how others define us. To that end, we will eventually arrive at a definition that embraces our historical roots and defines our vision for the future.

An additional aspect of institutional identity came up when I was providing feedback to the campus. I mentioned the disconnect between the campus's view of itself and the general public's impression of the campus, which came as a surprise to many members of the community. The campus prides itself on being a student-centered, innovative institution, with a unique mission and vision unlike most other institutions of higher education. And while that definition is entirely accurate, it is not how we depict or portray ourselves to the general public. Most of our printed materials and media are very conventional, as are our campus activities and celebrations. As an institution, we have not embraced the uniqueness of our programs, students, and community. As an example, at the first commencement that I oversaw, I commented on how stoic and traditional I found the ceremony. But when leaving the arena, I encountered members of one of our historically African-American fraternities outside in the parking lot. They were showcasing a step-show performance for their families and friends. There was cheering and clapping; it appeared to be a very joyous event. That is when I realized what was missing from the commencement ceremony—celebration. Our students are unique, often the first in their family to complete a degree. They have stories of hardship, struggles, and commitment. Our ceremony should not only acknowledge their accomplishments, but also celebrate their journey to achieve success. While we will still wear gowns and mortarboards at commencement, we will now honor the journeys that students take in order to arrive at that ceremony. We have started to engage students in defining what should be included in the celebration, and if that includes a step-dance performance, so be it. Additionally, we are looking at other traditional college activities, giving ourselves license to explore the possibility of creating our own unique version of them, so as to accurately represent our community.

Next Steps

Our institution is primed and ready to begin thinking and acting strategically. Here is a brief outline of how we will begin to address this process, ever aware of our need to stay true to our institutional values and mission, while preparing ourselves to continue our success in a dynamic and changing society.

Assess and Prioritize

The first step in the strategic planning process is to be sure that the institution is ready to engage in such a process. For that reason, we are gathering our various institutional plans, discovering which, if any, are disconnected. Each campus plan should be interconnected with the others, and should inform the next steps in the process. For instance, a student enrollment plan cannot stand alone, and must inform both the academic program and facilities master plans. How can you attract more students without academic programs or more classrooms? If you create new academic programs, where will the students come from and where will they study? Each individual plan should provide guidance to the other campus plans. The process of assessing and prioritizing these plans will assist in the development of a comprehensive campus strategic plan.

A Culture of Change

Whenever an organization brings on a new leader, it has a response. For most organizations, there is excitement and anticipation, while at the same time a fear of the unknown. How will this leader be different from the last? What will change? What will stay the same? As a new leader, one should prepare the community to embrace change. In order to achieve this, the leader needs to be direct with the community, focusing on what its various constituencies know about the past and how they envision moving forward. As mentioned earlier, the technique that I find most useful is simply listening to members of the community, in order to begin the all-important process of building relationships. These relationships are not only critical to the success or failure of any proposed changes, but can also ensure that they are grounded within community values. Often, people fear that leaders are making changes for no apparent reason. Connecting proposed changes to gathered data and formed relationships provides solid reasoning, but also nurtures the community value that change is positive and not something to be feared.

A Future-Focused Community

As professionals in higher education, we must accept the fact that our field is not static, but always evolving. As new technologies are introduced, new discoveries are made, and old knowledge becomes obsolete, people seek out new knowledge. Consequently, colleges and universities need to adapt if they wish to maintain their success. As student affairs professionals, we are very accustomed to the changing nature of society and have learned to adjust accordingly. This has required us to be present in the moment, providing care and service to our students, while simultaneously focusing on events that will impact our futures and the futures of the students we serve. To inform the planning process and assist with the introduction of new and exciting advances in teaching and learning, higher education communities should share this forward-thinking approach.

Reflection

Looking back on these past six months, I do not believe I could have predicted how it would turn out. I always try to be optimistic when venturing into the unknown, and I knew this experience was going to be unlike any in my past. But I discovered that I was better prepared than I had anticipated. I owe much of this to my experiences in student affairs, which provided me with a solid foundation and allowed me to grow and change throughout my career. In student affairs, I explored all aspects of the academy, including my passion for learning. As student affairs professionals, we are expected to not only have knowledge of the direct units that we oversee, but to understand the functions and purposes of all areas that affect students' lives. A colleague once reminded me that to successfully serve students, we, as student affairs professionals, must not only learn to speak the language of students; we must also be well-versed in the language of the faculty and staff. The analogy of being a multi-linguist in "campus-speak" addresses the fundamental principle of the student affairs profession, which is to create opportunities for students to fully develop their minds, bodies, and spirits. I have incorporated this perspective into each of my professional roles, and it has served me well as a campus leader. Student affairs has allowed me to become fluent in the multiple languages of higher education, providing me with a unique perspective on a student-centered approach to teaching and learning. It has also created opportunities for me to learn *about* students, *from* students. As a result, I became a more effective professional, a better leader, and a better person.

SECTION II

Frameworks that Shape Teaching and Learning

SECTION II

5

CULTURAL TRADITIONS AND ASSUMPTIONS ABOUT LEARNING

Jane Fried

Cultures tend to function like fishbowls (Fried, 2016). Within one's own primary culture, it is difficult to be aware of embedded norms, values, traditions, or belief systems. Every culture attempts to explain its origins through its *cosmology* (world creation story) and transmit its values through its *mythology* (symbolic stories that are told to the young and within the community to convey the collective wisdom). Cultural approaches to *pedagogy and epistemology* (methods for deciding what knowledge is reliable and methods for conveying that knowledge to the young) are used to teach children what to believe and how to think, while cultural *ethics* convey the rules of right and wrong that govern behavior within the community. We tend to absorb elements of our primary culture on an unconscious level and often are unable to articulate them when asked to do so (Polanyi, 1967). Awareness generally does not arise until a person from one culture tries to interact with a person from another and is unsuccessful despite the best intentions. A simple example from the dominant American culture is greeting style. Handshaking is normal for most Americans, but it is not acceptable across gender with observant Muslims. So if a naïve American sticks out a hand to a Muslim person of the opposite gender and the person refuses the handshake, confusion ensues and can lead to all kinds of misunderstandings.

Academia has its own dominant culture and innumerable subcultures as well. For people who have spent most of their adult lives working in higher education, the norms of the cultures may be both invisible and taken for granted. For historical reasons, the intellectual norms of higher education, particularly in most faculty cultures, are grounded in the epistemology of the Enlightenment, buttressed by the Cartesian mind/body split and embedded in the assumptions of positivism. Even though Heisenberg's uncertainty principle, first published in 1925, demonstrated that the knower inevitably interacts with and influences the known, on a mundane basis it seems as if most people believe that subject and object are separate and non-interactive. The common use of the phrase "high impact practices" illustrates this perspective, since it implies that a practice used on or with a particular student or population is an external event that moves consciousness like a billiard ball. High impact implies the subject object/split and uses the notion, embedded in English grammar, of subject-action-object. While perspective is often taken into account when describing situations, there is still the assumption that objective truth, or accuracy, exists in an external world separate from perception and interpretations. Of course, there are exceptions to this framework, particularly the post-modernist schools of thought in the social sciences and the humanities, but these are at variance with the dominant belief system. Briefly, the dominant positivist academic belief system includes separation of subject and object or the knower and the known, the assumption that cognition can be separated from emotion in the learning process, and that context should be irrelevant to facts as they are learned. This is an oversimplification, but provides the skeleton for understanding.

Western Cultural Assumptions about Learning

The notion of how accurate information comes to be known is a major aspect of what is considered learning. If subject and object are separate and emotions interfere with cognition, then teaching and learning should be framed by this set of assumptions. Every effort should be made to keep personal perspectives or ideas based on individual experience out of the learning process; they are assumed to interfere with accuracy of perception. Belief in autonomy is also foundational to American culture and to most pedagogical approaches. The assumption of individual autonomy governs most elements of American life, including the way that most universities operate. Despite the pervasive assignment of group projects, most key elements of a student's postsecondary experience are individual, from admission, to assessment, to awarding of degrees. Therefore, one of the ways that the culture of academia can be described is that of separation and, inferentially, competition for dominance. If there is only one right answer or accurate perspective, that perspective can be expected to "win" in any competition. Students are considered separate from the information they are expected to learn. They are separate from each other in their progress toward degree attainment, often set into competition for grades achieved and class rank. Ever since Ronald Reagan, as governor of California in 1967, declared that society could not afford to support intellectual curiosity (Berrett, 2015), achievement of degrees has been tied to autonomy. The purpose of college became one of job training, investment in one's personal financial future. Attendance was no longer a publicly supported investment in developing the skills and knowledge of the next generation of citizens and workers for the welfare of the larger society.

There are two groups of reasons that provide a foundation for challenging the assumptions about learning that tend to govern American higher education: 1) recent developments in the scientific understanding of the learning process including the roles of self-authorship (Baxter & Magolda, 1999) and metacognition; and 2) the increasing presence of students on our campuses who are members of non-Eurocentric cultures and have different ideas about teaching, learning, legitimate knowledge, and the roles of both peers and teachers as contributing elements to this process (Chavez & Longerbeam, 2016; Grande, 2004).

Self-Authorship

Self-authorship as a fundamental element of learning is a relatively recent idea. "It is an ability to construct knowledge in a contextual world, an ability to construct an internal identity separate from external influences and an ability to engage in external relationships without losing one's internal identity" (Baxter Magolda, 1999, p. 12). In addition, self-authorship implies "integration of cognitive and affective learning; and action to transform values" (p. 17). This notion closely parallels Mezirow and Associates' (2000) description of transformative learning as moving from "being psychologically 'written by' the socializing press to 'writing upon it'" (p. 59). Kegan's (2000) term for this process is "meaning forming," defined as, "the activity by which we shape a coherent meaning out of the raw material of our inner and outer experience" (p. 52). In describing the various elements of transformative learning, these authors imply that the intellectual process that human beings use to understand their worlds involves developing a sense of personal responsibility for constructing a coherent framework. This framework permits newly acquired information to be filed and integrated into pre-existing knowledge schema, including knowledge about one's sense of self. Such a complex process requires a relatively sophisticated level of cognitive development (Baxter Magolda, 1992). This integrated approach is supported by recent research in cognitive science (Zull, 2002; Siegal, 2007). Fried (2016) has asserted that meaningful learning has four key components: 1) cognition and the acquisition of new information; 2) affect, or a sense of caring about the information; 3) changes in behavior based on the new information and caring about it; and 4) metacognition, an ability to understand why knowing and understanding the information matters in a student's life. The notion of self-authorship requires integrated learning and is a far cry from Descartes's bifurcated idea, "I think therefore I am."

There is a cultural element to self-authorship as part of the framework of understanding how people learn. Baxter Magolda states that students learn to construct an internal identity in a contextual world. The process of self-authorship implies the construction of a separate self in a social or cultural context, but it retains the notion of separate self. This is generally appropriate for students from Eurocentric cultures, but is contradictory to the ways in which students from more collectivist cultures understand themselves in their cultural worlds.

These two assumptions about self that typically operate in the same academic setting lead to contrasting ideas about collaboration. One sense of collaboration is group learning and cooperation. The other is cheating.

Cultural Frameworks for Learning

There are many ways to compare and categorize different cultures. One of the most widely used frameworks establishes a continuum from individualistic to collectivist cultures. Cultures on the individualist side of the spectrum are shaped by the intellectual emphasis of Enlightenment thinking, rely heavily on written communication and contracts, and emphasize materialism, individual ownership, and property rights. Cultures on the collectivist end of the spectrum emphasize community, the power of the spoken word and verbal agreements, collective ownership, and collective responsibility for members of the group. Within each category along this spectrum there are also hierarchical designations to determine which respective elements of a category assume operational priority (Fried, 1995). For example, every culture has a definition of authority, but the designators of authority vary. In some cultures, elders hold authority. In other cultures, rich people or very smart people claim authority. The hierarchy of authority is based on cultural roles and values. Cultures also tend to vary in their notion of time (linear vs. circular), relationship to nature (harmonize or dominate), family structure (nuclear vs. clan or tribe), and assumptions about decision-making methods (hierarchical vs. egalitarian/participatory).

Chavez and Longerbeam (2016) have applied these various cultural assumptions about the ways the world works to the teaching/learning process, both epistemology and pedagogy. They describe the cultural continuum as individuated vs. integrated, which is roughly equivalent to the individualist/collectivist categorization. Their description of the purpose of learning in individuated cultures is "knowledge, individual competence, to move forward toward goals and the betterment of humanity" (p. 8). The purpose of learning in an integrated culture, they say, is "wisdom, betterment of the lives of those with whom we are connected—family, tribe, and community" (p. 8). In individuated cultures, intellect is the only reliable channel for knowledge acquisition. In integrated cultures, "mind, body, spirit/intuition, reflection, emotions, relationships (are) important aspects and conduits of knowledge" (p. 8). Even with this minimal description of cultural differences regarding epistemology and acquisition of knowledge, it becomes apparent that the culture of universities in the United States privileges students from individuated, Eurocentric backgrounds. Educators in American universities tend to teach the way students from Eurocentric backgrounds learn.

Chavez and Longerbeam (2016) also describe the applicability of various approaches to teaching (pedagogy) to the cultural continuum. For example, an individuated approach to describe the purpose of learning is to connect subject matter to future profession or career realities, practices, and expectations, while approaches more suited to integrated cultures would connect subject matter to needs, realities, challenges, or opportunities in local or the student's community, tribe, or family. Learning, in individuated pedagogy, is discussed in relationship to the information presented in class while learning in integrated pedagogy is discussed in relation to the broader context of a student's life, community, values, and career aspirations. Time is also a key element in understanding the range of learning approaches. Individuated learning requires focused, verbal processing of new information until the student can explain what she or he knows in written or verbal form, usually within a designated time frame like a semester. Integrated learning assumes a range of activities associated with the process, including "letting things settle" by walking or doing some other physical activity, imagining why this information might matter to the community, and how the implications of this knowledge might change over time. Integrated learning seems less focused and more contextual, less internal and more broadly applicable to both internal and external concerns of the student. It also happens on its own schedule and is not as amenable to assessment by time-defined examinations.

Learning as experienced by students from integrated cultures seems very closely connected to Baxter Magolda and King's (2004) description of self-authorship, and mirrors in many ways the understanding of learning that is being discovered through the cognitive sciences. Integrated learning is complex, multifaceted, and holistic. It is not linear and does not presume that a student must read Chapter 1 before being able to understand Chapter 2 in a textbook. Learning from written documents is sequential and linear. Learning from electronic media such as webinars, YouTube, or streaming media can much more closely resemble learning in the integrated style. A student can begin viewing at any point and then go to another section for clarification of something that is not understood. Perception and knowledge acquisition in this mode is holistic, visual, auditory, and interactive. Presumably a student who learns in this manner would begin with the subject that is most interesting and then go back for information that cannot be intuited from the presentation.

For example, if a science teacher wants to teach evolution or genetics to her students, she should probably start with sexual reproduction and back up into the variety of ways that reproduction can occur. Anyone who has ever taught 12-year-olds knows that sex, and any activity that provokes awareness of its pleasures, dominates much of 12-year-olds' consciousness for most of their waking hours. After the teacher has "hooked" the students on the intrigues of sexual reproduction across a wide range of species, she probably has a better chance of keeping the students' attention when she moves into the technicalities of genetics. The same approach is true for almost any subject. If a teacher wants students to learn anything meaningful, it is advisable to begin by grounding the learning in areas of student interest and motivation for learning. It is most helpful to identify a problem that a student is facing and relate whatever needs to be taught and learned to help the student solve the problem.

Vignette

I once purchased an instructional DVD about brain function. The teacher was excellent and had all kinds of brain models and animations to help the viewer understand what she was explaining. The problem was that I bought the DVD because I wanted to understand a particular aspect of brain function and dysfunction, particularly mental illness and learning. I had to view several hours of tedious explanations of neurology and physiology before I got close to psychology. I regularly fell asleep while watching this program. In fact, I never made it to the part that had motivated me to buy the DVD! I also realized that I simply could not hold that much neurology in my relatively uneducated brain while I watched and listened to the explanations of the subjects that truly interested me. If I had watched the sections on learning or dementia first, I would have gone back to the sections on neurology and development and learned that information more effectively because I could place it within the context of what I cared about at the moment—no more falling asleep!

In writing the explanation of cultural differences in learning style, I have realized that my own learning style is highly integrated even though I come from an individuated culture. As I have experienced this individuated approach to learning over my own lifetime, I have often been very bored and impatient as I waited for the teacher to get to the point. I have realized that "getting to the point" in my epistemology means telling me how to use the information, why it matters, and what problem it can help me solve. I have also become aware of why I decided that student affairs was a better profession for me than teaching, a personal epiphany!

Student Affairs as an Integrated Culture in the Individuated Academic World

Theoretically, student affairs professionals spend a lot of time and energy learning about and trying to understand cultural differences. Most graduate programs have courses in multiculturalism. Most field experiences involve conversations with and about students from many cultures and variations in approach that are tailored to be appropriate in work with students from contrasting cultural, racial, or religious backgrounds as well as persons of different genders or sexual orientations. We regularly construct educational programs and interpersonal dialogues about difference and support students in their efforts to understand each other.

I have long believed that the epistemology of student affairs is constructivist; that approach to knowledge acquisition and interpretation has disadvantaged the profession in the context of positivist academic culture (Fried & American College Personnel Association, 1995). For example, anybody who has ever attempted to untangle a roommate conflict knows that "truth" is not accessible to the mediator and may not be discoverable. All the mediator has to work with is the perspectives of the participants and a rough consensus about the "facts."

The implications and consequences of the facts are typically a matter of interpretation and negotiation. This type of normal work challenge forces most student affairs professionals into a constructivist posture when attempting to understand information in specific contexts. In the current iteration of this perspective, I can also see that the student affairs culture is integrated rather than individuated under most circumstances. Within the American tradition of dualistic, either/or thinking, knowledge that is acquired through intuition, inference, and observation, such as information about the behavior of individuals, is considered "soft" or anecdotal. Knowledge about facts, information that is acquired intellectually and can be demonstrated empirically, is considered "hard." In this system, hard is always better than soft, despite the fact that employers have told us repeatedly that new hires are more successful if they have the "soft skills" of effective group work than if they have perfect grade point averages in their academic disciplines (Huhman, 2014).

The reality is that student affairs is a bicultural profession. We are always responsible for counting and measuring the infinite numbers of details in student life—costs of events and activities, numbers of beds occupied, numbers of students who attend or participate in our activities and programs, income produced by various events, numbers of students who visit our offices for career or academic advising, and so forth. The current emphasis in higher education on assessment and accountability has forced student affairs as a profession to produce numbers and "facts" about almost everything we do. Of course, we are not opposed to accountability or even to counting. The problem is that producing and analyzing numbers is not the primary reason most student affairs professionals do the work we do. For many of us, that sort of analysis is neither motivating nor satisfying. And does it truly capture the value of our work? After 40 years in this profession, I take the liberty of generalizing to say that most people enter our profession in order to help students and improve the world, preferably both. This kind of motivation is a product of an integrated perspective where everything we do affects everything else we do. We know that when we provide academic coaching to students so that they can become more academically successful, we may not be addressing the real reason they are failing. They may know how to study but not have time because of pressing family issues, a medical condition, or loss of a job. All the skills training in the world won't solve that kind of problem. In some learning centers, advisors are not allowed to even ask about background issues. These advisors, and many of my own students have been in this situation, spend a lot of time trying to find and walk the line that divides academic coaching from counseling, which they cannot do because there is no such line.

Most academic faculty members have no such difficulties in the routine performance of their duties. A student is either passing or failing. She may need a tutoring session or better organizational or study skills. However, success in working with that student has only one measure from the academic side—whether or not the student passes the course. This can be described as a positivist or individuated epistemology. Data generated using this approach are considered far more reliable in academic settings. While it is one measure, it is often incomplete (and thus inaccurate).

Articulating a Pedagogy for Students from Integrated Cultures

When student affairs professionals attempt to share what they know about student learning with academic faculty, we face two challenges: 1) describing what we know about learning styles that are typical of students from integrated cultures; and 2) crossing the boundary between the ways that student affairs professionals teach and learn and the typical methods and epistemologies that academic faculty members use to organize and present content in their academic specialties. Neither of these conversations is easy. The first element must be explicit. The second may simply become awareness in the student affairs professional's mind. I suggest that student affairs practitioners take advantage of the integrated aspects of our own learning style as well as our knowledge of cross-cultural communication when discussing learning with faculty. Start by asking if faculty members have noticed any differences between students of color (or first-generation students) and white students or students from families where members of the previous generation are college educated. Then use the same techniques you would use with students as you develop a relationship and try to identify issues in faculty lives where you might have something to contribute. Student affairs professionals tend to operate as if they were members of integrated cultures. If we want to create connections with faculty members around the subject of learning and cultural differences, the first step is to understand the culture you are entering when you begin the conversation. Most student affairs professionals have this skill. We just don't think of using it when we connect with members of the academic faculty.

At this time, it has become widely accepted that rates of degree completion among students from different demographics tend to vary. White American students tend to graduate at higher levels within a designated period (typically six years) than their peers who are students of color (e.g., African American, Caribbean, Native American, Latino/a/x, etc.). Students from certain parts of Asia (e.g., India, Pakistan, Japan, China, and the Philippine Islands, etc.) tend to graduate at the same or higher rates than both of the previous groups. Typical university and college responses to differential graduation rates tend to focus on academic support (e.g., study skills, time management, the need for active involvement in and regular attendance at classes, etc.), financial aid, and creating peer support for studying. They rarely focus on pedagogy or conversations with faculty members about cultural differences in learning styles. This is an area where members of the student affairs staff can contribute to understanding retention of students from integrated cultures. We may not want to challenge programs that are in place, but using this individuated/integrated continuum, we may be able to contribute insights regarding elements of understanding regarding why the retention rates vary by demographic.

In other areas of pedagogical scholarship, there is a conversation about integrated learning. Palmer and Zajonc (2010) call for the transformation of the academy through conversation, by which they mean dialogue about personal implications of knowledge. They suggest that we should "get beyond the divided academic life" (p. 53) and introduce conversations among all elements of the academic community about the interconnectedness of knowledge; they further stress the importance of learning to live with the consequences and implications of knowledge acquired in a higher education setting. Baxter Magolda (1999) also calls for the creation of a constructive developmental pedagogy that allows students to use what they are learning to create their own understanding of what the knowledge means and how they want to use it in the development of their own sense of self. She particularly describes the use of narrative as a teaching tool to help students both learn to write effectively and to discover their own voices as they become "self-authors" of their own lives.

These authors are implicitly writing about the differences between traditional academic culture and an integrated approach to student learning. Their arguments can easily be supported by brain science and all the neurological information about learning that has appeared in recent decades (Zull, 2002; Jensen, 2000). What is missing in the work of Baxter Magolda and King (2004) and Palmer and Zajonc (2010) is any explicit reference to the various ethnic cultures whose learning styles (epistemology and pedagogy) overlap with the calls for transformation in the teaching learning process. This is not a flaw in their work by any means. It is simply a different focus that has a great deal in common with the work of Chavez and Longerbeam (2016). My suggestion is that student affairs professionals are in an ideal position to bridge this gap in conversations with academic faculty. We can use our knowledge of cultural differences, of learning styles, and of the differing norms of people in academic and student affairs to describe possible changes in pedagogy that have great potential to increase the success of students from integrative cultures—perhaps of all cultures.

The use of narrative in teaching writing provides an excellent example of this bridge. Baxter Magolda (1999) describes a course in narrative writing (pp. 167–203) that has the dual purpose of teaching students how to develop powerful writing skills and also to create the narrative of their own lives, as they have been and as they wish them to evolve. What follows is an example of the use of narrative therapy in a multicultural counseling course as it was used to improve teaching effectiveness.

Vignette

My colleague, who was born in Africa, was one of the most highly educated members of our department. I will call her Dr. Ngyo. She has a bachelor's degree in health from an African university, and three additional degrees in counseling and human resources from American universities. All of her involvement in higher education, both in Africa and the United States, was predicated on the Eurocentric model of teaching, i.e., information transmission. The students liked her, but they objected to many aspects of her teaching. The department decided to try to help her with her teaching, and I volunteered to be her coach. The project was to team teach a multicultural counseling course. We decided that this was a perfect venue because we were a multicultural team and could model what we were helping the students learn. This colleague is also an expert in narrative and group therapy. Her approach to teaching, particularly in theory courses, was the traditional impersonal fact and research based approach of lecturing, stopping to ask questions, and providing an occasional case study that the students discussed briefly before she presented the "academic" interpretation of the case. In class, she expected to be considered the expert and did not expect to have her authority challenged. When students objected to her style in class, she was at a loss about how to respond.

In our conversations, I asked her to identify the cultural assumptions that framed her teaching style, and she identified all the traditional ideas mentioned. I suggested that she explore the possibility of using narrative therapy techniques to teach this class, not simply to teach the students how to do narrative therapy, but to use those methods as the foundation of her pedagogy. She struggled with this idea because, in her experience, therapy and teaching were two different processes. Nevertheless, we began to use group and narrative techniques to teach the course together.

The first segment of this course addresses racism and privilege. She chose to emphasize micro-aggressions as an aspect of privilege that often goes unnoticed or ignored. In our conversations with students, micro-aggressions inevitably occurred. Initially, the students didn't realize the implications of what they were saying to each other. Because she had confidence in her skills as a narrative therapist, Dr. Ngyo had very little difficulty in pointing out micro-aggressions as they occurred in conversation and in helping students learn to believe each other's stories. Because of her skill as a therapist, she was able to create a non-threatening environment in the class that permitted students to examine their own assumptions and comments. At first, some students were frightened about being judged (a phenomenon often referred to as "white fragility"), but with support and their own courage they were able to recognize their own micro-aggressions as they happened, take responsibility, and examine the narrative of their own lives that supported the beliefs the comments expressed. She and I modeled inquiry into each other's cultures and encouraged students to ask each other questions across cultures. We also acknowledged the inevitable discomfort that accompanies this kind of integrated learning and gave students permission to discuss it in class. Dr. Ngyo kept a journal of reflections and we discussed her evolving insights into this new way of teaching. Finally, she told me that she realized I had asked her to make a paradigm shift in her pedagogy, and that she had basically made it. She now had two different methods for teaching and could shift back and forth with an increasing level of comfort and skill.

Learning happened on many levels in this experience. Dr. Ngyo learned an integrated method of teaching that came very naturally to her because of her upbringing and her experience with family storytelling. I learned, in explicit detail, how to explain the cultural assumptions that frame traditional teaching and learning and the reasons how and why our counseling students were uncomfortable with that approach. The students in the class were of African, European, and Latino descent, and came from Jamaica, Puerto Rico, Cuba, the segregated southern United States, and New England. They had the opportunity to learn "about" each other's cultures and also to experience the conversation without the need to defend themselves, which increased their understanding of the narrative process. Finally, we had an end-of-the-semester multicultural feast in which every person brought food from either their own culture or the one they had studied, shared the food with the class, and explained whatever they knew about its origins. Some students also brought music. This was a completely integrated learning experience. The students expressed their satisfaction with what they learned and how they planned to use it. I have been teaching this course for almost 20 years and there was no question in my mind that co-teaching with a person from another ethnic background made both of us better teachers and gave the students a much richer learning experience. The dialogue illuminated our cultures and the cultures of the students because of the conversational process and the narrative emphasis on understanding each other's experience rather than trying to find an elusive truth.

Culture and Learning

All of us live in our own cultural fishbowls. We have the opportunity to understand both ourselves and others when we realize that the fishbowls do divide us—but they are also transparent. Student affairs professionals have the advantage of being members of a non-dominant culture on most campuses. Typically, we complain about this situation, but we can also use it to understand the difficulties that our students often face in traditional classrooms. Empathy is one key to the process. Taking what you know about integrated cultures (e.g., Latino, African American, Caribbean, Indigenous and, to a certain degree, various Asian cultures), try to imagine what it is like for those students to learn from faculty who have a strongly individuated approach to teaching. If you have trouble imagining, ask some students you know about their academic experience on your campus. Then ask what works for them, what doesn't work, and what would make things better. Finally, think about what works and doesn't work for you as a student affairs professional when you try to engage with the larger campus culture (beyond your own office or work environment). Relate and apply your insights to what the students have told you. If you generally don't engage with the larger culture beyond your work with students and other student affairs professionals, ask yourself why. What do you have to learn from your own experience?

Our customary ideas about teaching and learning are deeply embedded in Eurocentric epistemology and pedagogy. It is the fishbowl of higher education (Fried, 2016). Deviations from this worldview are often referred to as "lowering standards." This frame of reference operates to the disadvantage of both students from integrated cultures and to the profession of student affairs. We are not talking about lowering standards. We are not talking about hand-holding. We are talking about expanding our ideas about standards and achievements so that we have a range of flexible and culturally appropriate methods for understanding and assessing learning. I recently saw a cartoon that had several animals standing in front of a large tree, preparing to be assessed for their tree-climbing ability. There was a monkey, a snake, a bird, an elephant, and a cow. The standardized test was the ability to climb the tree. Just think about it for a minute. Cow-ness has a powerful effect on tree-climbing ability. Monkey-ness has a powerful effect on milk-giving ability. If the bird flew to the top of the tree, would that be cheating?

References

Baxter Magolda, M. (1992). *Knowing and reasoning in college.* San Francisco: Jossey-Bass.

Baxter Magolda, M. (1999). *Creating contexts for learning and self-authorship: Constructive developmental psychology.* Nashville, TN: Vanderbilt University Press.

Baxter Magolda, M. & King, P. (Eds.). (2004). *Learning partnerships: Theory and models of practice to educate for self-authorship.* Sterling, VA: Stylus.

Berrett, D. (2015, January 26). The day the purpose of college changed. *The Chronicle of Higher Education.* Retrieved from http://www.chronicle.com/article/The-Day-the-Purpose-of-College/151359

Chavez, A. & Longerbeam, S. (2016). *Teaching across cultural strengths.* Sterling, VA: Stylus.

Fried, J. (2016). *Of education, fishbowls, and rabbit holes: Rethinking teaching and liberal education for an interconnected world.* Sterling, VA: Stylus.

Fried, J. & American College Personnel Association. (1995). *Shifting paradigms in student affairs: Culture, context, teaching and learning.* Lanham, MD: American College Personnel Association/University Press of America.

Grande, S. (2004). *Red pedagogy: Native American social and political thought.* Oxford: Rowman & Littlefield.

Heisenberg, W. (1927). *Uncertainty principle.* Retrieved from https://en.wikipedia.org/wiki/Uncertainty_principle

Huhman, H. (2014). The ten unique skills employers desire in new hires. *CareerBuilder Millennial Branding,* Retrieved from http//entrepreneur.com.article/234864

Jensen, E. (2000). *Brain-based learning.* (Rev. Ed.) San Diego, CA: The Brain Store.

Kegan, R. (2000). What form transforms? A constructive developmental approach to transformative learning. In J. Mezirow & Associates (Eds.), *Learning as transformation,* (pp. 35–70). San Francisco, CA: Jossey-Bass.

Mezirow, J. & Associates. (2000). *Learning as transformation.* San Francisco, CA: Jossey-Bass.

Palmer, P., & Zajonc, A. (2010). *The heart of higher education: Transforming the academy through collegial conversations.* San Francisco, CA: Jossey-Bass.

Polanyi, M. (1967). *The tacit dimension.* Garden City, NY: Doubleday.

Siegal, D. (2007). *The mindful brain.* New York, NY: W.W. Norton.

Zull, J. (2002). *The art of changing the brain.* Sterling, VA: Stylus.

6

THE USE OF INDIGENOUS WORLDVIEWS, REFLECTIVE PRACTICE, AND STORYTELLING TO PROMOTE INTEGRATED LEARNING

Stephanie J. Waterman (Onondaga, Turtle) and Seán Carson Kinsella (nêhiyaw/otipemisiwak/Nakawé/Irish)

Introduction

As we begin our contribution to this chapter, we do so acknowledging that we are guests of our relatives (most recently the Mississauga of the Credit) on the territory where Seán was born and continues to reside, and that this territory (Tkaronto) is subject to the Dish with One Spoon Wampum covenant between the Haudenosaunee and Anishnaabek peoples of this area—as well as the Huron, Petun, and other First Peoples. Stephanie is Haudenosaunee, Onondaga, Turtle Clan, visiting here from her homeland in Onondaga. While the Seneca lived in Tkaronto for a time, she acknowledges that this was not always the case and that the lives of Indigenous people in this area are complex. Next, we introduce ourselves, providing context to who we are and how our identities influence our teaching. If you are not familiar with this scholarly writing style, we are pleased that you are taking the opportunity to learn. Readers will also note differences between the ways the United States and Canadian governments currently deal and have historically dealt with Indigenous peoples. You are encouraged to research unfamiliar terms and historical references that are important but not central to the educational theme of this chapter.

Seán Kinsella

I introduce myself as I have been taught by my Anishnaabek and Haudenosaunee teachers: kîsikâw-kihiw nindizhinikaaz. mahihkan nindoodem. Tkoronto nindoonjibaa. Mississauga nindaa. nêhiyaw, Nakawêyiniwak, Métis, Irish, Scottish ndaaw. This introduction is a combination of some of the languages I carry small amounts of (I am learning), and is mainly Anishnaabemowin, the language of the territory in which I reside, and related to the nakawê language of my people.

My peoples are Gaelic (from Éire and Alba, respectively) who settled in what would become modern Montreal as well as those from the Iron Confederacy (nêhiyaw/ nêhithaw, Nakawêyiniwak, Métis) and share within them that collective history of those peoples in the northern woodlands of what was known as the Athabaskan region and Western Great Plains. In particular, my specific family was largely involved in the fur trade and was part of the 1885 Northwest Resistance. We were related to (and in some cases were) the original signatories of Treaties Four, Six, and Eight and were affiliated with several bands (including notably Muscowequan, Ketawayhew, Mistahimusqua, Kaquanum, and Peaysis), although many (including my family members and ancestors) took Métis Scrip when it was offered for reasons that have been captured at length in Heather Devine's book *The People Who Own Themselves: Aboriginal Ethnogenesis in a Canadian Family, 1660–1900* (2004, pp. 169–195, 207–8) and came largely from the Lac La Biche and Saddle Lake areas (p. 207) before settling in the Battlefords regions in the early 1900s. In this way, our Indigenous history has largely been one influenced by hiding due to the retaliation that was enacted on those perceived as disloyal to the newly formed state that would become Canada, as Devine (2004) notes: treatment of "rebels" and bands deemed "disloyal" was harsh, well in keeping with Hayter Reed's recommendations. Dissident bands were refused rations, or had their annuity payments held back. (p. 177)

This has led to a climate in which "there is still a lack of acknowledgement of Métis people, from both non-Native and Native peoples" (Schudeler, 2011, p. 191), and has created a dynamic in which "Métis scattered and lived life on the margins, many hiding their identities because of racism and the prevailing view of Riel" (Schudeler, 2011, p. 192). In her analysis of Métis poet Greg Scofield, Schudeler notes that "Scofield highlights the false divisions between First Nations or Status Indians and Métis, as Métis dark enough could be included in treaties while their fair-skinned relatives were written out of history by passing as white to escape racism" (2011, p. 192). She also refers to the work of Jo-Anne Episkenew (Métis) who asserts that "a significant constituency of Métis were almost impossible to distinguish from their Indian relatives, much to the dismay of the colonial officials with the responsibility of negotiating the treaties" (p. 192); this is a theme that Devine (2004) grapples with and extensively covers. One of the reasons to spend the time unpacking these identities is the concept of "resistance," as contained in the work of Cree/nêhiyaw scholar Neil McLeod (cited in Schudeler, 2011), noting that:

> The narrative memory of Cree-speaking people is also involved in a process of preserving a place in the world—a way of understanding reality. While the pressures of colonialism can crush the collective spirit of a people, it can also solidify resistance and allow people to conceive of an alternative mode of being. (p. 193)

Schudeler also applies the concept of Métis resistance as indicated in the work of Scofield. I will return to themes of resistance and survival as we explore what it means to be an Indigenous student affairs professional who also teaches.

Schudeler (2011) mentions two other concepts of note. First, the idea that "writing by Indigenous peoples, in this instance Cree Métis people, can be a form of resistance" (p. 193), for which I would argue that teaching can also fulfill this function when done by Indigenous scholars. This is especially true when teaching is approached from a perspective of âcimowina, which Episkenew defines as "everyday stories . . . the stories which are the foundation of contemporary Indigenous literature, although not spiritual, are nevertheless spirit" (as cited by Schudeler, 2011, p. 194). Second, she declared, "Writing our own stories is powerful maskihikîy—medicine—because not only does it educate non-Métis people, but more importantly it provides Métis people a sense of pride in their history" (Schudeler, 2011, p. 194). Simpson (2011) also explored storytelling, or Dibaajimowinan, our personal stories, which are critical because "our personal creation stories—our lives, mirror and reflect the Seven Fires of Creation" (p. 40). She reiterates that "Every Nishnaabeg has our own personal stories or narratives that communicate their personal truths, learning, histories, and insights. Dibaajimowin in this sense are personal opportunities to create" (p. 40). This approach allows us to both reflect on which stories we personally use to reconstruct our reality, and also question the Creation story of the Canadian state itself—an important part of decolonizing. As Simpson (2011) further articulates:

> the spiritual world is alive and influencing; colonialism is contested; and storytelling or "narrative imagination," is a tool to vision other existences outside the current ones by critiquing and analyzing the current state of affairs, but also by dreaming and visioning other realities. (p. 40)

I am very grateful to work in a faculty and at an institution where I can use storytelling as a methodology to facilitate course content. This is particularly important to me, given that the courses I teach are situated in the Indigenous Studies Program at Centennial College (located in Scarborough, Ontario, Canada) and by using this methodology we are able to try to explore building other realities together. Community survival, resistance to coercive power and social stereotypes, and finally the use of storytelling, and particularly âcimowina, are important for understanding my framework as both an Indigenous faculty member and in my own teaching methodology. Scholars such as Cherryl Smith make the argument that "colonialism, racism, and cultural imperialism do not occur only in society outside of the gates of universities" (as cited by Smith, 1999, p. 37). And as Schudeler and others point out, "Academic writing . . . is a way of 'writing back' whilst at the same time writing to ourselves" (Smith, 1999, p. 37). We argue that this approach can be applied to teaching in an environment that allows us as practitioners to centralize our stories and worldviews.

Stephanie J. Waterman

I cannot introduce myself in my language, as my parents were both impacted by the residential school legacy. Although my maternal grandfather spoke all six Haudenosaunee languages, he did not teach any one language to his children. My father was fluent in Mohawk, but spoke in his language only to his relatives and other Mohawks. Whenever I asked my mother for words, she would immediately respond, but then say, "Oh wait a minute. That's Seneca." Or "No, that's Oneida." I would become confused and eventually stopped asking. When we introduce ourselves in Onondaga, we specify our house and clan before our names. "I'm Longhouse, Turtle Clan, and my name is Guyyoñdisaye."

The Haudenosaunee are made up of six nations: Mohawk, Keepers of the Eastern Door; Oneida; Onondaga, the Keepers of the Fire; Cayuga; Seneca, Keepers of the Western Door; and Tuscarora who came under our protection around 1722 when they were driven out of the Carolinas. We live in our traditional homelands in what is now called New York, although these lands are greatly reduced in size due to encroachment and attempts at removal over time. Our lives are based on Thanksgiving, that is, giving thanks to all of Creation. It is our duty to give thanks to everything and for the continuation of our ceremonies and the "network of relationships" in which we live (Alfred, 1999, p. 42) so that we may continue as a people. We are responsible for our environment, which includes humans.

> The Creator planted us here.
> He planted lots of things.
> So our duty is to keep thanking the Creator.
> When we pray it's a greeting. We don't ask for anything.
> Church people ask for things in their prayers.
> We don't. We greet Him by thanking Him
> For all the things He has left for "human Beings" to survive.
> (Shenandoah, in Wall, 2001, p. 38).

In this tradition, we know that we need each other to survive. Bad relationships will not allow us to give thanks and to continue as a people. There is a goodness about our relationships and assumptions (Waterman, forthcoming).

> We come from the Creator and we go back.
> There's another circle you better not forget.
> Everything you do comes back to you.
> Do good and it comes back good.
> Do bad and it comes back, too.
> Try to do more good than bad.
> Your time here will be better (Shenandoah, in Wall, 2001, p. 82).

I strive to rely on the good, to make my time here better for those who follow, not only subsequent generations, but for those who wish to follow a Western-type educational path and work with post-secondary students, an environment that (for the most part) gives me joy and energy. The philosophy and wisdom shared here by Leon Shenandoah, who was our Tadodaho for most of my life, informs my life and work.

Before I discuss an example of how this life philosophy informs my teaching, and offer a short discussion of teaching in higher education, I must share another teaching by Leon Shenandoah. "The Creator is not a he or a she. It's just the Creator. Sometimes I say He, but Creator's not either. The Creator is both and neither" (Wall, 2001, p. 43). This is a complicated and sophisticated way of thinking about Creation and opens up the potential for an expansive, diverse outlook on life. I have always said that the work that we do as Indigenous scholars and student affairs practitioners is not about us, that it is more than us. So is this life and our work; it is more than us.

Applications to Student Affairs and Teaching in It

In the next section we share how our worldviews are embedded in our teaching. Chávez and Longerbeam (2016) discuss individual versus integrated cultural frameworks in teaching. Throughout the rest of this chapter, the reader will see how we both utilize integrated frameworks rather than individual student work such as a testing, so-called objectivity, and competition. We both use reflection, on the part of the student and for ourselves, group work, and assignments that have personal, concrete meaning.

We see integrated learning as a responsibility and as relationship-building. Responsibility and relationships are key concepts in Wilson's (2008) Indigenous Research Paradigm. While Wilson (2008) writes about a research paradigm, the axiology and ontology we employ in our teaching is deeply connected to who we are, with responsibility and relationship being central. The tension and dissonance that can happen in our work is what happens in life, including our work in student affairs. There is uncertainty. As student development theories claim, that is when the learning and growth happens. Caine, Estefan, and Clandinin (2013) write that the more you think about a story, the more it can change you. Wilson (2008) claims that research should change you. The learning is reciprocal. Archibald (2008) emphasizes the "work" in her concept of storywork. We do not passively receive knowledge, and through our integrated approach to the classroom . . .

Seán Kinsella

I do my best to embody the principles and values that I expressed in the previous section, as well as those that have been passed along to me by my traditional teachers, which are embedded in the worldviews of both the First Nation(s) I and they come from. These are also values that I do my best to apply in my work as a student affairs practitioner who has been working in the field of student housing for the past ten years.

One of the most important of these principles that I utilize in my practice is the concept of Aanjigone (Simpson, 2011):

> a concept that promotes the framing of Nishnaabeg values and ethics in the positive. It means that if we criticize something, our spiritual being may take on the very thing we are criticizing. It promotes non-interference by bringing forth the idea that if someone else does wrong, the implicate "order" will come back on that person and correct the imbalance in some other way. (p. 54)

In the classroom and in academia more broadly, this complex concept can be a difficult notion to balance, something Simpson talks about extensively, as the perception of the role of faculty, particularly in a Western educational model, is to offer objective criticism. She advises,

> we need to be careful with our criticism. We should not blindly follow the academy's love affair with criticism . . . Instead, we should highlight the positive within each other's work, and save our criticism for the forces that continue to rip us apart. (2011, p. 55)

While she is speaking here specifically about the concept of criticism in regard to critical analysis of the work of Indigenous scholars, I believe this is a lens that can and should be applied in our work with students as well. How might we use criticism to create a safe and holistic environment? Are there better, more affirming ways of providing feedback and guidance? Another critical component of Aanjigone is the idea of independent learning as a foundation. Simpson references:

> Our culture placed a profound importance on individuals figuring out their own path, or their own theoretical understanding of their life and their life's work based on individual interpretation of our philosophies, teachings, stories, and values. In combination with their own interpretation of the name or names they held within their society, clan responsibilities, and personal gifts or attributes, individuals were afforded a high level of autonomy within the community for exploring and expressing their responsibilities. This is sometimes framed as an "ethic of non-interference" on the part of other community members. It is also coupled or twinned with individual responsibilities of figuring out one's place in the cosmos and how to contribute to the collective while respecting oneself and one's inner being. (2011, pp. 53–54)

This passage is one that I have taken to reading to my students in my first few classes, as I believe it articulates well the type of learning I expect from them and gives an important framing to the Indigenous approach I will take in the classroom. Another one of the ways that this enacts itself is through my own care as a faculty member to balance a sense of safety in the classroom. This is especially important during student discussions. I have learned that, without directly confronting a student's perspective as being wrong (unless it is harmful to others in the classroom space), this approach allows students to work through where they are for themselves. To this end, I do my best to provide alternative perspectives, solicit feedback from the other students in the class, or point to course materials that may give other evidence, without specifically telling students they are incorrect. If a student violates our "classroom commitments," I will address that specific behaviour. Sometimes this works more effectively than others, and in the case of conflicts, I need to address the concerns to the broader class while acknowledging my role in creating the environment. In such cases, I try to model the idea that I have learned from observation with my own traditional teachers who often utilize this principle in the way that Simpson (2011) describes as:

> In a sense, critique is an internal process and the outcome is an individual action rather than an attack on another. Indeed, when an Elder is displeased with an action of one of his or her students, the Elder does not criticize that action, but is silent. Often at a later point, the Elder will use a story of an activity to convey a particular teaching in an indirect manner. (p. 54)

Admittedly, this is an area of growth for me and is not entirely possible in practical application due to the requirement of grading reflection journals and assignments. I have noticed that some very positive discussions with students have resulted from me engaging in this way, as they will often come and try to clarify or understand my comments upon receiving a grade. These conversations also prompt me to reflect on my own praxis and make alterations to ensure that I am balancing the critical aspect of my role as a teacher, while ensuring that I am recognizing what their differing skills sets and approaches might be. Another term that captures these concepts in nêhiyawewin is the idea of "pêahtihk," which means "to walk softly, to give something great thought and consideration" (Scofield, 2009, p. 4), specifically because all of our actions and words have consequences.

Another important concept is the idea of "Debwewin," often translated as truth, and which is derived from odebwewin, meaning "the sound of the heart" (Simpson, 2011, p. 59). It is further defined as "a wholistic way of knowing and being that involves one's heart and mind working together" (Gehl, 2012, p. 30) and speaks to the idea of a self-directed learning journey in which

> individuals travel on a personal knowledge-seeking adventure where it is their responsibility to learn the history of colonization, such as the criminalization of our culture and the history of the oppressive and sexist Indian Act, for example. In learning the circle of the mind knowledge and in connecting it to the circle of heart knowledge, an individual is able to come to a wholisitic understanding of who they are. (Gehl, 2012, p. 32)

This personal journey also recognizes that specifically "my truth will be different from someone else's" (Simpson, 2011, p. 59), and allows for the fact that there will be different interpretations based on our social locations. Simpson notes that her interpretation comes from her location

> as a Nishaabekwe from the gdigaa bizhiw doodem (bobcat clan) of the Michi Saagiig Nishnaabeg territory, as a mother, as an intellectual and a language learner. For me, gender plays an import role in my own perspective, but my understandings of gender are not fully shared by other members of my nation. (2011, p. 60)

For me, what this means as a faculty member is that my social locations presenting as male, mahihkan (wolf) clan, my national identity (being nêhiyaw/nêhithaw, Nakawêyiniwak, Metis, Irish, Scottish), urban, mixed, Indigenous, Two-spirit/Queer, and disabled is inseparable from who I am as a teacher as they are keys to my own journey and truth and therefore a source of, rather than a determent to, my knowledge. I use the word "location" rather than "identities" very intentionally, as I believe it references more of a land-based idea. Where I am, and who, is influenced by this, as well as my kin, etc. What understanding truth from this location also means is that I must do the work to ensure that other âcimowina, Dibaajimowinan, and truths are used to represent the viewpoints that I cannot. Simpson (2011), Driskill (2016), and Gehl (2012) discuss the ways heteropatriarchy and sexism have influenced our communities and specifically that "homophobia, transphobia, and misogyny, then, are part of colonial projects intent on murdering, removing, and marginalizing native bodies and nations" (Driskill, 2016, p. 35). This perspective is critical in interrogating which parts of curriculum we showcase and whose voices we ensure have weight in the classroom. In praxis, for me, this means ensuring the voices of Indigenous youth, women, and other Two-spirit folks—especially those who are not cis gendered—are centralized.

The final area is the nehiyaw concept of kinship or wâhkôhtowin, or kinship that speaks to the idea of embedded relationships among all of us as humans, but also with the wider world, encompassing the spiritual (McAdam, 2015; Stonechild, 2016). When we introduce kinship into the teaching equation, it brings the idea of responsibility and to whom I am responsible into the discussion. It further introduces the broader understandings of our creation stories and our ceremonies, including my specific responsibilities to the laws of my nations, such as the manitow wiyinikêwina (or Creator's laws) that McAdams (2015, p. 38) writes of with regard to the nêhiyawak. This is about coming to terms with what Ryan McMahon shares as passed along by his Kookum: "Our beadwork told our story. Our beadwork named us. Our beadwork put us in relation to each other" (McMahon, 2016, para 25). For me, it is the moccasins and small beaded flowers passed along to me that were made by my nicîpan and carried by my mother and sister that now hold a place in my bundle. If we can try to understand where we come from, it gives us a strong basis to try to relate to the differing identities, nations, and places our students do as well, and to explore where they fit into this relationship of kinship with me and all of creation.

Stephanie J. Waterman

I have taught the core student affairs courses at the graduate level for about ten years. This includes Student Development Theories in Higher Education, Contemporary Issues in Student Affairs, the History of Higher Education, and Access and (In)equity in Higher Education, to name several. I do not explicitly share my life philosophy when teaching, but do have a teaching philosophy (Waterman, 2013). I cannot teach anyone unless they are ready. I provide the tools—theories, for example—for students to use to "see" injustice, racism, or development. Then students must teach others about what they have learned as a way to help students "own" their learning (Waterman, 2013). I developed this philosophy while teaching a diversity course.

In my student development theory course, students are expected to learn about a specific group of students and then, using the NASPA: Student Affairs Administrators in Higher Education national conference call for programs, review process, and session format in order to propose, review, and present an analysis of their group to the classroom, as if they were attending the NASPA conference. Students can also choose to use the Canadian Association of College and University Student Services annual conference guidelines. Students select a group to study by examining Andrew Garrod's series of books that include personal narratives written by students at Dartmouth about who they are in the context of that college (see a sample title, Garrod, 1999, included in references). In discussions with a colleague from Syracuse University, I settled on these books as a resource through which to apply theory—the narratives are life stories of post-secondary students from diverse backgrounds, including immigrants, who tackle different identity development challenges.

Students are put into groups according to the book they have chosen and work in this group for the entire semester. I introduce group work concepts (Colbeck, Campbell, & Bjorklund, 2000) as a way to address conflict management and remind them to think about their group work and group reward as they progress through the class. Groups must write a mission statement and code of conduct. My syllabi all include an inclusivity statement so they know we will have a respectful classroom environment free of hate speech.

I also share how theory can be limiting. On the first night of class, I share a PowerPoint slide with the content shown in the following bulleted list as a warning and ask students to list their own lenses through which they interpret the world. While the first statement needs context, the others can stand on their own. Sally Roesch Wagner researched the suffragettes in the United States. In a world in which men literally owned their wives and children, Dr. Wagner searched for many years for how these women could have acquired the idea that they could have equal rights. She discovered that the suffragettes were friends with the Haudenosaunee, a matrilineal society, in which women had power, a voice, and freedom. While this link was right in front of her for many years, however, the patriarchal and Western dominant lens of Dr. Wagner's upbringing and the academy interfered with her ability to see the connection.

- "Always be aware of that filter." Sally Roesch Wagner
- "Whether or not you can observe a thing depends on the theory you use. It is the theory that decides what can be observed." Albert Einstein
- "Many theories can be used to explain experiences and data, but they do not do so equally." (Patel, 2016, p. 60).
- Your own level of complexity "filters" how you view the world (students).

Students not only analyze their particular book group using theory, they must analyze what they, personally, have learned about their identity or development in a final reflection paper. Students list the different tasks each group member performed for the final presentation and then must reflect on that process in their learning. I included this assignment after a student, who was an administrator, wrote an addendum to her final theory paper about her own learning. She wrote that she was a "boss" during the day and carried that behavior with her into the classroom. She had an epiphany one day in class that she did not have to "boss" the group, that there was learning she could experience if she consciously stepped aside and listened and allowed herself to be guided, to be vulnerable. Since I have incorporated this personal last group reflection, students have used theory in their analysis of conflict and personal growth. Their essays show that they have become aware of their strengths and weaknesses, areas they might want to work on to improve their work with students, and ways they could improve their programming.

Because the narratives in the books are diverse, students can critically apply the various development theories we use in student affairs. Racial and gender identities are in the narratives as well as complicated spiritual intersections. The books help me to guide students in understanding the complexities of the narratives, but always with a thought toward how we can use this new understanding with current students. Interestingly, students have not used the final reflections as an opportunity to speak badly about others. Even when there has been serious conflict, group members were able to reflect on their own personal understanding of the situation, rather than blaming others. There are times I think they handle the conflict better than I do, and when those times come, I write my own personal reflection.

Student affairs is a person-centred profession. My own experiences as an Indigenous undergraduate and then graduate student, mother, auntie, grandmother, practitioner, and faculty member, inform all of my work. We need to work together for the benefit of all students, to support our colleagues, and to strengthen the academy and our communities. I mention the environment in class especially during our discussion on moral theory as these theories do not include non-humans, yet we depend on them for our survival. I strive to emphasize the good; we work on ways in class to be good, and we discover ways to work with conflict constructively. This does not mean we are not critical. I model what I expect from students. I share triumphs and setbacks, because we all experience good and bad. While I am careful to not overshare, I do so as a way to humanize the classroom and the academy.

I am not always successful in the classroom, but I need to grow also. I make mistakes and sometimes wish I had responded to an issue or student in a different way or had addressed more time on an issue. I am human, after all.

Discussion

We are from different nations and teach very different types of courses in student affairs professional preparation and Indigenous studies at the community college level, respectively. There are, however, several key themes that come out of both narratives contained in this chapter that new and future student affairs practitioners who are teaching, in any context, would do well to keep in mind.

As Stephanie explained, she is unable to teach students who themselves are not ready to learn. This is echoed by Seán in the concepts of Aanjigone and Debwewin explored earlier in this chapter, as they are both speaking about the concept of learning as being the responsibility of the learner and indeed the "ethic of non-interference" that surrounds this process. The specific journey that each learner will take is based on his or her own social location, including the affiliating of physical location, social class, gender, race, immigrant status, Indigenous status, clans, and nations (Wilson, 2008). If we are to help our students to learn, then, we must provide opportunities for them to do so, but recognize that they are also human, as are we. This is where our Indigenous worldviews and perspectives overlap with that of student affairs, which as Stephanie has referenced, is a people-centred profession. By centering both the learner and teacher as people who are on separate, but for the time we are interacting, overlapping journeys, we are able to explore their individual responsibilities and where they fit within the collective. We are in relationship with our students (Wilson, 2008).

Another important theme centres on the recognition of our own social locations, and limitations that occur from them in teaching. Seán talks about this in the context of using Dibaajimowina and âcimowina to provide perspectives on what he is teaching, ensuring that there are a variety of voices, particularly those who are marginalized, present in course content. This is something that Stephanie speaks to in her choice of texts, noting particularly the way that the complex narratives and life stories utilized in Andrew Garrod's books provide a space for growth and, importantly, application for what has been learned. This application piece is a part of the personal journey of each student, and will be different for everyone. Archibald (2008) emphasizes the work the listener engages in when hearing a story; a hunter will interpret a story in a different way than a basket maker (p. 97). This happens in our teaching as well, especially in student affairs when our students can work in such a wide range of offices from student health, residence life, judicial affairs, assessment, to athletics, for example.

Finally, there is the theme of self-reflection as part of the learning process for both students and faculty. In both courses discussed in the chapter, reflection serves as a tool to assess learning and understanding for students, while allowing an opportunity for their own life stories, Dibaajimowina, and âcimowina to be part of the course and the learning process, and further to define what action steps they want to take based on this learning. Reflection allows students, as articulated in Simpson (2011), to construct meaning for themselves based on their own understandings and experiences. And for us as instructors, courses we teach become a part of each individual's âcimowina and allow further analysis of growth and learning in both an individual and collective sense.

Implications

As noted, self-reflection is important for both us. Keeping a reflection journal, or utilizing other reflective practices to analyze when things do not go as expected (or when they did) is utilizing the concept of Debwewin in an effective way. Reflection can offer a balance of using both an intellectual and spiritual approach as outlined by Gehl (2012) to better understand how we are having an impact on our students and can better approach the practice of teaching. Chávez and Longerbeam (2016) suggest keeping a teaching journal (p. 112). We assign journals to students; we should write them, too. Researchers keep research journals; use the journal as a way to stay in reflective conversation with yourself regarding the many ways you as student affairs professionals enhance student learning.

References

Alfred, T. (1999). *Peace, power, righteousness: An Indigenous manifesto*. Don Mills, ON: Oxford University Press.

Archibald, J. (2008). *Indigenous storywork: Educating the heart, mind, body, and spirit*. Vancouver, BC: University of British Columbia Press.

Caine, V., Estefan, A., & Clandinin, D. J. (2013). A return to methodological commitment: Reflections on narrative inquiry. *Scandinavian Journal of Educational Research, 57*(6), 574–586.

Chávez, A. F. & Longerbeam, S. D. (2016). *Teaching across cultural strengths: A guide to balancing integrated and individuated cultural frameworks in college teaching*. Sterling, VA: Stylus.

Colbeck, C. L., Campbell, S. E., & Bjorklund, S. A. (2000). Grouping in the dark: What college students learn from group projects. *The Journal of Higher Education, 71*(1), 60–83.

Devine, H. (2004). *The people who own themselves: Aboriginal ethnogenesis in a Canadian vamily.* Calgary, AB: University of Calgary Press.

Driskill, Q. (2016). *Asegi stories: Cherokee queer and Two-Spirit memory.* Tucson, Arizona: The University of Arizona Press.

Garrod, A. (1999). *Souls looking back: Life stories of growing up black.* New York, NY: Routledge.

Gehl, L. (2012). *Anishinaabeg stories: Featuring petroglyphs, petrographs, and wampum belts.* Southampton, ON: Ningwakwe Learning Press.

McAdam, S. (2015). *Nationhood interrupted: Revitalizing Nêhiyaw legal systems.* Saskatoon, SK, Purich Publishing Limited.

McMahon, R. (2016, December 30). What colour is your beadwork, Joseph Boyden? Retrieved from https://www.vice.com/en_ca/article/what-colour-is-your-beadwork-joseph-boyden

Patel, L. (2015). *Decolonizing educational research: From ownership to answerability.* New York, NY: Routledge.

Schudeler, J. (2011). Gifts of Maskihkîy: Gregory Scofield's Cree Métis stories of self-acceptance. In Q. Driskill (Ed.), *Queer indigenous studies: Critical interventions in theory, politics, and literature* (pp. 190–210). Tucson, AZ: University of Arizona Press.

Scofield, G. (1997). *Love medicine and one song.* Cape Croker First Nation: Kegedonce Press.

Simpson, L. (2011). *Dancing on our turtle's back: Stories of Nishnaabeg re-creation, resurgence and a new emergence.* Winnipeg, MB: Arbeiter Ring Pub.

Smith, L. T. (1999). *Decolonizing mythologies: Research and indigenous peoples.* Dunedin, NZ: University of Otago Press.

Stonechild, B. (2016). *The knowledge seeker: Embracing indigenous spirituality.* Regina, SK: University of Regina Press.

Wall, S. (2001). *To become a human being: The message of Tadodaho Chief Leon Shenandoah.* Charlottesville, VA: Hampton Roads.

Waterman, S. J. (2013). Using theory to tell it like it is. *The Urban Review, 45*(4), 335–354.

Waterman, S. J. (forthcoming). They won't do it the way I can: The role of relationality and goodness in the work of Haudenosaunee administrators.

Wilson, S. (2008). *Research is ceremony: Indigenous research methods.* Halifax, NS: Fernwood.

7

INTEGRATING SERVICE-LEARNING INTO STUDENT AFFAIRS PEDAGOGY

Barbara Jacoby

Well before service-learning became prominent on college campuses, student affairs professionals in many functional areas facilitated volunteerism and other community-based experiences for and with students (Jacoby, 1996). We know that engaging in such activities for the common good is associated with a number of indicators of well-being for college students, including optimism, self-efficacy, self-esteem, and a sense of meaning and purpose (Flanagan & Bundick, 2011). As service-learning grew dramatically since it took root in higher education in the mid-1980s, student affairs professionals continued to bring our considerable skills and experience to bear on developing service-learning experiences inside and outside the formal academic curriculum.

Although there are definitions of service-learning that clearly state that service-learning must be part of the formal curriculum (Clayton, Bringle, & Hatcher, 2013), I define service-learning more broadly. Service-learning is a form of experiential education in which students engage in activities that address human and community needs together with structured opportunities for reflection designed to achieve desired learning outcomes (Jacoby, 1996). This definition offers a broader umbrella that intentionally includes experiences facilitated by student affairs professionals, campus chaplains, community partners, and student leaders, as long as those experiences incorporate the fundamental elements of service-learning: reflection and reciprocity.

In service-learning, unlike volunteerism, opportunities for learning and reflection are fully integrated into the structure of the program or course. Service-learning is explicitly designed to promote learning about the historical, economic, political, and cultural contexts that underlie the needs or issues the students address. Different programs or courses emphasize different types and combinations of learning goals: intellectual, social, civic, ethical, moral, spiritual, intercultural, career, or personal. Other learning outcomes include deepening understanding of academic content, applying theory to practice, increasing awareness of the complexity of social issues, understanding human difference and commonality, exploring options for future individual and collective action to solve community problems, and developing a wide range of practical skills.

The other key element of service-learning is reciprocity. Reciprocity means that we, as service-learning educators, relate to the community in the spirit of partnership, viewing the institution and the community in terms of both assets and needs. Participants in reciprocal service-learning relationships seek to avoid what Thea Hillman (1999) refers to as the "provider-recipient split" that all too often occurs in volunteerism and community service (p.123). Sigmon (1996), one of the early proponents of service-learning, emphasized that:

> Each participant is server and served, care giver and care acquirer, contributor and contributed to. Learning and teaching in a service-learning arrange-ment is also a task for each of the partners in the relationship . . . each of the parties views the other as contributor and beneficiary. (p. 4)

Reciprocity implies that the community is not a learning laboratory, and that service-learning should be designed *with* the community to meet needs identified *by* the community. Service-learning activities can take place at or away from the community site and may or may not engage students in interacting with community organization leaders or clients.

As a pedagogy, service-learning is education that is grounded in experience as a basis for learning and on the centrality of critical reflection intentionally designed to enable learning to occur. Service-learning educators select service experiences, as they would select texts or other learning activities, that they believe will be most effective in enabling students to learn and apply knowledge and develop skills. Reflection in service-learning stimulates learners to integrate experience and observations with existing knowledge and to formulate questions to deepen understanding of the world, the root causes of the need for service, and learners' *a priori* assumptions and beliefs (Jacoby, 1996).

Most service-learning scholars believe that the theoretical roots of service-learning are in the work of John Dewey. Often viewed as the father of experien-tial education, Dewey sought to understand how experiences can be educative. He observed: "The belief that all genuine education comes about through experience does not mean that all experiences are genuinely or equally educative. Experience and education cannot be directly equated to each other. For some experiences are mis-educative" (Dewey, 1938, p. 25). Dewey believed that learning is situational and proposed that learning from experience occurs through reflective thinking. Based on this proposition, reflection has become one of the core elements of service-learning.

David Kolb's Experiential Learning Model (1984) also serves as one of service-learning's theoretical foundations. The model consists of four elements: concrete experience, observation of and reflection on that experience, formation and synthesis of abstract concepts based upon the reflection, and active experimentation that tests the concepts in new situations. These four elements form a cycle, or spiral, of learning. Individuals can enter the cycle at any point, but service-learning and other forms of experiential education are often designed to begin with concrete experience. Learning occurs when the cycle is repeated as service-learners test their newly developed concepts in concrete experience and continue through the other elements. Service-learning engages students in concrete experience followed by reflection on the service experiences. Reflection is designed with the intention of leading to deeper understanding of the complexity of social issues that underlie the need for service as well as potential future actions within the context of the service-learning experience and beyond.

Principles of Service-Learning Pedagogy

The *Principles of Good Practice for Combining Service and Learning* (Porter-Honnet & Poulsen, 1990), commonly known as the Wingspread principles, have served as indispensable guides to the design of service-learning initiatives since the 1990s. The Wingspread principles, which are reproduced in Exhibit 1.1, emphasize structured reflection, clear goals and responsibilities for all participants, careful program design, and sustainability.

EXHIBIT 1.1 PRINCIPLES OF GOOD PRACTICE IN COMBINING SERVICE AND LEARNING

An effective and sustained program:

1. Engages people in responsible and challenging actions for the common good.
2. Provides structured opportunities for people to reflect critically on their service experience.
3. Articulates clear service and learning goals for everyone involved.
4. Allows for those in need to define those needs.
5. Clarifies the responsibilities of each person and organization involved.
6. Matches service providers and service needs through a process that recognizes changing circumstances.
7. Expects genuine, active, and sustained organizational commitment.
8. Includes training, supervision, monitoring, support, recognition, and evaluation to meet service and learning goals.
9. Insures that the time commitment for service and learning is flexible, appropriate, and in the best interest of all involved.
10. Is committed to program participation by and with diverse populations.

(Porter-Honnet & Poulsen, 1990, p. 40)

Sigmon's (1994) Service and Learning Typology is a frequent companion to the Wingspread principles. Sigmon proposes that there are four variations, depending on the primacy of service in relation to learning: *service-LEARNING*, which implies that learning goals are primary and service outcomes secondary; *SERVICE-learning*, in which the service agenda is central and the learning secondary; *service learning*, in which the absence of the hyphen indicates that the two are essentially separate from one another; and *SERVICE-LEARNING*, in which the service and learning are of equal weight with each enhancing the other.

Two of the conceptual foundations that undergird the principles and practices of service-learning partnerships are the asset-based community development approach of Kretzmann and McKnight (1993) and the Community-Campus Partnerships for Health Guiding Principles of Partnership (Community-Campus Partnerships for Health Board of Directors [CCPH], 2013). According to Kretzmann and McKnight (1993), institutions seeking to develop service-learning partnerships should ensure that they build on community assets and meet community needs *as defined by the community*. The first principle they put forth is that community development starts with what is present in the community and the capacities of its residents and workers, rather than what is absent or problematic. Secondly, they state that community development is internally focused and thus should concentrate on the problem-solving capacities of local residents and institutions. The role of external forces, such as colleges and universities, is not minimized but should complement the primacy of local definition, control, creativity, and hope. If a community development approach is to be asset-based and internally focused, it also needs to be relationship driven. Therefore, it is essential to constantly be in the process of building and rebuilding relationships among local residents, organizations, and institutions (Kretzmann & McKnight, 1993).

Reciprocity implies that campus-based service-learning educators seek to develop trusting, mutually beneficial relationships with clearly defined outcomes for all participants. The Guiding Principles of Partnership promulgated by the Community-Campus Partnerships for Health (CCPH) are easily generalizable to partnerships outside the health field. They are not intended as prescriptive but rather as a guide for developing one's own principles of partnership. They emphasize respect, commitment, communication, and sustainability.

Service-Learning Pedagogy in Practice

As student affairs professionals, we bring much to service-learning. We are knowledgeable about student development and learning styles. We have skills in networking, developing partnerships, and facilitating group process. We have experience in program administration and logistics. Above all, we enjoy strong relationships with students and student leaders. However, we may wonder: What does it look like to put the principles of service-learning into practice in student affairs work? This section will examine the core principles and practices of reflection and reciprocity in greater detail and provide a guide to their implementation.

Facilitating Critical Reflection

While there are different types of reflection, the primary form of reflection service-learning educators strive for in service-learning is *critical* reflection. Critical reflection is the process of analyzing, reconsidering, and questioning one's experiences within a broad context of issues and content knowledge. We often hear that "experience is the best teacher," but Dewey and many others who have written about reflection remind us that experience can be a problematic teacher. Experience without critical reflection can all too easily allow students to reinforce their stereotypes about people who are different from themselves, develop simplistic solutions to complex problems, and generalize inaccurately based on limited data. For example, students who do community service in a homeless shelter without critically reflecting on their experience may come away with unfortunate and inaccurate impressions like these, which I have personally encountered: "Homeless people would be able to get off the street if they would just get a job" or "Homeless people are lazy or crazy."

I find that Dewey's (1933) definition of critical reflection is more useful in practice than the one previously presented: "Critical reflection is the active, persistent, and careful consideration of any belief or supposed form of knowledge in the light of the grounds that support it and the further conclusions to which it tends" (p. 9). It is guiding students through the process of considering and reconsidering their values, beliefs, and acquired knowledge that enables them to question and challenge their stereotypes and other *a priori* assumptions. Critical reflection gains depth and breadth as students challenge simplistic conclusions, compare varying perspectives, examine causality, and raise more challenging questions. Mezirow (1990) posits that the most significant learning experiences for adults involve critical reflection in which we reassess the way we have posed problems and our ways of perceiving, knowing, and acting.

According to Eyler, Giles, and Schmiede (1996), critical reflection in practice is continuous, connected, challenging, and contextualized. These "4 Cs" have guided many service-learning educators in developing and facilitating reflection in both course-based and co-curricular experiences.

For the deepest learning to occur, reflection must be ongoing. *Continuous* means that reflection must occur before, during, and after the experience. Reflection prior to the service, or "pre-flection," prepares students by introducing them to the issues, the community, the organization, and the population that their service will address. Reflection during the service experience enables students to record their observations, to apply theory in practice, to process the dissonance they may find between their expectations and the reality of their experience, and to consider how to resolve issues as they arise. When it follows the service experience, reflection can help students realize what they learned, how their learning relates their previous thinking and experiences, and what it might lead them to explore in the future.

Reflection must connect the service-learning experience with other areas of participants' learning and development. New ideas must be placed in a broader context, connected to a student's sense of identity and firmly embedded in their meaning-making, or metacognitive system. Connected reflection leads students to build bridges between content learning, personal reflections, and first-hand experiences. It is often demanding too much of students, particularly those new to service-learning, to assume that they will make these connections on their own. In Kolb's (1984) experiential learning model, reflection follows concrete experience and connects it to abstract conceptualization and generalization. Without structured, connected reflection, students can become overwhelmed by the needs and problems they see and become frustrated by a sense of hopelessness. Conversely, student participants in both curricular and co-curricular service-learning may fail to understand why they need to engage in reflection if it is not integrally connected to their service experience.

Challenging reflection poses old questions in new ways, is designed to reveal new perspectives, and raises new questions. Service-learning educators engage students in difficult conversations and activities in which they consider unfamiliar and often uncomfortable ideas. Nevitt Sanford's (1966) notion of balancing challenge and support is important in understanding this component of reflection. If the reflection is too challenging and if adequate support is not available, students may retreat inside themselves and, thus, will not take the risks necessary for them to try on new ideas and perspectives. However, if the reflection is not challenging enough or if the environment is too supportive, then students are less likely to leave their comfort zones and, as a result, are unlikely to learn and grow.

Contextualized reflection engages service-learners in activities and with topics that are meaningful in relation to their experiences and appropriate for their developmental levels and life situations. Contextual considerations include whether the reflection will occur on campus or at the community site, whether community members should participate, and whether reflection should occur individually or collectively. Another contextual factor to consider is what else is going on in students' lives and thoughts. For example, students are not likely to possess the mindfulness necessary for critical reflection when stressed by family or work situations as well as on the day before final examinations or spring break. Current events, such as natural disasters or terrorism, can also profoundly affect students emotionally and intellectually, creating either distractions to critical reflection or enriching it by providing a context of immediacy and relevance.

Service-learning reflection can take place individually or in groups and has many forms. *Speaking*, or oral reflection, can include directed discussions, presentations, interviews, storytelling, debate, deliberation, preparing oral or written testimony, or a creative form such as a poetry slam or enacting a play. *Writing* challenges students to organize their thoughts in order to make coherent arguments. It generates a permanent record of how they think about the service experience that can be used as part of future learning activities. While journaling is the most recognized form of written reflection, other examples include problem analysis, case studies, essays, press releases, drafting legislation, and letters to officials, editors, or oneself. *Activities*, or reflection through action, provide variety and, when done in groups, also help to develop team spirit and relational skills. Many team-building activities used throughout student affairs work can be adapted to include reflection. Role plays and other simulations are particularly effective in preparing students to enter the service site and to process what occurs there. Reflection through *media* and artistic creation includes individual or collective collages, drawings, photos or video essays, musical compositions, and other art forms. Creative means of reflection recognize students' various talents and learning styles and provide opportunities for students whose strengths are other than verbal.

Developing Community Partnerships

One of the most perplexing things about service-learning for individuals new to the work is how to initiate a community partnership. In response, many institutions have established a point of contact for both potential campus partners and representatives of community organizations seeking to develop service-learning partnerships, usually an individual in the service-learning center or community engagement office. This approach simplifies the process significantly for both parties, particularly because community partners often find it difficult to find the right person at a college or university to help them connect with a campus partner. More important than who should initiate campus-community partnerships is *how* to initiate and sustain them. The following steps are based on the principles for partnership development shared earlier in this chapter.

Step 1. Learn everything you can about potential partners through online, media, and personal sources. Sources for information about potential community partners include the service-learning center, institutional outreach office, service-learning faculty, local United Way, community volunteer clearinghouses, mayors' offices, and churches—all are sources of potential community partner contacts. Once you have identified a potential partner, you should consult the organization's website, local newspapers, and social media for useful background information and recent activities. Word-of-mouth can be the most helpful source of all in locating potential partners and learning about them on both the professional and personal levels.

Step 2. Carefully consider the commitment you are willing to make. Although it may seem obvious, I feel it is important to state clearly that service-learning educators and students should take making a commitment to a community organization seriously. Take the time to determine the amount of your own time and energy that you can contribute to the partnership. Because most community organizations operate with too few staff and limited budgets, their leaders may make resource or service delivery decisions based on your commitment of time and expertise, both your own and your students'. One of the first questions a potential community partner is likely to ask is about the duration and frequency of the intended commitment. Limited commitments are likely to be less useful from the community perspective. Unless short-term service projects, perhaps ten hours or less over the course of a semester, are specifically designed to target particular needs, they may actually result in a net loss to the community organization. If you want your students to have deeper, more meaningful experiences, consider making a deeper commitment to the partner organization.

Timing is an issue to consider in planning intensive experiences such as alternative breaks. Spring break may be a convenient time for colleges and students, but it may not be best for communities. Some communities have found that they cannot accommodate all the alternative spring break participants who seek to do their service-learning during the same week. In addition, needs are generally ongoing and important community events do not necessarily coincide with the academic calendar. It is also possible that a conflict may arise between the work that alternative spring break students would like to do and the work that must be done at that time. For example, a community may need health screenings and education, but not when their crops have ripened for harvest.

Step 3. Start early. Potential community partners appreciate being contacted well in advance of the start of the course or program. Volunteer coordinators usually try hard to be obliging and to avoid saying "no" to a college or university. However, imposing on them without adequate time to develop meaningful placements for students, particularly if intensive service or a significant number of students is involved, can be disruptive and time consuming.

Step 4. Remember that communication is essential in starting and developing any relationship. While the first communication can certainly be through email or by telephone, there is no substitute for face-to-face communication at the community site. Potential partners should engage in preliminary conversations that are both personal and professional. Informal conversations about families, hometowns, and backgrounds over coffee or lunch lay the foundation for frank interchanges about what each of you brings to the partnership and what each needs from it. The primary reason that most community organizations take on service-learners is to increase their capacity and productivity; however, most do not think only in terms of their self-interest. Community partners are interested in contributing to students' education about the issues and populations they are passionate about and in learning how to engage with the college or university in regard to their organization's priorities and social issues.

Step 5. Determine if there is compatibility. Any partnership, especially a service-learning partnership, is a collaborative process. Compatibility in a collaborative process means that the individuals or organizations involved can accomplish more by working together rather than separately. Compatibility in a service-learning partnership should exist on several levels. First, the desired learning outcomes for the service-learners should be compatible with the organization's mission and the tasks or projects the organization requires. The schedules and number of hours also need to be compatible. For example, if the course or program is one semester in duration and the time of the community's greatest needs do not fall within that time frame, there could be a lack of compatibility. A third compatibility issue is whether the students will have the knowledge and skills for the work that the organization would like them to perform.

Step 6. Ask the right questions. Once you have determined that there is a match between your desired outcomes and those of your community partner, there are specific questions to discuss. These include: How many students are needed? With what knowledge and skills? How much service is needed? How frequently? Over what time period? What are the specific tasks? What role would the community partner like to take in selecting the students to work with the organization? Where will the service take place? Would the community partner like to participate in reflection? Will you do service with the students or, if not, regularly visit the service site? Who will provide the necessary training? What security procedures are required, such as inoculations, fingerprinting, or background checks? Will there be a written agreement?

Step 7. Stay in touch. Determining the best and most productive way to communicate on a regular basis involves finding a delicate balance between consistent communication and placing an unwanted burden on either partner. Regardless of how you decide to do it, regular communication is essential to keeping things running smoothly, to prevent small issues from becoming big problems, and to continue to develop the relationship.

Step 8. Ascertain how you will know the extent of the success of your partnership. Based on your earlier conversations about the outcomes each of you seeks from the partnership, you will need to determine the measures and other criteria that you will use to assess the extent to which the desired outcomes were achieved for both partners. Assessment of student learning is often done through the products of reflection. As far as the community, objective measures such as the number of hours of tutoring or the completion of a project to pre-determined specifications may be complemented by subjective measures such as surveys that reflect increased client satisfaction.

Step 9. Celebrate success. It is important to take time to recognize and celebrate successes, large and small, along the way as well as at the end of the course or program. This can be accomplished through reflection, "shout outs" as service-learners leave the community site, or social media. As the experience concludes, celebration can occur at gatherings in the community or on campus, through coverage in community and campus publications, or as recognition by local and campus officials (Jacoby, 2015).

What is Unique about Co-Curricular Service-Learning

While it can be challenging to develop high-quality service-learning experiences outside the formal curriculum, carefully designed and implemented co-curricular experiences enable student participants to achieve learning and developmental outcomes other than those related to a discipline or academic course content. While the student and community outcomes, as well as the service and reflection activities, may be different from those of curricular service-learning, the fundamental principles of reflection and reciprocity apply to all service-learning. Co-curricular service-learning does not benefit from the structures inherent in academic courses, such as established learning outcomes, required class meetings and assignments, credits, and grades. As a result, service-learning educators must put in place structures that ensure that the experience, even a one-time experience, embraces the principles and practices of high-quality service-learning.

Because most co-curricular service-learning is not directly related to an academic discipline, its benefits to students generally fall in the areas of personal growth and interpersonal development. Among the potential psychosocial and identity development outcomes for students engaged in co-curricular service-learning are self-efficacy; emotional maturity; clarification of values and life purpose; deeper awareness of their own identities related to such elements as race, class, gender, sexual orientation, and ability; increased tolerance and empathy; and greater sense of their roles in local and global society. Student participants in co-curricular service-learning can also show gains in complex thinking, ethical development and moral reasoning, and clarity about their faith and spirituality. Student communities, such as residence halls and student organizations, also benefit from working together on meaningful projects in terms of stronger relationships, shared purpose, and a sense of community. Participation in service-learning and other forms of community engagement also contribute to satisfaction with the college experience and a higher likelihood of degree attainment (Jacoby, 2015). In addition, recent research on adolescents and young adults indicates that those involved in volunteerism and collective action for the common good are associated with a number of indicators of psychosocial well-being, including hope and optimism, self-efficacy, self-esteem and self-confidence, sense of meaning, and sense of living up to one's potential (Flanagan & Bundick, 2011).

Co-curricular service-learning can be more flexible than course-based experiences, because it is not necessarily bounded by the course schedule or semester time frame. Service and reflection can readily occur during evenings and weekends. Often subjective rather than objective, reflection in co-curricular experiences generally focuses on gaining a deeper understanding of oneself, relationships with others in the context of local and global communities, and examining one's values and beliefs. A potential drawback is that students may not take reflection seriously, since it is not part of a course. As a result, it may be more challenging to achieve the delicate balance of service and learning that Sigmon's (1994) typology illustrates. While academic service-learning may be more likely to emphasize learning over service (sL), co-curricular service-learning may tend to emphasize service over learning (Sl). While I challenge this belief, there are some who view co-curricular service-learning as lacking the legitimacy of experiential education because it is not integrated into an academic course. There is no necessary connection between the infusion of academic or empirical information into conversations and reflection and participation in a formal course. Perhaps learning needs to be more broadly defined in this context (Fried, 2016)

From the community perspective, if service is not part of a course, students are more likely to be able to take on tasks that are not directly related to academic content or course-based learning outcomes. Because their service experience is often not limited by the academic calendar or related to a specific course project, student participants in many forms of co-curricular service may choose to continue working with a community organization or issue over time, sometimes in more complex and challenging ways. On the other hand, a particular challenge of co-curricular service-learning is sustaining student commitment to projects and organizations unless their motivation is intrinsic.

Service-learning outside the curriculum is more likely to be initiated and led by students than course-based service-learning. Student service-learning leaders are usually passionate, committed, and creative. Some facilitate service-learning in paraprofessional roles including resident assistant and orientation advisor. Others coordinate service-learning experiences through the service-learning center, offices of diversity and inclusion, and student organizations. They are often excellent at recruiting peers to join their efforts. Students who are trained as reflection facilitators can engage and hold their peers' interest in ways that older adults cannot. In most cases, the effectiveness of student leaders is enhanced when they can rely on faculty and staff advisors and mentors for support. However, providing such advising and mentorship can require substantial time and energy. It involves walking a fine line between maintaining accountability to outcomes and partnerships on the one hand and allowing students the freedom to make and learn from mistakes on the other. Some advisors find it difficult to relinquish authority, to live with the ambiguity that student leadership often entails, and to sustain community partnerships as student leaders move on (Fisher & Wilson, 2003).

Incorporating Service-Learning Across Student Affairs

Student affairs professionals in all functional areas, as well as campus ministers and student leaders, can and do facilitate high-quality co-curricular service-learning experiences. It is also important to note that many of these individuals also teach courses that include curricular service-learning. In addition, student affairs professionals who may not be directly involved in facilitating service-learning experiences can engage students in reflection based on their service-learning experiences.

Student groups can address a number of organizational issues, such as developing shared purpose; improving internal and external communication; working together across differences, group dynamics, and recruitment and retention of members, by planning, organizing, and engaging in service-learning. For example, I was consulted by officers of an English honor society who were concerned about how difficult it was to retain members because the organization's primary activity was the induction of new members. We developed a service-learning project in which the members worked with a local Title I elementary school to develop an after-school reading enrichment program for struggling readers. As the project took root, the honor society's member participation and retention increased. The group's meetings became purposeful as they engaged together in reflection about how to enhance their work in the school and how their experiences informed their thinking about graduate school and career choices.

Students who live together in a residence hall or on a floor can develop a sense of community, shared interests, and a commitment to one another and to a cause by participating together in service-learning. The living environment facilitates group reflection through scheduled and impromptu discussions. Something as simple as placing large sheets of paper on the walls containing prompts for verbal or artistic reflection can encourage ongoing engagement.

Orientation programs engage new students in service-learning to achieve many purposes, including introducing students to peers, to communities surrounding the campus, and to experiential learning and reflection. Outcomes can also include exploring the meaning of community, exploring self in relation to others, civility, and community standards of behavior.

Staff and student leaders who work with diversity and inclusion programs or with students of a particular race, ethnicity, or sexual orientation can develop service-learning experiences that allow students to explore their identities in deep ways. In an example related to me, two student leaders, one African American and the other African, worked with a staff member in the diversity office to develop a mentoring program for black youth. Their group reflections centered on the similarities and differences among the black college students based on whether they were U.S.-born and on how they could share their experiences with the youth. Intercultural and interfaith service-learning experiences enable students to work together in community settings and explore their similarities and differences through group reflection.

Chaplains and advisors of faith-based organizations engage students in service-learning experiences ranging from one-time to intensive, including international mission trips. They may or may not be directly related to religious dogma. For example, service-learning experiences could be designed to enable students to consider Luke's preaching that "From everyone who has been given much, much will be demanded" (Luke 12:48, New International Version) or "what's Jewish about service" (Repair the World, 2016). Prayer or silent meditation may be incorporated into reflection. Career development professionals can advise students to consider careers in the private, public, and nonprofit sectors that would enable them to pursue the values they have acquired through their service-learning experiences. Many students who are committed to social justice believe that they should limit their career search to nonprofit organizations. However, career counselors can help students locate for-profit companies that value corporate social responsibility, social value creation, social entrepreneurship, and employee community service. They can seek to deepen their relationships with corporations that embrace the triple bottom line of profit, community enhancement, and sustainability. They can also guide students in comparing careers in all three sectors, as well as to consider graduate programs and post-college national and international service opportunities where they can pursue their social interests. Programs like Careers for the Common Good at the University of Connecticut are based in collaborations between the career center and the service-learning center and enable students to explore career interests through service-learning experiences (University of Connecticut Center for Career Development, 2017).

Professionals in wellness and health education often train peer leaders who provide educational programming to students in classes, groups, and residence halls. They could work with these student leaders to expand their offerings on topics such as safe sex, substance abuse, and sexual assault awareness and prevention to high schools, community centers, and churches in neighborhoods where pregnancy, crime, and drugs are prevalent among youth. The peer educators could then engage together in reflection about how these issues are affected by poverty and what future actions they can take to address them.

Judicially mandated community service is a common sanction that student conduct officials and courts impose on students found responsible for violations. Often, the student who has committed the violation is required to submit verification of completing a certain number of service hours and an unrelated, so-called "reflection paper" about the consequences of the violation. Student conduct officers and student judicial board members can instead engage violators in well-designed service-learning and reflection that are based on situation-specific learning outcomes such as the rights and responsibilities of citizenship, self in community, and issues specific to the nature of the violation.

Leadership development programs often engage emerging and experienced student leaders in service-learning to enable them to develop leadership competencies such as effective communication, resilience, building trust, empowering and developing others, goal setting, problem solving, and valuing and leveraging diversity. Service-learning can also be a powerful means of engaging with the concepts and practices of leadership for social change, including socially responsible leadership, servant leadership, and social entrepreneurship. An outstanding example is the APPLES service-learning program at the University of North Carolina-Chapel Hill, a student-led program under the Carolina Center for Public Service. Among its numerous initiatives, APPLES offers a fellowship to student teams to create an innovative social-impact project that addresses a community-identified need (Carolina Center for Public Service [CCPS], 2017).

Conclusion

King and Baxter Magolda (1996) observed that a successful educational experience "simultaneously increases cognitive understanding and a sense of personal maturity and interpersonal effectiveness" (pp. 163–164). Whether it is inside or outside the formal curriculum, service-learning enables students to learn both affectively and cognitively. By developing and facilitating service-learning experiences that embed the principles of reflection and reciprocity, student affairs professionals assume their rightful place as educators.

References

Clayton, P. H., Bringle, R. G., & Hatcher, J. A. (Eds.). (2013). *Research on service-learning: Conceptual frameworks and assessment* (Vol. 2). Sterling, VA: Stylus.

Carolina Center for Public Service. (2017). *APPLES Service-Learning Robert E. Bryan Fellowships.* Retrieved from http://ccps.unc.edu/apples/bryan-social-innovation-wfellowships-3/

Community-Campus Partnerships for Health Board of Directors. (2013). Position statement on authentic partnerships. Retrieved from https://ccph.memberclicks.net/principles-of-partnership.

Dewey, J. (1933). *How we think: A restatement of the relation of reflective thinking to the educative process.* Boston, MA: D.C. Heath and Company.

Dewey, J. (1938). *Experience and education.* New York, NY: Collier.

Eyler, J. S., Giles, D. E., & Schmiede, A. E. (1996). *A practitioner's guide to reflection in service-learning: Student voices and reflections.* Nashville, TN: Vanderbilt University Press.

Fisher, I. & Wilson, S. H. (2003). Partnerships with students. In B. Jacoby (Ed.), *Building partnerships for service-learning* (pp. 85–105). San Francisco, CA: Jossey-Bass.

Flanagan, C. A. & Bundick, M. (2011). Civic engagement and psychosocial well-being in college students. *Liberal Education, 97*(2), 20–27.

Fried, J. (2016). *Of education, fishbowls, and rabbit holes: Rethinking teaching and liberal education for an interconnected world.* Sterling, VA: Stylus Publications.

Hillman, T. (1999). Dissolving the provider-recipient split. *Academic Exchange, 3*(4), 123–127.

Jacoby, B. (1996). *Service-learning in higher education: Concepts and practices.* San Francisco, CA: Jossey-Bass.

Jacoby, B. (2015). *Service-learning essentials: Questions, answers, and lessons learned.* San Francisco, CA: Jossey-Bass.

King, P. & Baxter Magolda, M. (1996). A developmental perspective on learning. *Journal of College Student Development, 37*, 163–173.

Kolb, D. (1984). *Experiential learning: Experience as the source of learning and development.* Englewood Cliffs, NJ: Prentice Hall.

Kretzmann, J. P. & McKnight, J. L. (1993). *Building communities from the inside out: A path toward finding and mobilizing a community's assets.* Evanston, IL: Center for Urban Affairs and Policy Research, Northwestern University.

Mezirow, J. (1990). *Fostering critical reflection in adulthood: A guide to transformational learning.* San Francisco, CA: Jossey-Bass.

Porter-Honnet, E. & Poulsen, S. J. (1990). Principles of good practice in combining service and learning. In J. C. Kendall (Ed.), *Combining service and learning: A resource book for community and public service.* Raleigh, NC: National Society for Experiential Education.

Repair the World. (2016). Retrieved from http://www.repairtheworld.nyc

Sanford, N. (1966). *Self and society: Social change and individual development.* New York, NY: Atherton Press.

Sigmon, R. L. (1994). *Serving to learn, learning to serve: Linking service with learning.* Washington, DC: Council of Independent Colleges.

Sigmon, R. L. (1996). *Journey to service-learning: Experiences from independent liberal arts colleges and universities.* Washington, DC: Center for Independent Colleges.

University of Connecticut Center for Career Development. (2017). *Careers for the common good.* Retrieved from https://career.uconn.edu/careers-for-the-common-good/

8

PEDAGOGY

What Is That?

Jane Fried

When was the last time you talked about *pedagogy* or even used the word in a conversation? It's not part of the typical student affairs discourse, yet it has implications for almost everything we do. If we are about helping students learn some of the most important elements of personal and community life, the time has come to describe what we do in these areas as teaching. *Pedagogy* is a word that describes teaching, but has much broader implications than the word usually carries. Student affairs professionals need to know what pedagogy is and how to discuss it with faculty colleagues. If we say we teach and we can't describe our own teaching process, we will be unable to communicate our educational role to the other educators in our institutions.

The Greek origin of the term *pedagogy* refers to teaching children. A closer look at the historical use indicates that pedagogues taught children life skills and were their caretakers throughout the day, including those times of day when they were in school under the supervision of instructors who taught them academic subject matter. *Pedagogy* is a complex idea because it integrates processes that we have disaggregated in modern universities. *Pedagogy* refers to what Dewey (1938) called experiential education, including the process of creating challenging experiences that students must participate in, discuss, and integrate into their understanding of the world. *Pedagogy* involves information acquisition, creation of a context in which that information is meaningful, and development of methods that help students learn how to use and speak about the information they have learned. Ultimately, *pedagogy* is concerned both with character development and application of information and skills to real-life problems in social settings. In most modern colleges and universities, we have separated information transfer and many aspects of analytical thinking from character development and the teaching of skills related to interpersonal activities and personal values. The organizational representation of this phenomenon is the academic/student affairs divide.

What is Student Affairs Pedagogy?

Student development education is another term for student affairs pedagogy. When Esther Lloyd-Jones (1954) wrote *Student Personnel Work as Deeper Teaching*, she was describing student affairs pedagogy. She described "educating students as whole people, teaching them to reflect on their own experiences as a means of developing the skills of democratic equality in interpersonal and community relationships" (as cited in Fried, 2012, p. 16). More recently, Crookston (1973) suggested,

> What is needed is to transform education so that it neither focuses on subject matter requirements and syllabi nor attempts to fit the student into a cultural heritage, but becomes a model of human development that teaches students the processes of discovering what is known and applying that knowledge to a deeper understanding of self, of enhancing the quality of relationships with others and of coping effectively with their world. (p. 52)

Student affairs pedagogy is the process of helping students learn content, skills, and attitudes in a context that pertains to the subject matter so that they can become more effective in achieving their goals. The process of understanding student affairs pedagogy is mostly a phenomenon of translating what most student affairs practitioners do from academic language to student affairs language. Once we realize that what we typically call "training design" is pedagogy in other terms, the entire project becomes far less intimidating. Everybody who conducts RA training, teaches leadership skills, helps students write résumés, or make good academic and career decisions is using some kind of pedagogy. Even when we mediate roommate conflicts or help student groups make decisions about programs or budget, we are teaching and we use pedagogy. As student affairs professionals become a more visible part of the educational staff of our institutions, we should be describing the pedagogy that underlies the work we do with students that helps them learn all of the elements that are in our curriculum (e.g., decision making, life planning, leadership etc.).

Pedagogy as Epistemology

Pedagogy is more than the design of learning experiences. It is based on epistemology, or "ways of knowing" (Belenky, Clinchy, Goldberger, & Tarule, 1985). The dominant epistemology of teaching in Western education is positivism. Positivism is the theory that all reliable knowledge is based on phenomena that can be observed, and by implication, described and counted or measured (Fried, 2016). Positivism can be thought of as the old adage, "seeing is believing." The presumption is that if a person can't see something, either through their own sensory apparatus or the many kinds of instruments that measure and make physical phenomena visible, then it is not to be considered real. There are many consequences of seeing the world through positivist epistemology. The one that is important to student affairs professionals is the assertion that feelings cannot be considered valid sources of information precisely because they can't be seen or measured. Another assumption of positivism is that when people observe the same phenomena, they all see precisely the same thing. Time, place, and context are irrelevant (Fried, 1995). Anyone who has ever attempted to resolve a roommate conflict or negotiate a decision about which band to invite to a campus event has ample evidence that while all involved may know the same facts, not everyone comes to the same conclusions about what they mean. Positivism provides the foundation for much of Western science and many other elements of Western civilization. It is typically an accurate but incomplete description of consensual reality.

A contrasting epistemology is constructivism. Constructivism has many definitions even in the field of education. At its most basic, constructivism is the epistemological system that asserts that information cannot be understood separately from the people and the situation in which it is being understood. A consensus can typically be achieved about "facts," but interpretations are profoundly influenced by context, language, and a host of other personal, cultural, and social factors. Constructivism has deep implications for teaching and learning. Working on the assumptions of this philosophy, one is obligated to give credence to many interpretations and learn to ask questions about the facts that support the interpretations. "Constructivism rejects the idea of a universal perspective and the discovery of facts in favor of the selection of facts from context with an acknowledgment of perspective" (Fried, 2016, p.16).

Student affairs professionals typically operate on constructivist assumptions because most situations in which we work are complicated, social, and ambiguous. There is often no right answer to a question. Sometimes even achieving consensus about the definition of the question is difficult. Every person in student affairs who is helping students learn needs to be able to describe and discuss constructivism and its implications, because most academic work and many outcomes of empirical assessments are based on positivism. If we don't explain that we are operating on a different epistemology, many academics will simply dismiss our arguments and discussions about our educational work with students as "soft." In this culture, soft is never as good as hard, and words are considered soft while numbers are considered hard. Think about this process as translation. For example, if you say *Are you hot?* in English, you might be asking about physical temperature or sexual interest. In German, if you say *Ich bin heiss,* you are describing sexual interest and there is another grammatical construction for comments about the temperature. Imagine if you were speaking German and made that grammatical error. Similar types of misunderstandings occur all the time in higher education when student affairs professionals describe our educational work to faculty. We are speaking to people who operate on different assumptions about teaching and learning, and translation is very important so that we can understand each other. It is often very interesting to have a conversation with faculty members about their definition of learning, what kinds of learning matter, and how they know if students have learned. The purpose of such a conversation is to understand how other people define the terms we are using and how close we are in achieving consensus about meaning.

Assessment of Learning Outcomes

Student affairs professionals have become quite skilled in assessment of learning outcomes in the past decade. The distinction between positivism and constructivism is important in this context as well. We know how to describe learning outcomes. Now we must learn how to think about how we define learning outcomes based on either one of these two systems, or possibly both. A learning outcome described in *Learning Reconsidered 2* (Komives, 2006) is, "Students will be able to articulate the pros and cons about a complex issue and formulate their own position regarding that issue" (p. 22). How does one assess whether or not a student has learned how to do this? A student has to learn to express the perspectives involved and take a position in support of one perspective based on facts. This is a verbal process and should be assessed in a constructivist, qualitative manner. In contrast, a learning outcome from a math course might be that a student can complete ten geometry problems in half an hour and arrive at correct answers for 80 percent of the problems. That is a positivist outcome. Nobody is interested in the student's state of mind while completing that task. One of the first things I learned in college is that before we can have a meaningful conversation, we must define our terms and be sure we mean the same thing when we use the same words. Otherwise, we will never understand each other, no matter how much we care about doing that.

Becoming Systematic in Your Educational Work

I was completely surprised when I looked up *pedagogy* and discovered the connections to what I have always called training design. I was also very pleased to discover how much research there is about pedagogy and how much we in student affairs have to learn from the folks who have investigated the most effective approaches to pedagogy. Here are several methods for conceptualizing the way you organize your training programs and other educational activities.

Robert Gagne (Instructional Design, 2015) discusses the conditions of learning.

1. *Gain attention*—This usually involves food, gongs, and ice-breakers;
2. *Identify objective*—We tend to call this learning outcomes. What do you want the students who participate to learn? If you are doing a mediation or other kind of conversation, you still have some kind of learning outcome, even if you haven't thought about what it might be;

3. *Recall prior learning* —It is always useful to connect what you are helping students learn with what they already know. Metaphors are also useful, such as examples from local sports teams, other activities you know the students are involved in, etc.;

4. *Present stimulus*—This can mean your whole program, or whatever you are using to focus student attention and structure new learning;

5. *Guide*—Is there anybody in student affairs who doesn't know how to do this? Ask questions, connect thoughts and experiences, present other ideas that might make this experience more meaningful;

6. *Elicit performance*—If there is a skill involved, ask students to show you how they would do whatever you are teaching them to do. This might mean learning to provide non-judgmental feedback, organizing an agenda, or creating a draft résumé;

7. *Provide feedback*—This is also a widely-used student affairs skill. Tell students how they're doing and what they might do differently to be more effective;

8. *Assess performance*—We are up to our earlobes in assessment methods. Go back to your learning goals and ask what performance would look like if the students had learned what you taught;

9. *Enhance retention*—In later conversations, refer back to the learning experience; ask students to write journal entries before they leave; ask them to think of one place where they can use what they have learned and make a commitment to practice it within a day or relatively short period of time; check in with students.

These steps can provide a convenient checklist for any program as part of the planning process; they are often in use in student affairs, even when planners are not aware of the process. If most of what you do educationally involves unscripted conversations with students, take a few minutes after the conversation is complete and review what you did as a personal assessment.

Teaching Tolerance is a project of the Southern Poverty Law Center (SPLC). In order to support culturally responsive pedagogy, *Teaching Tolerance* has created "Five Standards of Effective Pedagogy" (*Teaching Tolerance*, 2017). The SPLC provides many educational resources for teachers at all levels to support work on social justice issues. These standards can be applied to lessons in social justice, and include:

> *Standard 1—Joint Productive Activity.* All constructivist methods emphasize the role of language in helping people understand and make meaning of what they learn. Joint productive activity is a way to describe the creation of a collaborative task that students have to address, complete, and discuss. Creating these activities requires taking into account the numbers of participants, the seating arrangements, the time available, and all other factors in typical training design.

Standard 2—Language Development. Students may need to develop new vocabulary to discuss both the task and to speak to the other participants. Participation of the trainer in this process is crucial in order to support interpersonal respect, creation of effective terms for the work at hand, and mutual understanding if all participants do not use the same primary language.

Standard 3—Contextualization. The trainer is responsible for helping students connect the activities to their lives in other contexts. All meaningful learning must have some connection to areas of life that are important to students. Trainers should ask appropriate questions like "Have you ever seen this happen anyplace else?" as they observe the learning process.

Standard 4—Challenging Activities. Challenging activities are closely related to the support of cognitive complexity. Challenging activities require students to understand the big picture as well as the details. Teachers are also expected to set standards for acceptable performance and tell students what they should achieve and how they will know when they have done so. An example of a challenging activity is the tower building exercise, which has been in use for decades. Groups of students compete to build a tower that is tall, strong, and attractive. All groups receive the same materials and planning instructions. Groups must think about achieving all three standards simultaneously. The tallest tower will not win, nor will the strongest or the prettiest. Students must find a way to meet all three standards at the same time.

Standard 5—Instructional Conversation. Instructional conversation is dialogue that occurs between the teacher and the students during and after the activity. It focuses on interaction. The teacher should ask questions to push students to think further about the consequences of their choices, provide corrections if the students have misunderstood information, and expect that the students will respond to questions and converse with each other using whole sentences and complete thoughts. This aspect of effective pedagogy requires students to develop accurate language, learn to listen carefully, and ask questions when they don't understand. Dialogue also encourages the development of mutual respect. Generally, these kinds of dialogues may require time out to develop the rules of conversation in the activity. This is easily done by asking students how they want to be treated, how they expect to treat others, and what they want to do if they feel disrespected. Often, these rules are written on newsprint and taped to the wall.

Effective Student Affairs Pedagogy: Two Examples

Student affairs training programs range from the simple to the complex, from one-time programs to year-long curricula, as have been developed for residence hall systems. Going back to the tower exercise mentioned earlier, it is evident that it follows the format of Gagne's "Conditions of Learning" (Instructional Design, 2015).

The trainer gains attention by placing students in groups. She then informs the students about the judging criteria, and presents the stimuli that are the materials and instructions. Before beginning the activity, instructions are presented and questions answered. Students then engage in the activity. In this program, the trainer may stop the activity at one or more points to provide feedback, change the directions, or do whatever seems necessary to enhance the complexity of the task. Finally, the towers are judged and the students have the opportunity to discuss leadership, decision making, competition, and anything else that may have arisen during the program (Pfeiffer & Jones, 1973).

A much more complex program for a 15,000-student residence hall system at a public university is designed to provide educational activities that support the educational goals of the residential life system for resident students. The educational priority is "for students to grow personally, interpersonally and intellectually through engagement in inclusive learning communities" (University of Connecticut, January, 2017, np). This program is based on the "ten essential elements of a residential curriculum (Edwards & Gardener, 2015), including direct connection to the institutional mission, a clear statement of educational priorities and educational outcomes derived from those priorities, inclusion of developmental theory, learning goals, a variety of educational strategies and contexts, a scaffolded process of activities and interventions that are sequential and based on student development theory, inclusion of non-staff stakeholders and procedures for feedback, formative evaluation, and summative assessment. The learning goals and outcomes describe in behavioral specifics what each student should be able to describe or do at the completion of the program. The program includes a narrative that describes what place each goal occupies in the total process and context. To achieve each goal, the curriculum designers create a variety of individual programs tailored to the cognitive complexity levels of the target populations. A rubric is created for each learning community, and programs and interventions are placed on the chart to support appropriate sequencing and temporal context. The entire program takes into account both the level of development of the student participants, and the time in the academic year when particular interventions are implemented. It is only at the end of this planning process that specific lesson plans or training designs are created. This program is probably best understood by referring to the *Teaching Tolerance* principles of effective pedagogy, which has slightly more emphasis on context and language (2017).

Summary

Student affairs professionals typically don't talk about pedagogy, but we use pedagogical principles all the time. We do so every time we create a training program or teach students how to do something that will improve their ability to navigate challenging life circumstances. Pedagogy isn't part of the student affairs vocabulary, but it is a key element of faculty conversation and contributes strongly to the way faculty members think about teaching. If we want to improve the quality of our conversations about learning with faculty colleagues, we need to learn both the vocabulary and the epistemology of pedagogy. Pedagogy is very similar to training design. Epistemology is another word for "ways of knowing." We must do our own translations so that we can talk across our borders and increase our mutual understanding for the benefit of students.

References

Belenky, M., Clinchy, B., Goldberger, N., & Tarule, J. (1985). *Women's ways of knowing.* New York, NY: Basic Books.

Crookston, B. (1973) Education for human development. In C. Warnath (Ed.). *New directions for college counselors* (pp. 47–65). San Francisco, CA: Jossey-Bass.

Dewey, J. (1938). *Education and experience.* New York, NY: Collier Books.

Edwards, K. & Gardener, K. (October, 2015). Residential curriculum overview (PPT slides). Indianapolis, IN: Residential Curriculum Institute.

Fried, J. (2016). *Of education, fishbowls, and rabbit holes: Rethinking teaching and liberal education for an interconnected world.* Sterling, VA: Stylus.

Fried, J. (2012). *Transformative learning through engagement: Student affairs practice as experiential pedagogy.* Sterling, VA: Stylus.

Fried, J. & Assoc. (1995). *Shifting paradigms in student affairs: Teaching, learning, culture and context.* Alexandria, VA: American College Personnel Association.

Instructional Design. (2015). Conditions of learning (Robert Gagne). Retrieved from http://www.instructionaldesign.org/theories/conditions-learning.html

Komives, S. (2006). Developing learning outcomes. In R. Keeling (Ed.) *Learning reconsidered 2.* (pp. 17–42). United States: American College Personnel Association, Association of College and University Housing Officers International, Association of College Unions-International, National Academic Advising Association, National Association for Campus Activities, National Association of Student Personnel Administrators, and National Intramural Recreational Sports Association.

Lloyd-Jones, E. & Smith, R. (1954). *Student personnel work as deeper teaching.* New York, NY: McGraw Hill.

Pfeiffer, J. & Jones, J. (Eds.). (1973). *The 1973 annual handbook for group facilitators.* Iowa City, IA: University Associates.

Teaching Tolerance. (2017). Five standards of effective pedagogy. Retrieved from http://www.tolerance.org/supplement/five-standards-effective-pedagogy

University of Connecticut Department of Residential Life. (2017). Retrieved from http://reslife.uconn.edu

9

BACKWARD DESIGN

Beginning with the End in Mind

Daniel Murphy and Ruth Harper

Introduction

Virtually all student affairs professionals are involved with program planning and training. Teaching can be considered program planning, too—though typically more sequential, longer in duration, and broader in scope than most student organization events or floor programs. How do you approach program development? Do you use a planning model? Do you look at your programs as *teaching and learning*? That is what Daniel P. Murphy, an area coordinator at Rhode Island School of Design (RISD), suggests. Murphy's undergraduate degree in education and knowledge of lesson planning prove highly useful in his career in student affairs. He recommends a pedagogical process called backward design (Wiggins & McTighe, 2011).

In this chapter, you will be introduced to the backward design model and gain a practical understanding of its use through a template for program planning. You will learn the basic components of the model, how to draft learning outcomes, how to identify appropriate evidence, and thus how to craft an authentic learning experience firmly rooted in student understanding. These questions are addressed:

- What are the components of backward design?
- How can you use this model to support the mission of your institution, division of student affairs, and particular program/service unit?
- How can you more effectively create and assess learning opportunities for students?
- How can backward design lesson planning be used to develop authentic, inclusive learning experiences?

Professional Context for *Backward Design* in Student Affairs

The primary role of student affairs professionals is to support the learning and development of college students, according to the *Student Learning Imperative* (American College Personnel Association [ACPA], 1996). In recent years, the student affairs profession has faced greater accountability and a deeper need to validate the impact of its programs and services. Relevant research, theory, and demonstrated achievement of learning outcomes are now priorities (Schuh, Jones, Harper, & Associates, 2011). Although developed for K-12 curricula, backward design inherently enhances accountability and provides a research-supported method from which to create more intentional student learning and developmental experiences in higher education. This approach also reinforces important elements of the ACPA/NASPA (2010) professional competencies, specifically: assessment, evaluation, and research; and equity, diversity, and inclusion. In other words, backward design can better equip you to be a stronger student affairs practitioner and more effectively meet the standards of the profession. When implemented, this model provides solid planning, which can help provide differentiation and scaffolding to address the various learning styles of today's diverse students. Backward design encourages professionals to be purposeful, creative, and collaborative.

The conceptual framework of backward design explicitly aligns with three benchmarks of the National Survey of Student Engagement (NSSE): level of academic challenge, active and collaborative learning, and enriching educational experiences (McTighe & Seif, 2003). Additionally, this framework aids in heightening personal inquiry and critical thinking skills, highly desired learning outcomes.

What is Backward Design? What are the Components of this Model?

Backward design, also called understanding by design, places an emphasis on student comprehension. Understanding, in this context, refers to a student's ability to 1) make meaning of acquired knowledge; and 2) transfer this learning to a new context (Wiggins & McTighe, 2008). Rooted in the identification of learning outcomes and broad, overarching ideas (called "enduring understandings"), this approach intentionally guides the development of learning activities. Studies in cognitive psychology show that learning is based in both comprehension and appropriate application. Newmann and Associates (1996) found that students who learned based on broad understandings were more successful in transferring their learning to new situations when compared to students whose learning required mere recall.

Backward design provides a rubric for professionals to push students beyond basic knowledge acquisition and memorization into more complex ways of thinking. Utilizing Benjamin Bloom's Taxonomy (1956; see Figure 9.1), this

```
┌─────────────────────────────────┐
│          Evaluation             │
│          Synthesis              │
│          Analysis               │
│          Application            │
│          Comprehension          │
│          Knowledge              │
└─────────────────────────────────┘
```

FIGURE 9.1   Bloom's Taxonomy of Educational Objectives. (From Bloom, Englehart, Furst, Hill, & Krathwohl, 1956.)

method requires professionals to be innovative when developing learning activities that support higher-level cognitive skills, such as application, understanding, and analysis, rather than focusing on lower-level thinking. This method also calls for the differentiation of instruction to meet the needs and abilities of all students, supporting Gardner's (1983, 1993) and Kolb's (1984) notions that students learn best when instruction allows them to use their emotional (and other types of) intelligence and work with their preferred learning styles. Differentiation helps professionals avoid "one-size-fits-all" approaches and allows for customization of instructional methods.

Beginning with the end in mind makes a lot of sense. In fact, some semesters I (Harper) distribute final exams right along with syllabi at the first class meeting. While not trained in backward design, I intuitively saw the advantages of creating learning outcomes (final case study applications) at the same time as outlining the means of acquiring the knowledge and skills to do well on that assessment—and in being transparent with students about the process. Doing this also helped me winnow interesting but extraneous topics from the syllabus and weave in learning activities and resources that focus and strengthen student learning. In sharing this example, I am illustrating curriculum design, which student affairs professionals utilize, like me, often on a "common sense" basis. Gaining awareness and adding design strategies allows us all to become more intentional and effective in guiding student learning.

So how do you approach backward design? Let your ends drive your means. Think of learning outcomes and assessment from the very start. See how this might impact your program planning.

Curricular Priorities: Mental Health Training

Take the example of designing mental health training for new resident or peer or community assistants (for consistency, these students will be referred to as RAs throughout this chapter, though many colleges use other terms). Obviously, mental health is an enormous and important topic, but you will likely have just one day (or part of a day) of training to devote to it. Immediately, you know that you will need to make judicious choices about what to cover and how to cover it.

Backward design helps set curricular priorities by placing topic-related ideas into one of three levels: 1) worth being familiar with; 2) important to know and do; and 3) enduring understanding (Wiggins & McTighe, 2011) (see Figure 9.2).

Many things are worth being familiar with relative to the topic of college student mental health. Student staff in residence halls might want to know how widespread psychological and emotional concerns are among the college population, and which disorders in particular are frequently encountered. A very quick overview of prevalent mental health issues is probably sufficient for this training. In the category of more important knowledge are behavioral warning signs and relevant resources (e.g., contact information and knowledge of services available from the campus counseling and health center, university and community mental health and law enforcement, etc.). So the focus narrows, and more time would be spent on providing this information and making sure that it is understood. Perhaps most important at this level is participants' thorough understanding of residential life protocols for helping a student experiencing crisis, as this knowledge is crucial to an RA's ability to perform his or her responsibilities in an appropriate manner (see Figure 9.2).

The third level is what drives program-planning decision making and is defined by those enduring understandings. These are the issues that *must* be addressed and comprise the program's essential take-away messages that *must* be retained by participants. To center in on what these might be in the program

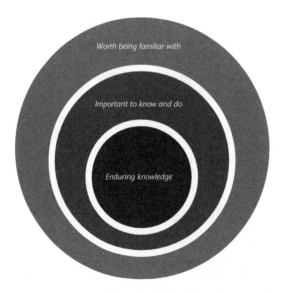

Worth being familiar with:
• college student mental health issues
• prevalent disorders and their signs

Important to know and do:
• familiarity with signs of student distress
• knowledge of campus and community resources
• initial intervention skills
  • talk with student privately
  • be accepting, attentive, nonjudgmental listener
  • refer appropriately (e.g., counseling, law enforcement, etc.)
  • follow up with student respectfully
• stress management: self and others

Enduring knowledge:
• ethically follow institutional and departmental protocols and policies
• suicide assessment and prevention
  • assessing potential for harm to self or others
  • keeping everyone safe
• record keeping re: all incidents of concern

FIGURE 9.2 Nested Circles. (Adapted from: Wiggins, G., & McTighe, J. 2011. Gaining Clarity on Our Goals. *Understanding by Design* 2nd ed., p. 71. Alexandria, VA: Association for Supervision and Curriculum Design.)

under consideration, Wiggins and McTighe (2011) pose four questions (slightly adapted for use in student affairs and this example):

- First, to what degree is the information essential to the RA performing his/her job responsibly? How will it help to ensure that a disturbed or disturbing student is safe and connected with appropriate support? How will it aid in protecting all students and building community and trust within the floor or hall?
- Second, to what extent does the topic or knowledge lie at the heart of being an ethical, effective RA?
- Third, these authors ask about what needs to be "uncovered." What in this topic might not be obvious—or might even be counterintuitive? Student employees often struggle a great deal, for example, with what information they can share with parents during a crisis, or even what they can reveal to roommates, suitemates, or floor residents. Regarding student mental health, what misconceptions might student staff harbor? Do they realize that depression and anxiety are highly treatable conditions, and that a student who experiences psychological crisis might well return to school and the hall and be just fine?
- Finally, how are you going to engage learners in the process of acquiring important information about supporting residents with mental health challenges? Fortunately, this topic lends itself to active learning with scenarios, case studies, vignettes, simulations, film clips, discussions, and more.

Working from the big subject area of mental health raises many questions and issues that will involve student staff learners. What *is* mental health? Which behaviors might be concerning? Backward design requires us to consider our population and utilize theories of student development. For instance, how might cultural differences impact understanding (e.g., if a middle-class white student is giving away all her possessions, that might indeed be something to look into; if an American Indian student mentions participating in a giveaway of valued possessions, it may signify a cultural gesture of generosity or gratitude)? What is the difference between a developmental issue (e.g., trying on a new identity in college that might involve a dramatic change in appearance) versus a mental health issue (e.g., social isolation and depression, excessive sleeping, crying, etc.)? How do RAs tell the difference (especially when they might be going through some of the same things themselves)? What exactly is an RA's responsibility here?

Continuum of Assessment

This example shows how the backward design model helps prioritize the content of the learning experience. Just as important is assessment. Sometimes student affairs practitioners are a bit leery of assessment. Many may fear that it is too time consuming; others may discover a favorite assessment tool and stick with it, even when it is not very meaningful. Backward design expects you to consider from the outset 1) what will constitute acceptable evidence of learning; and 2) how to deploy a variety of assessment methods. By identifying these two elements, you are effectively coming up with a usable assessment rubric. Wiggins and McTighe (2011) move beyond summative assessment to a *continuum* of assessment that incorporates many ways of checking in on participant comprehension, including preformative and summative assessments.

Formative assessments facilitate learning and guide the achievement of learning goals. Obtaining feedback along the way allows instructors to keep a finger on the pulse of student attention and comprehension—without which, a final, summative evaluation is relatively meaningless. Both forms of assessment are imperative: one guides the person(s) leading the learning and allows for adaptation and genuine learning; the other provides bottom-line evidence of changes in thinking or behavior.

In-Progress Assessments

Pre-assessment can happen prior to the session or as it begins. For instance, staff members can conduct a quick survey at the outset of a meeting to find out what participants already know about the issue at hand. An alternative to this is to draw upon existing information, such as incident reporting difficulties among RAs at the institution that indicate a problem area to be addressed.

Formative assessment is done throughout training in order to see what participants are struggling with or perhaps to confirm what they know very well. Review or clarifying questions are a good way to determine how well students comprehend material. Or students can use their cell phones to respond to an interactive live poll throughout the presentation. There are many ways to check in on student learning in the midst of any activity. The purpose of formative assessment is to verify that students understand the material as you go along, and if not, to identify the misunderstanding and address it before moving on.

An easy method to use at various points of the training is to simply ask those in attendance, "What questions do you have?" or "Let me know what is unclear at this point." Student affairs professionals are quite accustomed to asking for participant feedback on an ongoing basis. Open-ended questions involve learners and explore what is being learned while minimizing facilitator bias. As in inquiry-based teaching, this practice urges instructors to pose questions that require learners to investigate and uncover information themselves, making it more likely that the students will both understand and retain content. Familiar to many in student affairs is the "KWL" chart (know, want, learn). At the outset, the facilitator asks students: What do you know about this topic? What do you want to learn? And later, the question is: What did you learn?

Moving into more formal assessment methods, you can engage participants in topic-related dialogues and observe their interactions. Offering discussion prompts and brief scenarios requires participants to comprehend and apply what they are learning. And remember that faculty members don't hold the copyright on quizzes! Student affairs professionals also can use quizzes to identify what is being understood—or not. Even a quick, self-scored quiz can reveal areas that would benefit from further clarification or examples. Quizzes can serve as a pre-assessment evaluation and planning tool. Pre-tests often increase participant interest and buy-in to the learning experience. Both chapter authors have built discussions and quizzes around student assessments at the institutional level (e.g., CIRP, NSSE, etc.) and asked students to guess, for example, certain characteristics of entering students. When survey information is shared, students are often startled at the accuracy or inaccuracy of their assumptions, and this can lead to good discussion, with many implications for student affairs programing. At RISD, students were asked to estimate what percentage of the student body identifies as LGBT. Responses ranged from 5 to 50 percent; the actual figure was 20 percent. This grabbed students' attention, piqued their interest, and made them want to know more.

Wiggins and McTighe (2011) offered a useful assessment called an academic prompt. These are case studies, real-life examples, or more complex open-ended questions that compel participants to think critically, analyze situations, evaluate possible options, and apply what is being learned. Assessments like these address the "important to know and do" category of information, and draw students into the topic more deeply. Bloom's taxonomy theory, referenced earlier, endorses learning activities that require higher levels of application, analysis, and synthesis. An academic prompt on the topic of college student mental health could consist of a case study in which a student acts out under the influence of alcohol, shows up defiant at the student conduct meeting, and begins to cry when asked why a person who seems like a really good guy most of the time is suddenly treating friends and staff members with abuse (Laker, Harper, & Wilson in Harper & Wilson, 2010).

Summative Assessments

All of these assessments are formative; that is, they occur before and/or during the learning experience. What often comes to mind most readily regarding assessment is summative, or a culminating evaluation at the end of a program. Summative assessments are also valuable for many reasons: they can document overall learning, lead to ongoing program enhancement, or support the development of an action plan. Oftentimes, when departments or deans request proof of learning, they are referring to summative assessments. These assessments link the overall activity to the mission, goals, and objectives of the institution and/or the student affairs division or program unit. In other words, a traditional final evaluation, if constructed well, can provide clear evidence of learning and program value.

Returning to the example of an all-day training for RAs on the subject of college student mental health and how this issue will impact their work as student employees in residence halls, how might you start with identifying needed learning outcomes? Backward design asks you to list *all* desired learning outcomes related to the activity. In this case, outcomes might mirror Maslow's (1943) hierarchy of needs, starting with the psychological and physical safety and security of all individuals as well as the overall community, working through needs for love and belonging (e.g., residing in a caring community), through esteem and self-actualization (e.g., privacy and respect, learning to be helpful, supportive, and nonjudgmental). Specific phrases from the institutional, divisional, and residential life department mission statements could be included here. One example is: students in State University's residence halls will feel safe and secure in asking for help, as needed, from their community assistants. RAs will be knowledgeable of basic interventions (e.g., mental health first aid, etc.) regarding emotional or psychological distress, will follow established departmental and university protocols in the event of a crisis, and will communicate all incidents in a timely and accurate manner to a supervisor.

Toward or at the end of the program, a summative assessment that requires participants to apply the material and think more deeply about it is appropriate. In the context of this example, participants could be asked to create a community development plan and present it to others, using relevant theories and policies presented in the session. Another option is to ask students to observe a scenario, write up an incident report on the spot, and turn it in to their supervisors for discussion at an upcoming 1:1 meeting. "Behind Closed Doors" is a widely used, interactive series of residence hall scenarios that can serve as an excellent summative assessment. Some educators ask students to also write a "ticket out" of the session, such as "name one key concept you learned today" or "write down one way you plan to further your knowledge in an area we covered today." Wiggins and McTighe (2011) call such intentionally designed assessments "teaching targets" that lend focus as the learning activities are developed. With reference to the mental health training described earlier, a "ticket out" might be a written commitment to check the university's student health and counseling center's web page to become more familiar with its services and programs. Or a key concept could be two ways to help a student in crisis connect with an appropriate professional.

The residential life department at RISD uses backward design to construct all of its training sessions. Assessment often begins with a pre-planning survey. Next, staff members identify the learning outcomes and objectives for the upcoming activity, including institutional, departmental, and session-specific outcomes. Examples for RA training might include: 1) building mutually supportive relationships with your residential community; and 2) students will be able to identify key components of community development within their community.

The next step is to come up with the essential questions. These questions are broad and complex (with no one right answer); participants should be able to articulate a strong response by the end of the training. Examples of these types of questions are: How can active listening skills help RAs address the concerns of residents? What is the importance of being inclusive in program planning practices? How do we effectively create and assess learning activities for student staff? These are broad, open-ended questions that guide overall instruction and thinking.

Becoming increasingly specific, student affairs professionals then focus in on the knowledge they intend participants to be familiar with by the end of the session in question. For example, desired knowledge might entail traits of active listening, such as intentional body language, open-ended questions, and paraphrasing feelings and thoughts. Participants should also know relevant departmental policies and procedures.

But what should those in attendance be able to *do* as a result of this training? Goals in this area could include RAs being able to 1) effectively have conversations with students in distress by using active listening skills; and 2) ethically respond to residence life policy violations. Note here that planning for learning outcomes moves from knowledge to behavior.

Ongoing assessment is a crucial piece of backward design. In this scenario, how will student affairs practitioners know that participants have learned the material? What performance tasks will participants complete to demonstrate evidence of learning? Whatever is assessed here must tie back closely to the stated knowledge, behavior, and learning objectives previously identified. And, ideally, assessment is conducted before, during, and after the learning activity. In essence, identifying the learning outcomes, knowledge, and corresponding behaviors outlines what one is looking for in an assessment.

Differences Among Learners

Backward design also encourages program planners to consider the concept of differentiation, that is, to address the needs of the specific audience. For example, RISD is an art and design school with a liberal arts core. How could student development and related theories help accommodate the learning styles and preferences of art and design majors? Kolb (1984) might suggest that many are Convergers who like to think and then do; Gardner (1983; 1993) would indicate that these students are likely to be visual learners. Considering audience characteristics in this way can prompt trainers to be sure to offer clear and attractive visual presentation of the material and to provide an activity-based lesson that allows students to become involved in creating their responses. Not to stereotype, but students attending the Midwestern land grant institution of the other chapter author might tend to be Assimilators, in Kolb's terms, who prefer to think and observe before committing to action. Attending a university that is strongly oriented toward STEM fields, these students might also be more logical-mathematical in their conceptualizations. Creating programs for students at this institution might call for opportunities to reflect privately; instructional materials should engage students' interests in investigating or experimenting.

Another example of drawing on theory is in presenting to a campus LGBTQ organization, bearing in mind Cass's (1979) theory of sexual identity development. Realizing that some students may be in a stage of identity confusion while others will be in identity pride will help those designing learning experiences to anticipate the possible range of student issues, questions, and concerns. Knowing the audience and planning for students' full involvement in the learning activity is the goal.

Figure 9.3 is the program planning template that Murphy uses in the RISD Residence Life Office. Figure 9.4 is an empty backward learning template. How might you use this approach in the next learning activity you lead? Does it help you be more intentional if you focus on outcomes first? How does it aid in program development to determine assessment measures prior to constructing your presentation? Backward design can hone your program development skills, strengthen your training activities, and, best of all, enhance student learning.

Title/Topic:

Time:

Section 1 – Identify Desired Results

Learning Outcomes/Objectives: *List all desired learning outcomes for your activity. This can include institutional, departmental, and session-specific outcomes.*

    Examples:

- Building mutually supportive relationships with your residential community (RISD Departmental Outcome)
- Students will be able to identify key components of community development and practice it in their community (RA Training Outcome)
- Identify effective leadership skills and employ them in the RA position (RA Training Outcome)

Essential Question(s): *This is an overarching question that should be answerable as a result of attending the session. This should not be a yes or no question, but rather an open-ended question.*

    Examples:

- How can active listening skills help RAs address the concerns of residents?
- What's the importance of using inclusive programming practices?
- How do we effectively create and assess learning activities for our students?

Knowledge: *As a result of this session, participants will know…*

Examples:
- Residence life policies and procedures
- Skills of active listening, such as body language, asking open-ended questions, and paraphrasing

Behavior: *As a result of this session, participants will be able to…*

Example:
- Ethically respond to residence life policy violations
- Effectively have difficult conversations with students in distress using active listening skills

Section 2 – Determine Acceptable Evidence

Assessment: *List how you will assess learning. What performance tasks will participants partake in to demonstrate and provide evidence of proficiency? How will you, the facilitator, know they've learned the material? These should directly relate to the knowledge, behavior, and learning outcomes.*

Pre:

Examples:
- Quick survey at beginning of session to see what participants know about the topic
- Incident reporting by RAs prior to session demonstrates that students do not know proper writing techniques

Formative:
- Ask for participant questions throughout the session
- Using an interactive live poll with cell phones, ask participants questions on the material throughout the presentation

Summative:
- Participants create a community development plan and present it utilizing community theories discussed in presentation
- Students observe a scenario, write an incident report, and turn it in to supervisor to discuss during next 1:1

Differentiation: *Consider who your audience is. What theories can you use to guide modifications for different students in your audience? What accommodations can you provide to those with differing ability levels?*

Examples:
- Art majors: Provide an active activity that allows students to enact their learning; provide visual representations of information (Kolb: Converging, Think then Do; Gardner: Multiple Intelligences, Visual)
- Presentation to LGBTQ student organization, considering stages of sexual identity development and anticipating potential issues/responses (Cass: identity confusion vs. identity pride)

(Continued)

Section 3 – Plan Learning Experiences
Learning Activities: *List instructions of how to facilitate this session. Learning activities should relate directly to the identified desired results and identified acceptable evidence.*

FIGURE 9.3 Backwards Design Lesson Plan Template. (Adapted from: Wiggins, G., & McTighe, J. 2005. *Understanding by Design* 2nd ed. Alexandria, VA: Association for Supervision and Curriculum Development.)

Title/Topic: The First 6 Weeks (New RA Training)
Time: 1.5 hours, April 17, 2015
Section 1 – Identify Desired Results
Learning Outcomes/Objectives: *List all desired learning outcomes for your activity. This can include institutional, departmental, and session-specific outcomes.* •
Essential Question(s): *This is an overarching question that should be answerable as a result of attending the session. This should not be a yes or no question, but rather an open-ended question.* •
Knowledge: *As a result of this session, participants will know…*   **Behavior:** *As a result of this session, participants will be able to…* •
Section 2 – Determine Acceptable Evidence
Assessment: *List how you will assess learning. What performance tasks will participants partake in to demonstrate and provide evidence of proficiency? How will you, the facilitator, know they've learned the material? These should directly relate to the knowledge, behavior, and learning outcomes.* **Pre:** • **Formative:** • **Summative:** •

Differentiation: *Consider who your audience is. What theories can you use to guide modifications for different students in your audience? What accommodations can you provide to those with differing ability levels?*

Section 3 – Plan Learning Experiences

Learning Activities: *List instructions of how to facilitate this session. Learning activities should relate directly to the identified desired results and identified acceptable evidence.*

FIGURE 9.4   Backwards Design Lesson Plan Template. (Adapted from: Wiggins, G., & McTighe, J. 2005. *Understanding by Design* 2nd ed. Alexandria, VA: Association for Supervision and Curriculum Development.)

References

American College Personnel Association & National Association of Student Personnel Administrators (ACPA/NASPA) (2010). *Professional competency areas for student affairs educators.* Retrieved from https://www.naspa.org/images/uploads/main/Professional_Competencies.pdf

American College Personnel Association (1996). *The student learning imperative.* Retrieved from http://acpa.nche.edu.sli.sli.htm

Bloom, B., Englehart, M. Furst, E., Hill, W., & Krathwohl, D. (1956). *Taxonomy of educational objectives: The classification of educational goals. Handbook I: Cognitive domain.* New York, Toronto: Longmans, Green.

Cass, V. C. (1979). Homosexual identity formation: A theoretical model. *Journal of Homosexuality, 4,* 219–235.

Gardner, H. (1983, 1993) *Frames of mind: The theory of multiple intelligences.* New York, NY: Basic Books.

Harper, R. & Wilson, N. L. (2010). *More than listening: A casebook for using counseling skills in student affairs work.* Washington, DC: NASPA.

Kolb, D. A. (1984). *Experiential learning: Experience as the source of learning and development.* Upper Saddle River, NJ: Prentice Hall.

Maslow, A. H. (1943). A theory of human motivation. *Psychological Review, 50*(4), 370–396.

McTighe, J. & Seif, E. (2003). *A summary of underlying theory and research base for understanding by design.* Retrieved from jaymctighe.com

Newmann, F. M. & Associates. (1996). *Authentic achievement: Restructuring schools for intellectual quality.* San Francisco, CA: Jossey-Bass.

Schuh, J. H., Jones, S. R., Harper, S. R., & Associates. (2011). *Student services: A handbook for the profession* (5th ed.). San Francisco, CA: Jossey-Bass.

Wiggins, G. & McTighe, J. (2005). *Understanding by design* (2nd ed.). Alexandria, VA: Association for Supervision and Curriculum Development.

Wiggins, G. & McTighe, J. (2008). Put understanding first. *Educational Leadership, 65*(8), 36–41.

Wiggins, G. & McTighe, J. (2011). *The understanding by design guide to creating high-quality units.* Alexandria, VA: Association for Supervision and Curriculum Development.

SECTION III

Learning Contexts and Locations

10

ENHANCING STUDENT LEARNING THROUGH GLOBAL ENGAGEMENT

John M. Howe

Introduction

One would be hard-pressed to find a mission or vision statement of a college or university today that does not acknowledge the increasingly global nature of education in modern society. As stated by the American Council on Education (2012), "graduates must possess intercultural skills and competencies to be successful in this globalized world, and higher education institutions must commit to helping students achieve these outcomes" (p. 3). To meet these lofty objectives, colleges and universities must work diligently to provide curricular and co-curricular opportunities in order to prepare students for successful entry into increasingly diverse and multicultural workforces. With this context, this chapter highlights strategies for student affairs professionals to enhance student learning through global engagement.

Overview of Global Movements

Though international education has received increased attention in recent years, it is important to remember that even the earliest institutions of higher learning were global in nature.

> From the beginning, universities represented global institutions—in that they functioned in a common language, Latin, and served an international clientele of students. Professors, too, came from many countries, and the knowledge imparted reflected scholarly learning in the Western world at the time. (Altbach, 2004, p. 4)

In a seminal piece on comparative education, Cummings (1999) reminded readers that Meiji oligarchs during Japan's feudal era and early American educators like Horace Mann and Henry Barnard utilized notions of borrowing and lending found through educational tours of other cultures. Internationalization of modern day academe is increasingly accomplished through the global exchange of students and scholars, or as Altbach described these academic sojourners, the "concrete manifestations of the ways in which the knowledge network functions" (1997, p. 207). Simply stated, "Academic mobility is a hallmark of the global age" (Altbach, Reisberg, & Rumbley, 2010, p. 3).

Annually, the Institute for International Education (IIE) publishes a report on the global exchange of students and scholars to and from institutions of higher education in the United States. Data presented in the *Open Doors 2015: Report on International Education* indicate record amounts of American students studying abroad as well as historic numbers of international students pursuing studies in the United States. During the 2014–2015 reporting period, 974,926 international students enrolled in U.S. colleges and universities, representing a 10 percent increase from the previous academic year (Farrugia & Bhandari, 2015). The top five countries of origin for these international students include China (304,040), India (132,888), South Korea (63,710), Saudi Arabia (59,945), and Canada (27,240). "The United States remained the leading study abroad destination for higher education students worldwide, hosting 22 percent of all globally mobile students" (p. 14). This report also noted that 304,467 U.S. students received academic credit through study abroad during 2013–2014, a 5.2 percent increase from the previous year. The leading destinations for U.S. students include the United Kingdom (38,250), Italy (31,166), Spain (26,949), France (17,597), and China (13,763). Student mobility is not unique to U.S. institutions of higher education, however. Since its formal launch in 1987, the ERASMUS (European Region Action Scheme for the Mobility of University Students) Programme (now called the ERASMUS+ Programme) has assisted over 4,400,000 students to pursue studies at universities of member states throughout the European Union (European Commission, 2017).

With these global movements of learners, student affairs professionals play essential roles in preparing students for international study and readying our campuses to welcome students from across the globe. As both American students abroad and international students within American collegiate communities involve elements of global exchange, the fundamentals common to the shared experience of transition of these international sojourners will be jointly examined in this chapter.

The World Is Your Oyster

While student affairs professionals have long heralded the benefits of student engagement, participation in certain educational activities such as service-learning, research partnerships with faculty, and study abroad have been designated as high-impact practices (HIPs) as they engage students in activities that elevate learning (Kuh, 2008). Participating in one or more high-impact practice, such as study abroad programs and campus-based cross-cultural activities, increases "the likelihood that students will experience diversity through contact with people who are different from themselves" (p. 15). Active engagement in these experiences allows students to view alternative perspectives and creates a better understanding of self within a global context. In this manner, student affairs professionals must work diligently to ensure that our campuses offer welcoming and receptive learning environments through assessment of our campus climates as well as thoughtful, sustained programmatic efforts to all students—international and domestic.

Climate

Preparation is essential for successful travel. Even the novice vacationer will likely check the weather forecast to determine which items to bring. Whether packing a suitcase for a short-term study abroad program or filling boxes for a semester or longer international transition, it is imperative to have knowledge of the climate of your destination. Just as poor weather might influence a traveler's holiday, environmental theories inform student affairs practitioners of the critical role welcoming and supportive campus climates play in facilitating student learning.

To best engage student learners, we must understand our campus environments. From an institutional perspective, effective leaders support recurrent studies of their campus climate. Campus climate surveys proffer the opportunity for a community of learners to examine its institutional reflection as experienced through the prism of diverse campus stakeholders. Through regular administrations of climate surveys, campus constituents are able to share their experiences regarding the extent to which their institution lives its stated values, aspects of their shared belonging (or lack thereof), and assess and evaluate campus standings over time.

The act of administering climate surveys alone bears no fruit. In reflecting on her experience as an international faculty member from Jamaica, Stanley (2006) presented how U.S. institutions of higher education promote diversity, yet "maintain systems of power and privilege by asking those who are 'different' to walk the assimilation line and be like the majority" (p. 337). Berry's (2006) work on acculturation demonstrates that sojourning individuals who maintain ties to their culture and heritage and are also able to create close connections with their new surroundings are most likely to be successful in their transition. For this to be possible, however, the dominant society must embrace multiculturalism and a willingness to see the value in others. Climate surveys are a platform for anonymous, straightforward, in-time feedback like that of Dr. Stanley that, in turn, provides institutions invaluable data to improve and amend practice.

Institutional, divisional, and departmental leaders must utilize and share results of climate surveys so that areas of concern and gaps in campus programs and services are addressed in order to enrich current practice. Understanding the campus climate and environment is essential as we prepare to send students abroad and welcome international students into our campus communities. Information gleaned through climate surveys assists institutions in properly meeting and informing student needs for pre-departure study abroad advising meetings and orientations as well as to ready, enhance, and supplement campus programs for incoming international students.

Beyond Orientation

It is common practice for study abroad and international student services offices to present and make information regarding culture and customs readily available prior to domestic students studying abroad or before the arrival of international students to campus. This information is foundational to the transition of students as they prepare to embark on journeys to join new learning environments in unfamiliar countries. While awareness of country-specific cultural contexts is essential to facilitate understanding of their new environs, it is it also vital that new members of the educational community have appreciation for the distinctive culture of their learning environment. Kuh and Whitt (1988) defined culture in higher education as follows:

> the collective, mutually shaping patterns of norms, values, practices, beliefs, and assumptions that guide behaviors of individuals and groups in an institute of higher education and provide a frame of reference within which to interpret the meaning of events and actions on and off campus. (pp. 12–13)

It would be beneficial to explicitly discuss and have students explore their current campus cultures prior to navigating new institutional contexts abroad.

As novices to their new academic communities in unfamiliar national landscapes, U.S. students abroad and international students in the United States often find themselves at the periphery of this culturally rooted shared frame of reference critical to their educational success and understanding. Though websites, texts, presentations, and brochures assist in the facilitation of explicit knowledge (such as needed immigration documents, processes for course registration, campus-based housing options, etc.) necessary for international transition, elements of implicit or informal practices (such campus resources not readily apparent from organizational charts or websites and means to navigating institutional gatekeepers) require continued support throughout the length of students' international sojourns. Student affairs practitioners are afforded a critical opportunity to connect and help transitioning students navigate their new and unknown environments through orientation programs, inclusive programming, and the continual offering of welcoming, easily accessible spaces to assist throughout their time of transition. These services are critically important to mitigating the stresses that are present when navigating new surroundings.

Stressors of Transition

While an essential role of student affairs professionals is to assist all students as they navigate their new campus context, the importance of this role is amplified when the learner crosses national borders and faces added acculturative stressors. Sandhu and Asrabadi (1994) measured acculturative stress of 86 international male students and 42 females in the U.S. through the administration of a survey. Their study found that mitigating factors of acculturative stress included perceived discrimination, homesickness, fear, guilt, perceived hatred, and change (Sandhu & Asrabadi, 1994). More recently, Lee and Rice (2007) examined the experiences of 24 international students in the American Southwest using the conceptual framework of neo-racism. Through this conceptual lens, the authors found direct and indirect factors influencing international students' abilities to engage fully as members of their adopted community, organizational policies that disadvantaged non-majority members, opposition toward cultural traits (specifically surrounding language barriers), and negative stereotyping of cultural and national groups. Regrettably, all these factors "hinder intercultural diplomacy and friendship and obstruct intellectual growth, which should be the outcome of exchange" (Lee & Rice, 2007, p. 405). As presented earlier, climate surveys would provide institutions pathways to capture such lived experiences of international students and avenues to remedy difficulties experienced in their transition.

Unsurprisingly, U.S. students abroad also encounter elements of culture shock when facing unfamiliar environments. While 53.3 percent of U.S. students abroad studied in Europe in 2013–2014 (Farrugia & Bhandari, 2015), domestic students overseas also face elements of acculturative stress and dissonance. Dobly's (2004) qualitative study examined the study abroad experiences of U.S. citizens and residents in Australia and offered insight into how 19 Americans from the Midwest navigated their transition from the majority culture in their homeland to being the "other." One student expressed this notion of otherness as follows: "It's weird to show up and be the one, I have an accent now, and everybody else speaks what they consider normal. And so it was weird at first because I didn't want to open my mouth" (Dolby, 2004, p. 163). As demonstrated by this study, if linguistic stressors are present in exchanges in which visitor and host country share a mother tongue, student affairs professionals must also be cognizant of the role language plays in the transition and learning of sojourning students.

Language Barriers

When examining international exchange, it is imperative to examine the impact of language. If the U.S. participants in Dolby's (2004) study experienced linguistic dissonance abroad in a land with a shared language, this element of transition is undoubtedly amplified when greater barriers to communication are present for U.S. students abroad or international students on our campuses. This point is illustrated by Jenkins's (2000) study in which the linguistic barriers among seven Chinese teaching assistants and their mathematics faculty supervisors at a large research university were studied. While findings from the case study proffer limited generalizability, the differences of perceptions between faculty and students provide critical insights into the impact of divergent cultural and linguistic interpretations. Jenkins found that Chinese teaching assistants offered "polite deference and concern for maintaining appropriate face for unequal status interactions" (p. 477). This deference was often presented as silence toward faculty members. In turn, U.S. faculty inferred the behavior as a "lack of motivation, isolationism and unwillingness to cooperate in ITA (international teaching assistant) instructional assignments, or in improving their English" (Jenkins, 2000, p. 477).

Not all linguistic and cultural miscues will be as pronounced as those found in Jenkins's study, but this demonstrates the importance of ensuring that campuses offer continued support to international sojourners through offices, personnel, and peers so that international students have a sustained sounding board to aid their efforts in transition to unfamiliar campus environments. Fortuijn (2002) presents this foundational need for language in transition as follows: "Communication, however, is critical in the academy as the problem of language is a problem of understanding" (p. 226). Student affairs professionals play a critical role in ensuring that all voices are heard and in offering assistance to bridge gaps across linguistic and cultural divides when inevitable misunderstandings occur.

Student Affairs Sustained Role

Student affairs professionals also play an essential role in encouraging and readily providing opportunities for consequential interactions amongst the diverse populations of our campuses. The importance of these exchanges for international students and domestic students preparing for international study is significant. Chapdelaine and Alexitch (2004) found that meaningful contact is less likely to occur as distance between host and visitor's culture increases. Examined through Furnham and Bochner's model of culture shock, the authors found that as interactions with U.S. students decreased, the likelihood for the international student to experience cultural shock increased (Chapdelaine & Alexitch, 2004). These findings are critical to learning in that "without meaningful social interactions with hosts, international students are unlikely to learn and develop the cultural specific social skills that would enable effective cross-cultural interactions" (Chapdelaine & Alexitch, 2004, pp. 180–181).

Brown and Holloway's (2008a) ethnographic study of postgraduate international students at a university in the south of England offered "the view of adjustment as a dynamic and multifaceted process, fluctuating throughout the sojourn as a result of a host of individual, cultural and external forces" (p. 242). The complex and changing elements of students' acculturative processes led the authors to conclude that structures to support and assist the adjustment of international postgraduate students are required beyond orientation and other front-loaded programs (Brown & Holloway, 2008b).

Connecting with campus peer groups is essential for students' successful transition. Though campus internationalization efforts are often encouraged and touted, institutional support through funding has not always been as forthcoming. Pedersen (1991) reports, "International students are likely to experience more problems than students in general and have access to fewer resources to help them" (p. 24). While international student populations continue to rise (Farrugia & Bhandari, 2015), institutional support structures have not risen proportionately (American Council on Education, 2012). Connecting international students to national peers through programs, residential communities, or shared tables in dining halls creates informal connections that aid students in transition.

As student affairs professionals, we understand the significant need to offer foundational supports through robust orientation programs for sojourning students, but also the importance to continue sustained services to students throughout their global transitions. Though support structures are essential to facilitate a positive student learning experience, McNamee and Faulkner's (2001) study of American faculty abroad offers some caution to the institutional role in mitigating elements of the acculturative process. According to the authors, "too little meaning disruption is likely to result in little or no personal growth. Too much meaning disruption, on the other hand, may be debilitating and interfere with the quality of the experience" (McNamee & Faulkner, 2001, p. 76). The delicate balance of challenge and support in enhancing student learning is familiar territory for student affairs professionals, but also serves as an important reminder of this foundational tenet of our profession.

Who Is Internationalization For?

Though research demonstrates all students benefit from high impact practices (Kuh, 2008), evidence suggests unequal participation within these educational opportunities (Kinzie, 2012). Farrugia and Bhandari's (2015) analysis of 2013–2014 study abroad data reveal the following characteristics: most students are undergraduate (87 percent), Caucasian (74.3 percent), female (65.3 percent), reporting no disabilities (94.3 percent), and participate in short-term (eight weeks or less) programs (62.1 percent). Luo and Jamieson-Drake's (2015) analysis of Cooperative Institutional Research Program (CIRP) cohort data from the classes of 2009–2011 from medium-size, private, highly selective research universities revealed similar findings along gender and race, with logistic regression analysis demonstrating a 1.94 increased likelihood for females to study abroad. Further analysis of CIRP data revealed "domestic off-campus study, involvement in a music or theatre group, the student government, a political club, and club sports may act as a barrier to study abroad" (Luo & Jamieson-Drake, 2015, p. 50). Data of study abroad participants reveal that first-generation college students (defined as neither parent with a bachelor's degree) were significantly less likely to have participated in a study abroad program than their peers (Kinzie, 2012).

In examining domestic students' participation (or lack thereof), it is also important to note that there are often significant impediments that must be overcome by international students in our midst. While the United States Department of State promotes U.S. tertiary education through the provision of informational resources and services, its Education USA (n.d.) site openly states the important role financing plays in international students' educational endeavors:

> When looking into studying in the United States, evaluating your finances should be one of the first things you do. As with any investment, you need to evaluate what's best for your educational and career goals and what you are willing to spend. (para 3)

While detailed financial disclosure is not part of the DS-160 (non-immigration visa) application, Haynie (2015) informed prospective international students that most U.S. institutions will require documentation demonstrating their ability to cover a year's worth of educational and living expenses prior to issuing an I-20 form in support of their visa application. Altbach and Engberg (2014) cautioned readers about the "commercialization of international mobility" (p. 12) in which the benefit of the global movement of students is seen as a revenue generator for higher education systems. As with our own citizenry, however, international students with access to resources are more likely to make their way through the narrow gate of college access.

Enhancing Learning Through Campus Global Engagement

The previous pages outlined the inherent challenges of global engagement found in cultural and linguistic differences, stressors of transition, and barriers to international exchange. These challenges are significant. As student affairs professionals, however, it is incumbent upon us to address shortcomings on our campuses and support student learning with intentional co-curricular offerings that enhance the experience of our international students and better prepare our domestic students for international exchange.

While study abroad experiences provide opportunities for transformative learning, the data shared earlier in this chapter demonstrate limitations of participation. In their study examining longitudinal data from 17 institutions of the

2006 cohort of the Wabash National Study of Liberal Arts Education (WNS), Salisbury, An, and Pascarella (2013) found that

> on-campus diverse interactions and integrative learning experiences can also influence intercultural competence development. In fact, the size of the estimated effects across multiple [WNS] subscales suggest that these experiences might be comparatively more effective in developing intercultural competence than study abroad. (p. 15)

This analysis is heartening and demonstrates the necessity of creating curricular and co-curricular opportunities that enhance global learning by ensuring avenues for exchange are available without actually crossing national borders. While not every student is afforded the ability to travel abroad, we have the opportunity and obligation to promote interaction with the international population available on the vast majority of our campuses.

The following suggestions are also couched in the lived experiences of the author as a global sojourner. I have had the great fortune to be a U.S. citizen born in India, reared in Germany, and provided the unique opportunity to work professionally in Taiwan, the United Arab Emirates, India, and Afghanistan. The struggles and joys of transition shared earlier reflect not only the literature of internationalization, but also often match my lived experience. The following proposed programmatic offerings are provided as examples to establish or enhance existing campus co-curricular educational offerings that truly engage all campus constituents.

As presented earlier in this chapter, Chapdelaine and Alexitch (2004) found that meaningful interactions between international students and U.S. peers were less likely to occur as distance between cultures increased. Sandhu and Asrabadi (1994) reported that international students seek support largely from fellow co-nationals over U. S. peers. It is certainly understandable that international students and U.S. students abroad would cluster and form connections with others who share common cultural and linguistic norms. Also, it is understandable that networks of students from very disparate countries and cultures might band together while attempting to navigate and grasp elements of a new culture in their shared transition to an unfamiliar environment. It is also immensely important for institutions to aid and support efforts of these educational sojourners in their process to make meaning in their transition.

While institutions should support international student organizations and so-called country clubs (such as the Korean Student Association, etc.) and their efforts to provide support for international students in transition, these clubs and organizations also generate invaluable opportunities for rich and vibrant exchanges within our campus communities. Zhao, Kuh, and Carini's (2005) study of international and American students paradoxically reported that despite increases in campus diversity outcomes, participants' perceptions of support for international students decreased with rising international student enrollments. The authors conclude that "a campus cannot simply recruit a critical mass of international students; it must also intentionally arrange its resources so that international students and American students benefit in desired ways from one another's presence" (Zhao, Kuh, & Carini, 2005, p. 225).

Unfortunately, Gareis's (2012) study of 454 international undergraduate and graduate students shows the impact of this campus clustering in finding that 38.11 percent of respondents had no close American friends and participants reported a general lack of satisfaction with the quantity and quality of their interaction with U.S. peers. "Of the responses attributing difficulties to host-national factors, 32 percent make reference to superficiality" (Gareis, 2012, p. 319). Cole's (2007) analysis of CIRP student data from 119 predominantly white institutions (PWI) likewise demonstrates the need for colleges and universities to strategically create campus infrastructures to promote diversity initiatives. Without such interventions and intentionality, many white students at PWIs could avoid interracial interactions (Cole, 2007). Rather than wait in hope that international exchanges organically occur, student affairs professionals must create and encourage intentional, strategic, and thoughtful institutional actions that truly promote and facilitate meaningful cross-cultural exchange.

Shared Celebrations

One method to bridge and encourage cultural understanding is through sharing elements of celebration. By encouraging and providing a platform for international students to demonstrate and observe tenets of their customs, cultures, and religions, our campus is not only acknowledging their value, but also offering opportunities for domestic students to learn and interact with students holding diverse views. On my home campus, our Center for Diversity and Community has sponsored and supported programs in recent months in which students shared how they celebrated the Asian Lunar New Year, Diwali, and Eid al-Adha in their home countries. By making these events inclusive in nature, members of the campus community were invited to learn how these important holidays were celebrated differently through brief presentations by individuals sharing traditions unique to their homelands. Student presenters not only explained the importance of the holiday, but also included rich opportunities for students to learn how these holidays were uniquely celebrated by countries, regions, and family units. Perhaps most memorable for student presenters and attendees alike, samplings of traditional foods were available to complete the celebrations. Through these gatherings, unfamiliar celebrations from afar suddenly became relevant to our U.S. students. International students were able to share important cultural touchstones and celebrate during an important time when distance might otherwise have caused them to grieve the missed gatherings with friends and family in distant homelands.

Although large-scale programs and international student festivals have the potential to promote campus internationalization efforts broadly across the wide spectrum of campus, the American Council on Education (2012) encourages more systematic programs, such as language partner programs or programmatic endeavors in residential communities, that encourage "sustained learning opportunities that can complement global knowledge acquired in the classroom" (p. 13). Engberg and Jourian (2015) also stress the importance of the systematic connection to students' cultural integration and their academic pursuits for U.S. students abroad. "Effective programmatic design needs to incorporate curricular, co-curricular and community-based experiences that both challenge and support students to step outside of their comfort zones and immerse themselves more intentionally in the host county" (p. 15).

Living-Learning Communities

A clear avenue for institutions to facilitate student learning and transition lies within our campus residence halls. Living-Learning Communities (LLCs) are also considered a high impact practice (Kuh, 2008) by providing natural pathways that connect the curricular and co-curricular by meeting students quite literally where they live. Creating residential communities that embrace global and international themes provides an environment that links international and domestic students through a self-selecting application process. Not only do such communities indicate a welcoming environment for international students, they also give interested domestic students the opportunity to interact closely and regularly with diverse individuals. This community and proximity provide an avenue to aid international students in their transition as well as domestic students who hope to gain or improve their intercultural competence.

With findings from their analysis of the 2006 Wabash National Study of Liberal Arts Education, Salisbury et al. (2013) suggested that institutions create co-curricular learning opportunities in which students continue to reflect upon and make meaning of their study abroad experiences. Intercultural programs and residing within a globally-focused learning community afford returning study abroad students support in their re-entry to U.S. culture by living with diverse individuals and also present opportunities to maintain or improve foreign language acquisition. Engberg and Jourian (2015) suggest, "Additionally, students need opportunities for both guided reflection and more informal opportunities to discuss their study abroad experiences with others" (p. 15). Such supports for returning domestic students are essential so that they can adequately process their experiences abroad and reacclimate to their home and campus culture. La Brack and Bathurst (2012) contend that the reentry and readjustment period for returning students is the most significant component of their international experience.

While connecting students in common residential spaces based on interest in global exchange and dialogue offers great promise to engage transitioning students, incorporating academic partners and truly bridging the curricular and co-curricular in this endeavor more truly model the ideals of living-learning communities. To increase interest in internationally focused living-learning communities, Hovland (2010) recommends organizing learning communities that are interdisciplinary and global in reach, around themes such as health and social justice; globalization, wealth, and poverty; religion in global contexts. These and many other topics would be enriched by including the mixture of international and domestic student, faculty, and staff voices into the discussion. While living-learning communities offer important and sustained avenues to create intentional and engaged globally focused co-curricular educational opportunities for diverse learners, intergroup dialogues offer similar opportunities to non-residential students.

Intergroup Dialogue

Gurin, Dey, Hurtado, & Gurin (2002) encourage higher education leaders to "set the vision to create in their institutions a microcosm of the equitable and democratic society we aspire to become" (p. 37). Institutions of higher education are presented exceptional opportunities found within our diverse student bodies. While proximity allows for robust engagement, interactions are not a guarantee. Gurin et al. (2002) fervidly state, "in order to foster citizenship for a diverse democracy, educators must intentionally structure opportunities for students to leave the comfort of their homogeneous peer group and build relationships across racially/ethnically diverse student communities on campus" (p. 38). As stated earlier, however, it is not uncommon for majority students at predominantly white institutions (Cole, 2007) or international students (Chapdelaine & Alexitch, 2004; Sandhu & Asrabadi, 1994) to maintain closest connections with like peers. To address and overcome this concern and intentionally create avenues for meaningful interaction amongst diverse peers, Gurin et al. (2002) propose that campuses employ the use of intergroup dialogues.

The process of intergroup dialogue brings together students from differing social identities and standings (e.g., as men and women; differing faith communities, etc.) for an extended period of time through guided discourse. Nagda, Gurin, Sorensen, and Zúñiga (2009) present the following outcomes for intergroup dialogues:

- to develop intergroup understanding by helping students explore their own and others' social identities and statuses, and the role of social structures in relationships of privilege and inequality;
- to foster positive intergroup relationships by developing students' empathy and motivations to bridge difference of identities and statuses;
- and to foster intergroup collaboration for personal and social responsibility toward greater social justice. (para 5)

Intergroup dialogues provide open and receptive spaces for students to interact over the course of multiple weeks on weighty topics with diverse peer groups. These sessions allow participants to increase understanding of themselves and their awareness of others as well as opportunities for students to reflect on their experiences over time through open, honest, and challenging facilitated conversations (University of South Dakota Office for Diversity, 2015).

This model has been utilized with great success at my home institution. Each spring semester, the Office for Diversity presents an intergroup dialogue program called *Voices of Discovery*. The Office for Diversity works with faculty partners teaching courses that would benefit from engaged intergroup discussions (e.g., courses covering topics of race, intercultural communication, multicultural education, etc.) and encourages professors to provide partial or extra course credit to student participants. Any willing student can sign up for the *Voices* program; however, there is no associated course requirement. Last year, groups were formed around issues including race and ethnicity, gender, Native and non-Native, U.S. and non-U.S. born, athlete and non-athlete. While I had the privilege of co-facilitating the U.S. and non-U.S. born group with a graduate student from India, all the groups would be enhanced with the inclusion of international voices.

Prior to the commencement of the program, facilitators receive training on the *Voices of Discovery* curriculum, group dynamics, and theoretical frameworks. Over the course of the multi-week program, facilitators are given foundational teambuilding exercises to build rapport and trust; deeper discussions that examine complex topics of identity and social structures are more likely to ensue in a safe group atmosphere. The program culminates with challenges for participants to apply the knowledge learned from their experience into actionable outcomes that lead to improved intergroup relations. Student learning and understanding might be assessed through pre- and post-test surveys of participants and/or through administration of focus groups. When conducting climate surveys, institutions might also inquire about the respondent's participation in and awareness of intergroup dialogues as a measure of analysis. While numerous avenues are available to encourage intercultural exchange on our campuses, intergroup dialogues offer unique and invaluable opportunities to promote intentional and sustained engagement. Though time intensive to operationalize, intergroup dialogues certainly present a rich and rewarding co-curricular learning experience that bridges communities that would likely otherwise not naturally interact or collaborate.

Life-Long Learning

While this chapter has largely focused on creating pathways to promote and encourage student learning through global engagement, it is also important that we as student affairs professionals lead by example. If our institutions endorse notions of internationalization, how is this manifested in our work? If we encourage students to engage with international students on campus or participate in study abroad activities, how do we model these behaviors with our student interactions and our sponsored programs? If our actions do not mirror our message, students will easily identify the discord. As the ancient Chinese philosopher Lao Tzu (trans. 2008) stated, "Remember, / A tree that fills a man's embrace grows from a seedling / A tower that stories high starts with one brick / A journey of a thousand miles begins with a single step" (p. 83).

National student affairs organizations provide great avenues for professionals to expand and enhance their global knowledge of the field as well as networks of peers from around the world. ACPA's (American College Personnel Association) Commission for Global Dimensions of Student Development and NASPA's (National Association of Student Personnel Administrators) International Education Knowledge Community actively promote global issues relevant to the field through supporting educational sessions and programs at national meetings and publications. Annually, NASPA hosts the International Symposium, a preconference of the national meeting. This event attracts student affairs and services professionals from around the world and provides a forum for global peers to exchange ideas, attend internationally focused sessions, and share fellowship. Founded in 2015, IASAS, the International Association of Student Affairs and Services, is a relatively new organization with a truly global reach and a membership of 1,200 student affairs and services professionals from over 75 countries and five continents. Through online meetings and shared resources, IASAS truly allows for a global network of student affairs professionals. These organizations all provide rich opportunities to expand our understanding of student affairs practices around the world.

There is also great value for student affairs professionals to personally travel and see parts unknown. Through visiting new surroundings, tasting new foods, and experiencing the dissonance of being surrounded in conversations and cultures other than our own, we personally might better empathize with the experiences of our students traveling abroad or international students and scholars on our campuses. Through continuous learning about others and our own hospitable behaviors, we model the outcomes we desire from our students to successfully navigate professionally and personally in an increasingly diverse and globally connected world.

Conclusion

In his classic novel, *The Innocents Abroad*, Twain (1869/1990) surmises that

> Travel is fatal to prejudice, bigotry, and narrow-mindedness, and many of our people need it sorely on these accounts. Broad, wholesale, charitable views of men and things cannot be acquired by vegetating in one little corner of the earth all one's lifetime. (p. 424)

For those fortunate enough to visit and experience cultures other than their own, this quote often resonates. For many others on our college campuses, however, time abroad is a not an option, due to financial or even academic constraints. With a record number of international students arriving at U.S. institutions of higher education, the world is truly coming to our institutional doorsteps. Student affairs professionals have the opportunity and unique obligation to create and support programmatic efforts and intentional, welcoming spaces as our campuses globally engage. As demonstrated through the literature and programs described here, the role of student affairs professionals in supporting international sojourners is fundamental to their successful transition to their new learning environment and is one important way that we enhance student learning.

References

Altbach, P. G. (1997). The university as center and periphery. In P. G. Altbach (Ed.), *Comparative higher education: Knowledge, the university, and development* (pp. 19–36). Chestnut Hill, MA: Boston College Center for International Higher Education.

Altbach, P. G. (2004). Globalisation and the university: Myth and realities in an unequal world. *Tertiary Education and Management, 10*(1), 3–25.

Altbach, P. G. & Engberg, D. (2014). Global student mobility: The changing landscape. *International Higher Education, 77*, 11–13.

Altbach, P. G., Reisberg, L., & Rumbley, L. E. (2010). *Trends in global higher education: Tracking an academic revolution.* Chestnut Hill, MA: Boston College Center for International Higher Education.

American Council on Education. (2012). *Mapping internationalization on U.S. campuses.* Washington, DC: Author.

Berry, J. W. (2006). Contexts of acculturation. In D. L. Sam & J. W. Berry (Eds.), *The Cambridge handbook of acculturation psychology* (pp. 11–26). Cambridge, England: Cambridge University Press.

Brown, L., & Holloway, I. (2008a). The adjustment journey of international postgraduate students at an English university: An ethnographic study. *Journal of Research in International Education, 7*(2), 232–249.

Brown, L., & Holloway, I. (2008b). The initial stage of the international sojourn: Excitement or culture shock? *British Journal of Guidance & Counselling, 36*(1), 33–49.

Chapdelaine, R. F., & Alexitch, L. R. (2004). Social skills difficulty: Model of culture shock for international graduate students. *Journal of College Student Development, 45*(2), 167–184.

Cole, D. (2007). Do interracial interactions matter? An examination of student-faculty contact and intellectual self-concept. *The Journal of Higher Education, 78*(3), 249–281.

Cummings, W. K. (1999). The institutions of education: Compare, compare, compare! *Comparative Education Review, 43*(4), 413–437.

Dolby, N. (2004). Encountering an American self: Study abroad and national identity. *Comparative Education Review, 48*(2), 150–173.

Education USA. (n.d.). *Financing your studies.* Retrieved from https://educationusa.state.gov/your-5-steps-us-study/finance-your-studies

Engberg, M. E. & Jourian, T. J. (2015). Intercultural wonderment and study abroad. *Frontiers: the Interdisciplinary Journal of Study Abroad, 25*, 1–19.

European Commission. (2017). *From ERASMUS to ERASMUS+: A story of 30 years*. Retrieved from https://ec.europa.eu/programmes/erasmus-plus/anniversary/30th-anniversary-and-you

Farrugia, C. A. & Bhandari, R. (2015). *Open Doors 2015 Report on International Education*. New York, NY: Institute of International Education.

Fortuijn, J. D. (2002). Internationalizing teaching and learning: A European experience. *Journal of Geography, 26*(3), 263–273.

Gareis, E. (2012). Intercultural friendship: Efforts of home and host region. *Journal of International and Intercultural Communication, 5*(4), 309–328.

Gurin, P., Dey, E. L., Hurtado, S., & Gurin, G. (2002). Diversity and higher education: Theory and impact on educational outcomes. *Harvard Educational Review, 72*(3), 9–42.

Haynie, D. (2015). Count on showing financial ability to U.S. colleges. *U.S. News & World Report*. Retrieved from http://www.usnews.com/education/best-colleges/articles/2015/07/14/count-on-showing-financial-ability-to-us-colleges

Hovland, K. (2010). *Global learning: Aligning study learning outcomes with study abroad*. Washington, DC: NAFSA: Association of International Educators.

Jenkins, S. (2000), Cultural and linguistic miscues: A case study of international teaching assistant and academic faculty miscommunication, *International Journal of Intercultural Relations, 24*(4), 477–501.

Kinzie, J. (2012). High-impact practices: Promoting participation for all students. *Diversity & Democracy, 15*(3). Retrieved from https://www.aacu.org/publications-research/periodicals/high-impact-practices-promoting-participation-all-students

Kuh, G. D. (2008). *High-impact practices: What they are, who has access to them, and why they matter*. Washington, DC: Association of American Colleges and Universities.

Kuh, G. D. & Whitt, E. J. (1988). *The invisible tapestry: Culture in American colleges and Universities*. Washington, DC: ASHE.

La Brack, B. & Bathurst, L. (2012). Anthropology, intercultural communication, and study abroad. In M. Vande Berg, R. M. Paige, & K. H. Lou (Eds.), *Student learning abroad: What our students are learning, what they're not, and what we can do about it* (pp. 188–214). Sterling, VA: Stylus Publishing.

Lao Tzu. (2008). *Tao Te Ching: The new translation*. (J. Star, Trans.). New York, NY: Penguin. (Original work circa 500 B.C.)

Lee, J. & Rice, C. (2007). Welcome to America? International student perceptions of discrimination. *Higher Education, 53*(3), 381–409.

Luo, J. & Jamieson-Drake, D. (2015). Predictors of study abroad intent, participation, and college outcomes. *Research in Higher Education, 56*(1), 29–56.

McNamee, S. J. & Faulkner, G. L. (2001). The international exchange experience and the social construction of meaning. *Journal of Studies in International Education, 5*(1), 64–78.

Nagda, B. A., Gurin, P., Sorensen, N., & Zúñiga, X. (2009). Evaluating intergroup dialogue: Engaging diversity for personal and social responsibility. *Diversity & Democracy, 12*(1). Retrieved from http://www.aacu.org/publications-research/periodicals/evaluating-intergroup-dialogue-engaging-diversity-personal-and-social responsibility

Pedersen, P. B. (1991). Counseling international students. *The Counseling Psychologist, 19*(1), 10–58.

Salisbury, M. H., An, B. P., & Pascarella, E. T. (2013). The effect of study abroad on intercultural competence among undergraduate college students. *Journal of Student Affairs Research and Practice, 50*(1), 1–20.

Sandhu, D. S. & Asrabadi, B. R. (1994). Development of an acculturative stress scale for International students: Preliminary findings. *Psychological Reports, 75*, 435–448.

Stanley, C. A. (2006). Walking between two cultures: The often misunderstood Jamaican woman. In C. A. Stanley (Ed.), *Faculty of color: Teaching in predominantly white colleges and universities* (pp. 328–343). Bolton, MA: Anker.

Twain, M. (1869/1990). *The innocents abroad.* Pleasantville, NY: Reader's Digest Association.

University of South Dakota Office for Diversity. (2015). *Voices of discovery intergroup dialogue program facilitators' handbook.* Vermillion, SD: Author.

Zhao, C. M., Kuh, G. D., & Carini, R. M. (2005). A comparison of international student and American student engagement in effective educational practices. *The Journal of Higher Education, 76*(2), 209–231.

11

INTERCULTURAL CENTERS

Holistic Learning Toward Social Justice

Constanza A. Cabello

Colleges and universities have articulated a commitment to student learning that embodies multicultural understanding and social agency. Institutions also demonstrate commitments to diversity through their mission statements, priorities, and/or strategic goals (Cuba et al., 2011; Wilson, Meyer, & McNeal, 2012). These commitments are driven by a world that is becoming increasingly diverse and interconnected. Higher education practitioners are challenged to create spaces and opportunities for students to encounter critical learning moments that enhance their multicultural understanding of self, others, and larger communities. As Mezirow (2000) has observed, the creation of critical learning moments is essential to the developing adult mind. Critical learning moments occur when a person engages with another person whose frame of reference is significantly different and begins to realize that their own framework is both limited and ineffective in helping that person navigate his or her evolving world. Mezirow considers the development of adulthood to be a learning process that is

> a phased and often transformative process of meaning becoming clarified through expanded awareness, critical reflection, validating discourse and reflective action ... Our identity is formed in webs of affiliation within a shared life in the world. Human reality is intersubjective; our life histories and language are bound up with those of others. (pp. 25, 27)

Work with diverse populations or conversations about the life experiences of members of those groups inevitably leads to social justice education. Differences between the life experiences of the dominant group and experiences of members of non-dominant groups often illuminates privilege and requires conversation about justice, equity, and fairness.

Students meet diversity in multiple areas of higher education. The enrollment management area often has goals related to admission and matriculation. Students may participate in multicultural recruitment events, such as overnight programs and other outreach and yield events. Study abroad and cultural exchange programs also provide avenues for students to gain exposure to different cultural communities. We hope that students also encounter multiculturalism in the classroom through courses that infuse topics of diversity and social justice in the curriculum. This chapter will focus on student learning about these topics through on-campus co-curricular opportunities.

There are many ways in which students affairs units create multicultural learning experiences. Whenever students from groups that are economically stable meet students whose backgrounds are less stable, once again, the justice issue appears. Training for students who lead orientation groups should include helping students become aware of the different, and unequal, backgrounds of potential students. This helps the orientation leaders think before they make assumptions about students, their families, their cultural belief systems, or their economic resources. Student activities departments may infuse social justice education in leadership development programs, or they may support and advise cultural clubs through training in culturally relevant leadership strategies. Residence life units may require resident assistants to engage in social justice education through their training and programming models. Many student affairs divisions have cultural centers and/or multicultural affairs departments that utilize their resources (time, money, staff, space, etc.) to create multicultural learning experiences. To focus this more specifically, I will discuss student learning that occurs in multicultural affairs units (at predominantly white institutions, or PWIs) that include the following imperatives in their mission:

1. To provide support and advocacy for historically underrepresented student communities with the goal of persistence and graduation;
2. To help students realize that historical underrepresentation is typically accompanied by lack of institutional and systemic privilege (on campus). Students from these groups tend to experience a "cultural mismatch," i.e., methods of teaching and expectations for student behavior are not easily aligned with the learning processes, expectations, and behaviors of students in these groups.
3. To provide diversity, inclusion, and social justice education for all students with the goal of creating compassionate, socially engaged global leaders.

It is important to clearly understand the goals and mission of multicultural affairs units and/or cultural centers on each campus. Here are a few questions to ask that will help to support greater understanding:

1. What events, groups, trends, or needs inspired the unit's creation?
2. Where in the institution does the unit "live" (physically and symbolically)?

3. Who does the unit leader report to (which division and/or cabinet member)?
4. Is there a particular social identity group that the unit primarily seeks to support and affirm?
5. Are there specific elements of the college mission that impact the unit (e.g., open access vs. selective admission, faith based, minority serving, etc.)?
6. How does the larger context of the institution impact the unit (e.g., geographic area, local and state government, demographics, etc.)?

Again, these are just a few questions. The answers will help provide clarity on the unit's function and direct and assess its impact on student learning.

Let's Take a Step Back: What Do We Mean by "Multicultural"?

Often, multiculturalism is thought of as exclusively relating to race and ethnicity. While race and ethnicity are dimensions of culture, multiculturalism is an umbrella term to capture many social identities and experiences. Here is a short list of multicultural identities that tend to be salient among today's college student population: race, ethnicity, socioeconomic status, class, gender identity and expression, sexual orientation, ability, veteran status, faith, disability, primary language, and citizenship/immigration status. You can see that these identities encompass far more than race.

Culture is embedded in social identity groups. Each identity has a complex set of values, norms, beliefs, and/or artifacts that align members who identify with that group. It can be argued that many groups beyond ethnic groups have culture (e.g., college athletes, chemistry majors, resident assistants, politically affiliated groups, etc.). The efforts of multicultural affairs units in American higher education (most often) focus on social identities that systemically and structurally are disadvantaged in the larger American context (see previous list), rather than individual identities. What does this mean? Keep reading.

Quick History Lesson

To give context to the roots of student learning in these spaces, it is helpful to have a basic understanding of how these spaces originated. The catalyst for cultural centers and multicultural affairs spaces can be traced back to the student movements that emerged during the Civil Rights Era. Brown v. Board of Education (1954) was the groundbreaking case that ended segregation in public schools. While this ruling created access to public educational institutions for non-white students, it did not guarantee safety or inclusion for students of color. Cultural centers and spaces emerged to provide havens for black students to gather for safety, community, advocacy, and/or strategy development in pushing their institutions to attend to their particular needs and concerns.

Concurrently and shortly after this effort began, other historically underrepresented and ignored groups sought similar spaces (e.g., Chicano, Asian, Native, and LGBTQ students, and feminists). In some ways, the focus of cultural spaces remains the same: to provide safe havens, resources, and community spaces for underrepresented students. However, many of these spaces broadened their focus to include the education of *all* students on the topics of diversity, inclusion, and social justice that were of concern to the people who founded specific centers.

On Oppression, Privilege, and Intersectionality

Multicultural affairs units provide support and advocacy for underrepresented student communities with the goal of supporting these students in persistence to graduation. They also provide education in diversity, inclusion, and social justice education for all students. The goal of the educational programs that centers offer is to create compassionate, socially engaged global citizens and leaders. Students who become involved with programs and activities offered by multicultural affairs centers often have the opportunity to experience both their privileged and their oppressed identities. For example, white students who participate in activities sponsored by a black cultural center may gain a very small awareness of what it feels like to be members of a minority group for the first time in their lives. They also become aware of their privileges in new ways.

Humans possess an array of privileged and oppressed identities that impact how we experience the world—this is the essence of intersectionality. We engage in our privilege and oppression daily. A male student may move from an oppressed, or non-dominant status in a women's studies class to a dominant status as an officer of his fraternity in a matter of minutes. Students typically experience discomfort when they move into non-dominant, unfamiliar, or oppressive contexts. Without introspection, they may not understand the source of their discomfort or the reality that members of other groups may experience this type of discomfort frequently on campus. Seeking to understand this kind of discomfort helps students who hold privileged or dominant status in any situation empathize with the others and support their inclusion. Attending higher education institutions is often the time when many privileged individuals and groups recognize their privilege for the first time. It is often a time when oppressed groups are reminded of and experience their oppression on a daily basis.

Our privileged identities represent majority and/or dominant group memberships. These identities allow us to experience the world in ways that make us feel "normal," accepted, and affirmed. Life is easier because systems (social, political, educational, economic, etc.) were created and are sustained for privileged identities to succeed. An example of a privileged identity I hold is my sexual orientation, as I identify as heterosexual. As a heterosexual person, I don't have to worry if my spouse will be able to access benefits offered by my employer, if I will be "outed" by well-intentioned friends inquiring about my partner, or if political platforms will advocate for the rights of heterosexuals. I can experience the world without these worries, and frankly life is a lot easier because I benefit from heteronormativity.

Our oppressed identities represent underrepresented, marginalized, minoritized and/or subordinated group memberships (Harper, 2012). Life is more difficult because systems were created and are sustained for oppressed identities to fail or be less likely to succeed. Examples of oppressed identities (in the North American context) I hold are my race and gender, as I identify as Latina. As a Latina in the United States, I am often the only person of my race in leadership meetings at work; people are often surprised at the level of academic and career progression I have attained thus far; and I am seen generally as "a good one" because of the stereotypes I currently defy:

1. I am currently not married and do not have children. Nor am I *only* seeking a partner for US citizenship.
2. I have "good" use of English and do not have an accent or "broken English," which allows me to literally and figuratively "speak the language."
3. I live in a safe, middle class community.
4. I am not *always* loud, "sassy," outspoken, or enjoy being the center of attention. In fact, I can be quite introverted!

These stereotypes are damaging for Latinas and white people alike. Not only do they create false narratives of those who align with these stereotypes, but they create added pressures (i.e., stereotypes threat) for those who identify as Latina. The United States' systems were not inherently built to be compatible with the needs of Latino/a/x people or women.

Who can benefit from engaging in learning through multicultural affairs? The short story: everyone. Oppressed groups may find community, safety, support, and affirmation in their shared experiences of identity, culture, and/or challenges with systems. Privileged groups become aware of their culture, systemic benefits, and ways in which they can use their privilege to create equity for all people. Everyone may learn about their identities, dynamics of privilege and oppression (on campus and beyond), and how individuals can create a more just world for all identities. This kind of learning is a slow and often painful process, particularly for privileged white students. Once a person realizes that she or he has benefitted from "white privilege" (MacIntosh, 1988), there are inevitable emotional disruptions. People with privilege often feel guilt, defensiveness, and frustration. If they are aware of having benefitted from privilege, they have to ask themselves if it is their fault, if they have any responsibility to do anything about it, and whether or not the whole idea is real. After all, most people with privilege haven't intentionally hurt a person without privilege, but their lack of unawareness may have caused pain even if they don't know about it. Learning about privilege requires a lot of observation, introspection, conversation, and many cross-cultural experiences.

Levels and Dimensions of Holistic Transformative Learning

Through multicultural affairs, students learn at the individual, group, and community level. At each level, they learn about different multicultural frameworks, such as diversity, inclusion, and social justice. Each of the levels and frameworks (individual, group, and community) builds on one another and aids in students' overall development of personal and societal awareness. The subsequent sections will further explore the levels and dynamics through explanations and examples.

Individual Level: Understanding Diversity and Difference

To understand social justice, one must have a deep understanding of self and identity on the intellectual, emotional, and behavioral levels. The ability to name one's own identities is key. At this stage, many students begin to realize that there is a long list of identities that they or others may possess. Many students will participate in activities that allow them to recognize their identities. For example, an upper middle class student may never recognize this dimension of identity because almost everyone in their home community exists within that same economic status. An able-bodied person may not realize that dimension of identity, lacking life experience as someone with a mobility difference. Privileged groups often fail to recognize parts of their identity because it is the norm in their space; also, the world was designed literally and figuratively for them. When students can name their identities, they then are able to understand how identity shapes their worldview and perspectives. At this stage, students begin to learn about their intersectional identities as well.

The Social Identity Wheel is widely used to give students a picture of their many intersecting identities. This activity, found online (http://www.odec.umd.edu/we/about/Multiversity/handouts/SocialIdentityWheel.pdf), is a circle that students divide into pie-shaped segments that are proportionate to aspects of identity that they find salient in one particular setting or in general. When filled out with the entire range of social identity groups, students see connections and complexities, often influenced by context, that they did not recognize before.

At this stage, students begin to learn about their intersectional identities as well. As high school students, young people may be very aware of their race or gender. However, they may never have considered how these identities interplay with their religion or sexual orientation. College is often a time when students become more autonomous in their thinking and decision making. This offers an opportunity for individuals to potentially explore fluid identities, such as religion and gender expression. Additional contexts, like academic discipline or institutional type, may impact students' reflexivity regarding intersectional identities.

For example, consider a woman of color in the sciences. Perhaps race and gender are salient, given the low representation of women of color in the sciences. We can also think about a queer Muslim student who perhaps becomes more aware of this aspect of identity while attending a conservative church-affiliated institution. These are situations that can offer opportunities to think about how identities and intersectionality are at play.

There are a number of ways in which multicultural affairs departments staffed by student affairs professionals can facilitate this level of learning. Some may sponsor identity-based clubs or groups that encourage identity exploration and development. Trainings and workshops are often offered to help students (particularly student leaders) gain an understanding of the diversity they and others bring. Cultural programs are a way to affirm and celebrate identities as well. These opportunities engage students in their introspective learning. This stage challenges students to learn that difference matters and should be recognized. This recognition aids students in developing understanding of how society is sustained for privileged identities to navigate the world more easily and why this experience shapes worldviews. It moves students beyond thoughts like "I don't see (insert identity); we are all human" to more complex thoughts or awareness of inclusion, like "I recognize that being (insert identity) has an impact on how I experience the world." This phase empowers students to know the various elements of who they are and recognize who others are. It is not uncommon that privileged groups may experience guilt or shame when they recognize this privilege, and the accompanying power. However, when these feelings can be transitioned to more productive actions, true social justice can occur. Critical self-reflection is essential to the understanding of self, diversity, and difference.

Group Level: Comprehending Dynamics of Inclusion and Exclusion

When students recognize their social identities, they are able to better understand how these identities impact their engagement with and in groups. They learn how spaces of inclusion and exclusion are created and maintained over time. By engaging in critical interactions, such as dialogue and listening, students come to better understand why members of some groups might feel excluded in spaces that were designed for members of other groups. With the goal of community building and inclusion in mind, students work to create spaces where cultural affirmation and visibility are priorities so that everyone feels welcome and also feels free to express any feelings of discomfort. Making space welcoming might be as simple as hanging posters representing different cultural activities on the wall or subscribing to magazines that reflect different groups in the student lounge. It should also extend, however, to hiring or inviting staff of appropriate cultural backgrounds to participate in center programs, showing films that reflect the diverse population, and always encouraging students to talk about what they are experiencing with students from different groups. At the core, students learn how their identities frame their experiences of being part of privileged and oppressed groups.

Multicultural affairs departments offer a number of experiences that assist students in their understanding of group dynamics and inclusion. Some may offer orientation programs and/or peer mentorship services that aim to welcome underrepresented groups to campus and provide culturally relevant spaces. Intergroup dialogue programs also offer students opportunities to listen to one another's narratives and explore dynamics of inclusion and exclusion in their lives. Other units may use their physical space as a "home away from home" for students and a place where they can feel safe and affirmed.

At this level, students learn that they are part of the inclusion and exclusion process. They move from thinking "I treat everyone the same" to insights such as, "people get treated/I treat people differently because of their identities." Privileged groups learn to create space and visibility for marginalized groups. Students learn the value of developing welcoming and affirming spaces for everyone on campus and beyond. Through this learning, values such as trust and commitment are developed and demonstrated. Students aim to create communities where all individuals can bring their authentic selves.

Community Level: Engaging in Social Justice Practices

At the community level, students begin to understand how they engage in social justice practices and help to create equitable systems. At this point, students have gained a solid understanding of their identities, and how these identities impact their engagement with groups. To carry out social justice work, students must expand their scope of perspective to understand that they, and their groups, are operating in larger systems of inequity. This is a process described by Mezirow (2000) as the ability to shift frames of reference. Baxter Magolda (1999) asserts that "Self-authorship is simultaneously a cognitive (how one makes meaning of knowledge), an interpersonal (how one views oneself in relation to others), and intrapersonal (how one perceives one's sense of identity) matter" (p. 10). Zull (2002) describes this learning process as an aspect of development of the prefrontal cortex. Students do not have the physiological brain development to understand that they are part of much larger systems until their brains develop the capacity for the cognitive complexity that these insights require. The process is difficult, even though a great deal of it is unconscious. It takes time to shift frameworks, and it is initially disorienting. Once the necessary changes have occurred, students see the new reality as normal. Their focus turns to shifting the status quo to ensure that all people, on campus and in the greater world, have equitable access to safety, resources, and opportunities.

Multicultural affairs departments are charged with facilitating social justice learning through a myriad of opportunities to engage in true social justice practices on campus and beyond. Leadership development programs may train students to name, notice, and challenge oppression and privilege in everyday life. Many departments offer practical experiences and skills that enhance students' abilities to advocate for marginalized groups to ensure equity, rather than equality. Some units may provide support, mentorship, and advising for students who seek to challenge systems through protest, demonstration, and additional advocacy efforts.

Students learn how to create systems in which *all* people are heard and valued for their unique talents, strengths, and contributions. Students elevate the voices of the silenced and work towards the liberation of the oppressed. They realize that the starting line for everyone is not the same. They move from thoughts like "the system is bad" to "the system is not working for everyone, and it's my responsibility to fix it." Shared social responsibility, risk taking, courage, and persistence are demonstrated to create systemic, lasting change.

Summary

Multicultural affairs units contribute to the holistic transformative learning of students in a multitude of ways. To best understand the learning that emerges from these units, it is helpful to have knowledge about the history and current mission of the individual units. Multicultural affairs aim to promote learning at the individual, group, and community levels. Students move from learning about the fundamentals of diversity and identity, to understanding the complexities of systemic inequity and social justice. This type of holistic learning promotes self-reflection, humility, critical thinking, empathy, and courage, thus creating individual, group, and community change.

References

Baxter Magolda, M. (1999). *Creating contexts for learning and self-authorship: Constructive-developmental pedagogy.* Nashville, TN: Vanderbilt University Press.
Brown v. Board of Education, 347 U.S. 483 (1954).
Cuba, L., Jennings, N., Lovett, S., Swingle, J., Lindkvist, H., & Howard, A. (2011). Diversity from the student's point of view. *Change, 43*(4), 32–38.
Harper, S. R. (2012). Race without racism: How higher education researchers minimize racist institutional norms. *Review of Higher Education, 36*(1), 9–29.
MacIntosh, P. (1988). *White privilege: Unpacking the invisible knapsack.* Wellesley, MA: Wellesley College.
Mezirow, J. (2000). *Transformative dimensions of adult learning.* San Francisco: Jossey-Bass.
Wilson, J., Meyer, K., & McNeal, L. (2012). Mission and diversity statements: What they do and do not say. *Innovative Higher Education, 37*(2), 125–139.
Zull, J. (2002). *The art of changing the brain.* Sterling, VA: Stylus.

12

USING SOCIAL MEDIA AND SCIENTIFIC TEACHING TO ENHANCE UNDERGRADUATE LEARNING

Greg Heiberger and Ruth Harper

Student affairs professionals are familiar with Arthur Chickering's seven vectors of college student identity development (Chickering & Reisser, 1994). What many may not know is that Chickering, a former professor of English, also set out to explore principles of effective undergraduate teaching—and these principles (another set of seven) can be quite useful to those thrown into teaching with no pedagogical preparation. Working with Zelda Gamson, a sociologist with appointments at the University of Michigan and the University of Massachusetts–Boston, Chickering claimed that these ideas were built on 50 years of educational research as well as experience and common sense. So just as you once learned about developing competence, managing emotions, moving through autonomy toward interdependence, and so forth, you can now consider what one of the foundational scholars of student development theory said about quality undergraduate teaching. These principles of good teaching practice were first offered in 1987 (before many current readers were born), yet they have not enjoyed the same prominence within student affairs as Chickering and Reisser's (1994) vectors.

This chapter presents these key pedagogical concepts and their applications in contemporary instructional practice. Specific context, in this case, is classroom applications within a technology-oriented first-year seminar (FYSEM) for students enrolled in majors and programs in biology and microbiology at a Midwestern land grant institution taught by Dr. Greg Heiberger. Co-curricular applications will be considered as well.

Heiberger is undergraduate program manager and comes to his teaching assignment after serving in student affairs roles with the student union and activities, new student orientation, university accreditation, and undergraduate pre-health advising. Drawing on this varied background, he uses Chickering's teaching principles to extend the boundaries of the classroom in order to expand student engagement in virtual and physical environments. This is notable because student affairs practitioners appreciate how students' psychosocial and intellectual development outside the classroom implicates their experiences within it. Thus, it is reasonable to suggest that the good teaching practices Heiberger employs within his seminar can inform work in campus programs and other interactions with students on and off campus. Neither academic affairs nor student affairs has mastered the reciprocity to which most educators aspire; therefore, it is fitting to begin with this instance wherein classroom applications extend to the broader campus and community locations where students live, work, and socialize.

The principles of good practice in undergraduate education can be adapted to fit the mission of a specific institution, the characteristics of its student body, and the nature of any disciplinary course content. They draw upon "six powerful forces in education: activity, expectations, cooperation, interaction, diversity, and responsibility" (Chickering & Gamson, 1987, p. 2). Note that these forces immediately cast the person leading learning into a highly interactive role.

The first principle is that good practice in undergraduate education *encourages contact between students and faculty members* (Chickering & Gamson, 1987). This principle is enacted by academic advisors every day, as they urge students to talk with professors about course material, engage in service-learning, research opportunities, and more. In the days when most current professors were in college, contact between students and faculty might have meant merely taking advantage of posted office hours. In today's highly linked society, students and faculty members can and should connect through multiple venues. For example, in Heiberger's first-year seminar, he uses Twitter and active learning pedagogy to foster student-instructor interaction.

In a study conducted in this first-year seminar (Junco, Heiberger & Loken, 2011), students engaged with faculty members outside of class through Twitter by clarifiying assignment-related questions, completing "Common Read" discussions, and posting to common hashtags. This engagement increased the time that students had access to instructor support and feedback and lowered the access barrier that can limit student–faculty interaction. Students and faculty members transcended traditional classroom walls by engaging with this form of technology outside of formal meeting times, and the impacts were far-reaching. These Twitter-based interactions utilized Chickering and Gamson's (1987) seven principles of highly effective teaching and showed a significant impact in students' levels of engagement (as measured by a subset of National Survey of Student Engagement, or NSSE, data), as well as higher semester grade point averages.

The second principle states that good practice *develops reciprocity and cooperation among students* (Chickering & Gamson, 1987). Any student affairs professional who has advised a student organization is familiar with the importance of helping students learn to trust and rely on each other and work together as a group. In a classroom setting, this principle can present a challenge. Heiberger's seminar meets in a specially designed active learning classroom with high levels of technology integration that organizes students into small groups by its very structure; each group uses iPads to respond to questions posed by the instructor as well as to share information with each other.

Another study conducted with this first-year seminar (Heiberger & Vos, 2013) examined the impact of using iPads to engage students in group case studies. Although having 1:1 technology in this setting had a small effect ($p<.001$ and an effect size [eta^2] = 6%) on classroom engagement, an interesting finding was that this effect was large when the case study was highly structured ($p<.001$ and an effect size [eta^2] = 14%), but non-existent when the case study was loosely structured (p=.006). This showed that engagement and reciprocity between and among students can be enhanced with 1:1 technology (i.e., one iPad for each student) if the case study is highly structured, but also revealed that this instructional strategy may not be particularly helpful if the case study has a more loosely organized role assignment. Such research demonstrates that the use of technology must not only be effectively integrated into the pedagogy of the course as a whole, but also designed to facilitate individual learning outcomes of each assignment and classroom activity.

For example, when students were asked to share technology with other students and the classroom activity was structured in such a way that students could navigate a role that did not require technology (e.g., becoming a recorder, supporter, or organizer in the group), technology was not needed at a 1:1 ratio—and 1:1 technology may have even slowed group progress. Requiring students to share their technology, in effect, forced Chickering and Gamson's (1987) principle of reciprocity and cooperation. But when a classroom activity was more highly structured and differing group roles were not so negotiable (e.g., a case study in which students have no previous knowledge, a project requiring them to all read the same text, etc.), there is great benefit to an individual student's access to technology. In other words, asking students to stop and share while they are effectively working on their own slows the entire group and disengages some high-performing students within the work groups.

This study (Heiberger & Vos, 2013) underscores the truth that technology in and of itself may not enhance student learning; the use of technology in instructional settings is highly nuanced and must be assessed in each instance. Any particular learning activity may not call for an all-or-none approach with regard to the integration of technology. Many instructional strategies, including appropriate technology, can be used to ensure that students develop habits of reciprocity and cooperation.

Active learning is endorsed by the third principle of good teaching (Chickering & Gamson, 1987). Much of student affairs professional practice is defined by active learning, mostly in venues beyond the classroom. From simple ice-breakers to planning complex programs such as leadership retreats, multicultural cultural activities, or community-based service-learning—student affairs professionals are leaders in the area of active learning. In the classroom, Heiberger engages students actively through problems that small groups must address through interaction and technology. The traditional lecture/passive note-taking mode is completely absent. Instead, students are intentionally involved beyond the classroom space and class time through social media that is focused on their learning.

Imagine a potential workplace of the future. Employees are not in cubicles or shuttered away behind office doors, but many are working in collaborative, multifunctional, and dynamic spaces. This interactive setting can and should be emulated in the college classroom. In fact, many institutions of higher education have designed new learning spaces to simulate this emerging reality.

Such spaces require instructional methods that are dynamic and engaging. Scientific Teaching (Handelsman et al., 2004) is a very useful pedagogical model that helps guide educators in these settings. As we prepare students to solve problems in dynamic and collaborative careers, the structure of this model helps even the novice teacher, in any content area, to formulate a plan to actively engage students throughout the learning process.

The pedagogy of Scientific Teaching "mirrors science at its best—experimental, rigorous, and based on evidence" (Handelsman et al., 2004, p. 1). The framework is supported by numerous field-tested research studies, and associated meta-analyses; on-site trainings are offered across the country. Even without intense training in the pedagogy of Scientific Teaching, new instructors can utilize its concepts. This approach walks the reader through the development of learning outcomes and related, intentional, *active* learning activities, as well as both formative and summative assessments. It also helps the instructor address the diversity of students as learners, taking into account, for example, a student's prior knowledge, learning styles/preferences, abilities, experiences (cultural and personal), and motivation to learn the material. Finally, the framework provides guidance on class time management, and aids those new to teaching in planning and carrying out their many classroom demands effectively. Additionally, this approach helps novice instructors become more intentional and mindful in their teaching. It urges a process of continual review and improvement, documents teaching plans, and creates a resource for future work.

The Scientific Teaching process is straightforward and includes a planning rubric composed of learning outcomes, required active learning activities, formative assessment, and incorporation of learning-related diversity. Heiberger's seminar has included activities as scientifically oriented as teaching transcription and translation through case studies on the 2014 Ebola outbreak. Yet it also addresses more general student success skills and student development concepts, such as time management, reading skills, professionalism, and identity development. Each lesson or unit is planned with a Scientific Teaching template (Handelsman et al., 2004) (See Figure 12.1) that guides the instructor through the process of developing active learning activities, incorporating problems, and reflecting an overall orientation of scientific inquiry. Through this process, instructors learn to help students create hypotheses and challenge preconceived ideas; it further includes hands-on testing of the hypotheses, and application of this way of thinking to real-world situations.

Title of Unit		
Abstract		
Learning Goals & Outcomes/Objectives	**Goal(s)**: what students will know, understand, and be able to do; includes content knowledge, attitudes, & skills (i.e. "understand natural selection;" "appreciate the role of biology in society;" "think like a scientist"	**Desired Outcome(s)/ Objectives(s)**: specific student behaviors or performances that will indicate they have successfully accomplished the goal(s)

Incorporation of Scientific Teaching Themes		
Active Learning	**Assessment**	**Diversity**
How students will engage actively in learning the concepts	How teachers will measure learning; how students will self-evaluate learning	How the unit is designed to include all participants
Activities outside of class: *Activities in class:*	*Pre-assessments:* *Post-tidbit assessments:* *Summative assessment:*	

Presentation Plan (detailed schedule with approximate timing for unit)

Session 1	
Preclass	
Enter approx. class time for learning activity preparatory material presentation	minutes
Enter approx. class time for learning activity #1	minutes
Enter approx. class time for learning activity #2	minutes
Enter approx. class time for learning activity #3	minutes
Enter approximate time for post-activity summing up or transition	minutes

Add additional activities information as needed for the unit.
Resources for Teaching the Unit
Summary of Feedback

FIGURE 12.1   Scientific Teaching Template

When student affairs professionals teach, or team-teach, in STEM-related fields (Science, Technology, Engineering, Math), Scientific Teaching (Handelsman et al., 2004) offers a good framework for planning, drawing on research-based content that is both useful and relatable. Its pedagogical methods allow instructors to do this efficiently and effectively in each class session.

Although the term "Scientific Teaching" may inhibit some readers, the pedagogy is sound and can be adopted by any professional who wishes to actively engage students in a learning activity. The straightforward approach, matched with its structured guidelines, makes it a highly adaptable pedagogy that facilitates Chickering and Gamson's (1987) principles of effective teaching.

Prompt feedback has been shown to enhance student learning and is the basis of the fourth principle of good practice in undergraduate education (Chickering & Gamson, 1987). In student affairs work, prompt feedback is often achieved through a timely conversation, a text or email message, or even an impromptu meeting. Technology of all types can assist in expediting feedback for those in any role in higher education. (It can also create the expectation for instant responses, which is another issue to be managed through effective communication.) An article by scholars at the University of Miami (FL) described the benefits of using clickers in class as a means of instantly assessing student understanding (Pai, Stenerson, & Gaines, 2013). Hand-held clickers have been replaced by mobile technology, available to almost all students via their cell phones. This means of formative assessment allows instructors to modify what or how they are presenting course material, as well as better evaluate student preparation for class.

In Heiberger's class, students receive timely feedback via an ever-changing array of technology. In 2009 it was Twitter, and in 2015 it became SnapChat. Students have the option to use Snaps to communicate with their peer mentors and instructors. The instructional team uses Snaps to help students connect to the material, remind them of upcoming assignments and events, and stay motivated. Additionally, students will participate in a research study that uses SnapChat to encourage healthy food selections and behaviors (those linked to student success). For example, students will have the opportunity to be rewarded financially for following and watching Snaps. They will be further incentivized to Snap back to the instructors with photos of their food choices that day.

In addition, video conferencing via Skype, FaceTime, Google Hangouts, and other free or low-cost options, is being employed increasingly in mentoring students, particularly those who are at a distance because of an internship or study abroad experience. Regular, synchronous communication allows for instant feedback to undergraduates regarding research, writing, methodology, or technical issues. Although much of this type of feedback could be accomplished via "track changes" in a document, or by email, in contrast, synchronous, virtual face-to-face sessions hold students accountable at a higher level and ensure that the feedback is both delivered and received in a timely manner. A drawback with the typical asynchronous digital feedback is the potential (likelihood) for the feedback to not be read until hours, or days later, even if it is promptly delivered by the instructor/ mentor. Video conferencing is a simple, accessible option for providing feedback and clarification when students are far from campus or when the instructor is away on professional travel.

Chickering and Gamson's (1987) fifth teaching principle deals with helping students focus their *time on tasks* at hand. Most college students, even the highly capable, need to learn how to better manage their time when transitioning to a postsecondary environment. These students may also be impatient learners who did not have to study as hard in high school as they do in a more competitive collegiate setting. Some have bad habits to unlearn (e.g., overreliance on Wikipedia, Google, etc., as well as multitasking). In student affairs work, time on task frequently means setting goals, establishing timelines and responsibilities, and managing the social interactions so that they are enjoyable yet productive.

In most cases, this principle asserts, focus and effort enhance learning; dealing with course or project content in meaningful, challenging, and dedicated ways will help students master the material or complete the task. Instructors sometimes struggle with creative ways to accomplish this "time on task" aspect, especially when it can no longer be measured by traditional means (which may never have been all that accurate). In his FYSEM, Heiberger uses technology with respect to *time on task*. Students are engaged in the class through *time* via an ancient yet effective form of technology: paper and pencil. They are required to attend class 26 of the total of 30 hours of face-to-face class time or they will drop four letter grades (i.e., they will fail the course). Students are also required to complete ten assignments, each requiring a real-world experience (e.g., shadowing a professional, attending tutoring, participating in relevant student organization events, etc.) and to write directed responses about those experiences. Technology is heavily integrated into all of these activities: students are constantly connected and interacting with each other and the instructor; they also access the Internet in the classroom and use online course management tools to complete reflections/discussions. Future uses of technology in the biology seminar include digital portfolio management software, and integration of professionally oriented social media (e.g., LinkedIn, etc.) to manage and communicate students' capstone experiences in research, internships, and scientific communication.

Although students must invest quite a bit of time and energy in this course, they view the content itself as not particularly difficult. The challenge in this seminar is far more developmental than academic because it forces students to begin to wrestle with who they want to become as they transition to becoming professional scientists in the workforce. A large commitment to *time on task*—to consume information and produce reflections, write major- or career-related papers, create goals, and design research papers and posters—is essential to students' personal and professional development.

Chickering believed that it was vital to **communicate high expectations** to students (the sixth principle of good instructional practice) (Chickering & Gamson, 1987). Chapter co-author Harper saw the importance of this principle in her work advising the Genders and Sexualities Alliance (GSA) on her campus. Communicating high expectations has helped GSA student leaders to respond with enthusiasm and professionalism when offered opportunities to provide Safe Zone training on campus and in the community, and to reflect before reacting when confronted by disappointing choices on the part of others (e.g., administration inviting a Chik-fil-A franchise into the student union; McDonald's refusing to allow the

GSA to paint its windows for homecoming, etc.). Respecting student maturity was rewarded when their immediate hurt and angry reactions became thoughtful and educationally oriented within the span of one meeting's discussion.

Often, the courses that student affairs professionals are called upon to teach are exactly those that would benefit from communicating higher expectations. First-year seminars at some institutions function as mere extensions of new student orientation. These seminars busy students through scavenger hunts rather than provocative reading and challenging assignments. Many are pass/fail only, and are constructed in ways that actually impede instructor efforts to set high expectations. In many instances, students fail to take such courses seriously, and sometimes even fail extremely easy classes for that very reason—they simply don't engage. Student affairs professionals can join with faculty members who insist on quality learning experiences and high academic standards that make students think, work, apply, and relate.

In Heiberger's department, *time on task* and the *communication of high expectations* go hand in hand from the FYSEM through the senior capstone research/ internship experience. At every step of the curricular pathway, time in labs, time required in activities, and time spent in the field or lab collecting data involves many hours *on task*. In addition, the department and each instructor communicate high expectations for quality writing and overall professionalism. These expectations assume prior knowledge from high school writing and science courses and effective communication skills, but are also paired with significant levels of support for remediation or review as necessary. Students are aware of both high expectations and resources to help them achieve the required level of performance. First-year students are required to engage those support systems. All are assigned peer mentors, who spend 30 hours in class with them, and additional hours in 1:1 meetings; mentors and mentees complete a service-learning project together. This balance of challenge and support for students as they prepare for professional school, scientific research, or teaching is crucial.

Technology plays a critical role in communicating high expectations. Heiberger constantly innovates and often co-opts technology that students previously regarded as completely non-academic. A study conducted in 2009 using Twitter (Junco, Heiberger, & Loken, 2011), for example, found that many students had never considered using Twitter for academic purposes. Doing so actually created a bit of a dilemma for many of them: create a new academic account, or shift their current Twitter account to reflect a more professional persona? Interestingly, most students chose to clean up their existing online presence and adopt a more mature and professional tone. High expectations extend to students' Facebook pages as well. Heiberger's academic advising team uses Facebook accounts to "friend" students and then deliver academic information via that site. At times, students' lack of professionalism must be directly addressed in this medium—yet this can be seen as another way of communicating high expectations for students entering the biology major. From the beginning of the FYSEM, students realize that professionalism is expected, and lack of maturity in class or online will have repercussions (e.g., less favorable letters of recommendation, fewer opportunities for internal or external department leadership opportunities, etc.).

The seventh and final principle of good practice in undergraduate teaching set out by Chickering and Gamson (1987) is that such teaching must *respect diverse talents and ways of learning*. Since the publication of this set of principles, higher education has come a long way in terms of operationalizing this principle, but much remains to be done. Diversity of all types, including neuro-diversity, is more widely recognized and valued than ever before, yet many challenges persist. Student affairs professionals possess knowledge of student diversity that many faculty members may lack. In this area, in particular, student affairs instructors or co-instructors can bring expertise with and appreciation for many ways of thinking, knowing, and being (e.g., Abes, Jones, & McEwen, 2007; Baxter Magolda, 2003; Kolb & Kolb, 2006; etc.). For example, all student organizations routinely recognize and take advantage of diverse talents among their members. In the previously-mentioned GSA, the graphic arts major becomes the student who designs posters for the drag shows; the communications major maintains the organizational social media pages; the human development major plans programs that discuss human sexuality; and all executive board members use their unique contacts and strengths in outreach efforts. Some colleges utilize StrengthsQuest™ or similar inventories to help with team building and specific assignments within groups.

While most colleges today offer faculty development programs and resources, not all faculty members participate or choose to develop their expertise in accommodating and honoring a variety of ways of learning. In fact, it has been noted that most instructors utilize their own preferred learning mode in their teaching (Yale, 2015), so being aware of your own learning style will help you be more intentional in incorporating a variety of teaching methods.

Recognized learning styles include verbal, tactile/kinesthetic, sensing, global, and sequential (Felder, 2007, as cited in Center for the Integration of Research, Teaching, and Learning [CIRTL] Network, n.d.). Depending upon the nature of the course, it can be difficult to employ teaching strategies that balance case studies and problem solving (sensing/tactile) with presentations of theoretical material (verbal, sequential). By varying teaching techniques, incorporating technology and social media, and asking frequently for student feedback, instructors can increase the effectiveness of their teaching.

Heiberger notes that within his academic department, as in many STEM curricula, student assessment is heavily based on lab work and high-pressure, multiple-choice exams. However, a pedagogical shift is occurring. In 2015, a record 22 credits in the biology and microbiology major curriculum were taught with active learning pedagogy and in an active learning classroom. These changes in physical space and instructional strategies will increasingly permit diverse sets of students to engage in multiple ways of learning, such as group work, problem solving, presentations, and/or high levels of technology integration in what were for many years traditional 50-minute "professor at the podium" lectures. Respect for learner diversity is central to Scientific Teaching pedagogy and, although within STEM fields the challenge is daunting, diversity of thinking is critical to solving the world's looming problems. The interactive classroom setting that incorporates technology will allow students to complete assignments and projects in varied ways to allow for individual creativity, learning preferences, and innovation.

Another example of acknowledging various ways of learning within Heiberger's FYSEM is the inclusion of peer mentors (junior and senior students) in curriculum planning and implementation. Although student affairs professionals as instructors see themselves as approachable and welcoming, some messages and media are better received from peers. In the biology FYSEM, peer mentors create and implement case studies and learning activities that address time management, study skills, reading strategies, and résumé development. In each case, technology is used, whether the task is managing calendars, annotating an online textbook, building a résumé, or constructing a LinkedIn profile. Although instructors *could* lecture on these topics, most students would rather navigate LinkedIn with a peer, or show their biology e-book notes to a fellow student and discuss what they understand and where they still have questions. In an active learning classroom setting, first-year college students can present from their desks to the entire class, showcasing edits, assets, and critiques of a résumé they worked on in a group, or sharing a test subject's LinkedIn profile.

Of course, not all teaching situations involving student affairs professionals are as formal as the science-oriented FYSEM presented here. However, as noted, the Chickering and Gamson (1987) principles for effective undergraduate instruction are useful in more traditional student activities and programs as well, and represent an asset that student affairs practitioners can bring to any teaching role.

Conclusion

This chapter offered a variety of examples based in a pre-professional FYSEM that utilizes technology and/or social media to enhance instructional impact and learning. These examples also demonstrate that Chickering and Gamson's (1987) principles of effective undergraduate teaching can be updated and enhanced through the use of appropriate technology. Student affairs professionals will find that familiarity and comfort with these venues (e.g., Twitter, wikis, etc.) is a strength they likely bring to instructional settings (formal or informal). Some faculty members with whom student affairs may partner will also be active consumers of all kinds of technology, but others may be more hesitant (Heiberger & Harper, 2007). While not all younger professionals embrace social media, many student affairs personnel will be using the same platforms as their students, and may enjoy the challenge of creating educational uses for emerging technologies.

As technology and teaching continue to evolve, you will want to consider how the "next big thing" can enhance student learning in ways not currently imagined—in both clearly academic as well as co-curricular contexts. In fact, your future role as an educator may not even exist as you read these pages. Given the Chickering and Gamson (1987) framework, illustrated through real-life class examples from Heiberger, student affairs practitioners are better prepared to become instructors who can operationalize knowledge of student development as well as principles of effective undergraduate education, using technologies (often literally) at hand.

References

Abes, E. S., Jones, S. R., & McEwen, M. K. (2007). Reconceptualizing the model of multiple dimensions of identity: The role of meaning-making capacity in the construction of multiple identities. *Journal of College Student Development, 48*, 1–22.

Baxter Magolda, M. B. (2003). Identity and learning: Student affairs' role in transforming higher education. *Journal of College Student Development, 44*, 231–247.

CIRTL (Center for the Integration of Research, Teaching, and Learning) Network. (n.d.) *Planning a course: Teaching and learning styles: The academic culture.* Retrieved from cirtl.net.

Chickering, A. W. & Gamson, Z. F. (1987). Seven principles for good practice in undergraduate education. *AAHE Bulletin, 39*(7), 3–7.

Chickering, A. W. & Reisser, L. (1993). *Education and identity* (2nd ed.). San Francisco, CA: Jossey-Bass.

Handelsman, J., Ebert-May, D., Beichner, R., Bruns, P., Chang, A., DeHaan, R., Wood, W. B. (2004). Scientific teaching. *Science, 30*(5670), 521–522. DOI:10.1126/science.1096022

Heiberger, G. & Harper, R. (2007). *Have you facebooked Astin lately? Using technology to increase student involvement.* In R. Junco & D. M. Timm (Eds.). Using emerging technologies to enhance student engagement. *New Directions in Student Affairs, 124*, Winter 2008, pp. 19–35. San Francisco, CA: Jossey-Bass.

Heiberger, G. & Vos, D. (2013). *iPad ratio's impact on student engagement in a FYS.* Research poster presented at the annual meeting of College Student Educators International National Convention (ACPA), Indianapolis, IN.

Junco, R., Heiberger, G. & Loken, E. (2011). The effect of Twitter on college student engagement and grades. *Journal of Computer Assisted Learning*, no. doi:10.1111/j.1365-2729.2010.00387.x

Kolb, A. Y. & Kolb, D. A. (2006). Learning styles and learning spaces: A review of the multidisciplinary applications of experiential learning theory in higher education. In R. R. Sims & S. J. Sims (Eds.), *Learning and learning styles* (pp. 45–91). New York, NY: Nova Science.

Pai, A., Stenerson, J., & Gaines, M. (2013). *Enhancing student learning through Web 2.0 and social networking technology.* University of Miami Faculty Research Network.

Yale Teaching Center (2015). *Teaching students with different learning styles and levels of preparation.* Retrieved from teaching.yale.edu

13

SOLDIERS IN THE CLASSROOM

Supporting Student Veterans

Aynsley Diamond

Introduction

Veterans have as many reasons for utilizing their educational benefits via the GI Bill as they had for enlisting in the United States Armed Services. Like the general student population, each student has a story, an individual identity, and a myriad of developmental and transitional experiences. This chapter will aid the staff and faculty members working with this student veteran population to better understand its learning needs and support services appropriate to foster veteran student success.

The Student Veteran

Former military service members bring countless positive attributes to a collegiate environment. Military learners are generally characterized by maturity and experiential richness (Starr-Glass, 2011). Rumann and Hamrick (2009) surmised that veterans return to academia with a greater resolve than the remainder of the student population, but those who have experienced combat are statistically more likely to suffer from mental health disorders. Positive mental health screenings in troops deployed to Iraq are nearly twofold of those obtained before deployment (Baker et al., 2009).

Seen as an asset, yet sometimes challenged by psychological and physiological issues, this student population is in need of structured and comprehensive assistance to help them learn to adjust to the relatively unstructured and informal demands of college life. Thompson (2011) states that faculty members and administrators in higher education share responsibility for veterans, and as veterans return to civilian life, the faculty and administration should be part of a cohesive social support system that assists in the transition and helps veterans learn survival and success skills for their new environment.

Psychological Transition

"They will be combat veterans for the rest of their lives" (Thompson, 2011, p. 2). Traditional college students have a variety of worries on a given day, e.g., course preparedness, personal issues, and financial worries. Student veterans may have difficulty relating to and connecting with traditional college students' perspectives. Campus life and concerns may seem trivial compared to those found in combat (Onestak, 2009). Peer relationships can be difficult to foster, depending upon the veteran's transition process from service to college. Age difference between veterans and traditional undergraduates may be a deterrent to the formation of peer relationships. As the veterans return to college, they are already in early adulthood (Donahue & Tibbitts, 1946). In the classroom, service members and veterans are challenged by finding importance and meaning in experiences and ideas that are not life or death (Onestak, 2009). Often these students exhibit behaviors that are not understood by college personnel. For instance, in order to feel safe in the classroom, service members may utilize a variety of coping techniques (e.g., choosing classroom seats that allow for monitoring of others and rapid escape, such as sitting with their back to the wall and near a door) (Onestak, 2009). Out of the classroom, they also are faced with negotiating the structural and procedural differences between the military and higher education bureaucracies (Onestak, 2009). These situations can exacerbate an already challenging transition from the military to academia. Previously effective coping methods may now be viewed as disruptive, and new strategies may need to be learned, particularly those that help to mitigate stress.

In order to ensure success, student veterans must obtain their benefits, secure accurate and appropriate academic advising, while attempting to create connections with their peers. These steps must be accomplished in a culture they are unfamiliar with and under strict timetables for completion. The first step to support student veterans is making it as easy as possible for them to determine who and where to go to obtain services. Many colleges and universities have found the creation of "one stop" centers for veterans to be extremely helpful by saving time and resources of staff and students. It is critical for the service member to have an academic advisor who is well versed in utilizing military benefits. Incorrect advice leads veterans into academic paths that have them wasting their time and benefits on credits not aligned with their plan of study. Familiarity with military transcripts can smooth the advising experience for service members and advising staff. Student activities and clubs and organizations can benefit greatly by the inherent leadership qualities this student population has honed over their years of service. Critical to the veterans' integration into campus culture and an asset to the structure, organization, and management of student clubs, veterans also bring experience traditional college students have not yet developed.

The United States Armed Services are very diverse, with many members of minority groups achieving officer ranking and women continuing to be promoted at unprecedented rates. Student veterans are familiar with and trained to cross cultural divides when working toward completion of shared purposes. Oftentimes their skill sets are stereotyped into categories portrayed in the movies or on the news, but there are thousands of soldiers needed to ensure daily operations with expertise as varied as accounting and facilities management. In addition to skill set stereotyping, many student veterans have to endure assumptions made about the possibility of post-traumatic stress disorder (PTSD) and traumatic brain injury (TBI).

PTSD is one of an array of disorders that can be directly linked with combat service or exposure. The population of student veterans is not comprised solely of combat veterans; many never saw war or served abroad during their service. Practitioners must not assume that all student veterans suffer from PTSD or TBI. Their enlistment experiences are varied and often misunderstood. Some of these include fear of their own death; having to see, smell, and handle bodies and body parts; extended sleep deprivation; harsh climate; cramped living conditions; and homesickness (Onestak, 2009).

As a result of the acute traumas and general stress that characterize life in a war zone, military personnel frequently encounter an array of symptoms and reactions during the transition back to their homes and civilian life (Onestak, 2009). Some combat veterans experience triggers that can inhibit the normal carrying out of day-to-day activities. Common symptoms and reactions experienced by returning war veterans include insomnia, difficulty in concentrating, hyper-alertness, grief, guilt, impatience, and anger (Onestak, 2009).

Higher education professionals can understand how the manifestation of even one of these symptoms would create a challenge for a service member or veteran acclimating to the classroom following a combat deployment. Not all veterans have PTSD, and although most educators are familiar with the term, few understand what it means or how to recognize it (American Council on Education [ACE], 2010). Often, an academic environment presents the veteran with daily challenges by creating triggers, which will push the student to experience many symptoms of past trauma.

Military to Academic Transition

Toven (1945), a noted authority on helping veterans transition to civilian life, focuses heavily on selection of vocation. He stresses the importance of a good fit between career choice and aptitude and attitude. Because the veteran who returns to college is primarily interested in education as a means of gaining a congenial livelihood and is interested to a lesser degree only in its cultural aspects, the traditional college curriculum will have to be modified for him/her (Toven, 1945).

In a study by American Council on Education (ACE, 2010), veterans reported issues with enrollment following enlistment. They talked about problems initiating their GI Bill benefits and discussed how important it is to have a point of contact on campus that can assist them in navigating the maze of veterans and campus benefits and services (ACE, 2010).

The management of GI benefits requires coordination between academic and student affairs. While many institutes of higher education still function in a so-called silo system, it is imperative that these separate departments work together in order to best assist service members and veterans. Strong support from campus leadership and administration is vital in order for programs to facilitate college success for veterans, military members, and their families.

Veterans are valuable members of a classroom environment. Task and completion oriented, their commitment to degree obtainment and their ability to implement course objectives makes them natural classroom leaders. Engaging teaching methodologies, such as problem-based learning and active learning techniques, are highly effective, as are opportunities for presentations or group work. Student veterans are characterized as being highly adaptable and acclimate to the integration of technology very quickly. Some student veterans who seek anonymity find great success with educational technology, such as iclickers or other classroom response systems. Learning management systems that incorporate multiple platforms for content delivery are very successful with this population. For instance, using a discussion board online in concert with asynchronous lectures is an opportunity for student veterans to express themselves with a level of separation from the classroom environment. Due to their age, experience, and developmental progression, these students often serve as role models for student behavior and academic rigor.

Transition support of student veterans can take many forms, and services and resources focused on this population foster student retention and degree completion. Great efforts have been made since the enactment of the post-9/11 GI Bill to be proactive in student veteran support. Many institutions have allocated spaces on their campuses devoted to military lounges where advising staff and certifying officials can work directly with students rather than the students trying to navigate the institution hierarchy to find the appropriate staff members. In addition, new onboarding orientations and military transition courses are growing at an exponential rate across the country. One challenge to the survival of these programs and services is that they are dependent on student numbers. With tight budgets and limited resources, critical programing that fosters student success can be an easy line item to cut. However, even with budgetary constraints, many practitioners have found creative ways to support their veteran populations. Educating the faculty, staff, administrators, and students is the most cost-effective and helpful way to do this. Most civilians are simply curious and do not intentionally ask inappropriate questions; nor do they consider problematic aspects of asking student veterans to speak not as individuals, but as representing the entire population of returning service members.

Context is key to any education program, and panels of veterans can be very helpful in facilitating discussion and creating an opportunity to offer perspective. Peer-to-peer mentoring programs are a low-cost, low-effort option to aid with information transfer and cultural acclimation. Service members talk to one another. Regardless of branch affiliation, student veterans will support one another with information and transition. Communication is key to the learning and adaptation process for returning veterans. Brief interventions by members of the student affairs staff to teach mentors active listening skills can make the support process much more effective. Making sure the students get the correct information they need in a timely manner is critical to retention and success. Collaboration between advising staff and certifying officials cannot be stressed enough. Resource information and opportunities are critical to adjustment and sense of belonging on our campuses. Organizations like Student Veterans of America, Iraq and Afghanistan Veterans of America, American Veterans Committee, Veterans of Foreign Wars of the United States (VFW), and the American Legion offer services and resources that individual institutions do not have access to and often cannot provide. These organizations should be advertised and offered in a suite of support options to the students during orientation and throughout their academic enrollment at the institution.

Many veterans who face challenges acclimating to higher education find camaraderie in joining paramilitary organizations. Veterans relate that joining a volunteer firefighting brigade, working as security personnel, and joining an emergency medical technician program gave them a structure and deeper purpose while they obtained their degrees. Paramilitary agency involvement can provide sought-after connection with a shared purpose that could be lacking in an academic environment. Transition courses and seminars help veterans learn college survival techniques.

Veterans' affairs offices can increase services to aid integration by creating curriculum initiatives; campus-wide education programs for faculty, staff, and administrators; and by cultivating support for veterans by the establishment of veteran-specific policies and procedures. Faculty members in history, communication, computer science, allied health, and other disciplines can collaborate with veteran affairs offices for guest speaker opportunities and have reported great benefits from both the student and the student presenter perspective. Integrating activities and opportunities for expression, both in dialogue and in writing, are very effective in creative writing courses, philosophy, and the visual and performing arts. Literature and communication courses can help veterans reflect on their own experiences and present the opportunity to discuss information in novels at a distance. This makes conversation possible and makes reliving trauma slightly less probable.

These initiatives support the inclusion of this valued student population and ease their transition into college culture. Learning about the military, war and combat, and service members' experiences could also become one element of a campus's broader commitment to diversity and social understanding (Rumann & Hamrick, 2009). Dedication to the success of student veterans does not end with resources and campus education. An important aspect of student veteran success takes place in the classroom. There are numerous ways to determine student learning styles that can inform faculty curriculum and aid in academic planning for students. When advising student veterans, there is value in learning about their extensive prior training regimens and to consider their wealth of experience with experiential education models.

In the Classroom: Experiential Learning Alignment with Student Veterans

Many faculty members and most student affairs professionals are familiar with Kolb's Experiential Learning Theory (1984). The core of Kolb's four-stage model is a simple description of a learning cycle that shows how experience is translated through reflection into concepts, which, in turn are used as guides for active experimentation and the choice of new experiences (as cited in Healey & Jenkins, 2000). The theory is based on feedback and reflection through which the individual is informed, reacts, and the cycle begins again based on the preceding information. Experiential learning at its core is learned behavior from action, including field work and laboratory sessions.

Veterans come to higher education with a wealth of training and an array of educational experiences. Many have management and supervisory experience with extensive reporting responsibilities. Military learners are likely to possess a rich experiential history, and understand organizational culture, leadership, decision making, and different management styles (Starr-Glass, 2011). Military academies like the United States Air Force Academy (USAFA) incorporate experiential learning into the curriculum, including service-learning components. Already utilized in a training capacity and at military academies, experiential education can be familiar and effective with students who are veterans.

Examples of Experiential Learning Criteria

Many student veterans' previous military training lends itself to success in experiential learning environments. The ability to learn from experience is typically a survival skill in combat zones, and the ability to communicate what has been learned quickly and effectively is critical. Those with management and leadership experience excel in internships, where maturity and self-reliance are sought-after characteristics. Individuals whose previous experience included practical data management are well suited to field research and possess organizational skills not yet developed by their civilian peers. Service-learning projects have the added benefit for a veteran recently separated from the military to serve a community organization while facilitating the transition to non-military culture. Chapman et al. (1995) explain criteria that define a method or activity as being experiential; these attributes include:

1. *Mixture of content and process:* There must be a balance between the experiential activities and the underlying content or theory.
2. *Absence of excessive judgment:* The instructor must create a safe space for students to work through their own process of self-discovery.
3. *Engagement in purposeful endeavors:* In experiential learning, the learner is the self-teacher, therefore there must be "meaning for the student in the learning." The learning activities must be personally relevant to the student.

4. *Encouraging the big picture perspective*: Experiential activities must allow the students to make connections between the learning they are doing and the world. Activities should build in students the ability see relationships in complex systems and find a way to work within them.

5. *The role of reflection*: Students should be able to reflect on their own learning, bringing "the theory to life" and gaining insight into themselves and their interactions with the world.

6. *Creating emotional investment*: Students must be fully immersed in the experience, not merely doing what they feel is required of them. The "process needs to engage the learner to a point where what is being learned and experience strikes a critical, central chord within the learner."

7. *The reexamination of values*: By working within a space that has been made safe for self-exploration, students can begin to analyze and even alter their own values.

8. *The presence of meaningful relationships*: One part of getting students to see their learning in the context of the whole world is to start by showing the relationships between "learner to self, learner to teacher, and learner to learning environment."

9. *Learning outside one's perceived comfort zones*: "Learning is enhanced when students are given the opportunity to operate outside of their own perceived comfort zones." This doesn't refer just to physical environment, but also to the social environment. This could include, for instance, "being accountable for one's actions and owning the consequences" (Chapman, McPhee, & Proudman, 1995, p. 243).

Each of these characteristics defines an experiential activity or method that aligns with the skills and maturity the majority of the veteran student population possesses, dependent on training and conditioning. That said, the success of these activities is largely reliant on students being solely responsible for their own learning. When veterans transition from the military, they often express disillusionment or anxiety with lack of structure or express a need for clearly identified guidelines and objectives. This can be mitigated by clear curricular design, set overall learning objectives, and timelines for check-ins or general task completion.

On Campus: Cultural Understanding

Compounding military to academic transition is the lack of foundational perspective on the part of staff, faculty, and the administration. From generational and societal perspectives, large numbers of current administrators and faculty members will not have experienced military or wartime service (Hamrick & Rumann, 2009). This lack of perspective of military culture, in addition to the potential traumas of wartime service, may inhibit initiatives aimed at supporting this population. In the past, veterans returned to college campuses with the knowledge that, while their military understanding was vastly different from their older peers who were drawing on experiences from World War II, Korea, or Vietnam, there was a contextual similarity upon which to draw. In order to perpetuate this perspective Washton (1945) recommended that counselors or advisors for veterans be appointed from the ranks of professors who were themselves military veterans. As Vietnam veterans near retirement, a fear is that the mentorship, which is highly effective with this population, may be quickly disappearing from college settings. DiRamio, Ackerman, and Mitchell (2008) found that respondents reported facing anti-military bias on their campuses, particularly among faculty members. Their study demonstrated that professors made inappropriate disclosure requests of student veterans in class or regarded student veterans as spokespersons for all veterans.

During and following the Vietnam conflict, military students had an even more challenging experience transitioning into higher education. In part because of changing public sentiment, veterans reported feeling unwelcome on campuses and attempted to maintain a low profile as students (Rumann & Hamrick, 2009). These feelings persist on some college campuses today, which cause many service members and veterans to choose not to disclose their military background in order to blend into the student population and to prevent unwanted attention to their past experiences. In response, college campuses have begun to educate their population by drawing upon the unique experiences and challenges facing this group of students. Thompson (2011) suggests that, where appropriate, professors should incorporate veterans' perspectives, beliefs, and opinions on policy issues and their military experience to add to the richness of discussion in the classroom, while being careful to not ask the student to speak as a representative for all veterans. Assignments can be developed that give a platform for veterans to reflect and express their experiences.

Conclusion

With the passage of educational acts, such as the post-9/11 GI Bill, colleges and universities have committed to the education of an increasing number of recently discharged service members. Many will face challenges upon reentry to academic/civilian life. The transition from military service to an academic environment is wrought with difficulties, both in and out of the classroom. The first step in supporting and retaining student veterans is the creation of an environment that fosters their success. Veterans enter colleges and universities seeking support for transitional challenges, mentoring needs, and academic integration. Their presence and how they are supported will directly impact campus culture. All campus personnel should make every effort to assess campus attitudes and policies that affect returning veterans and commit to learning how to serve returning veterans more effectively.

Seen as an asset to college communities, yet often misunderstood, veterans bring varied needs when they enroll in postsecondary education. They depend on a holistic approach by faculty, staff, and administration to create a streamlined process for access to support and academic alignment. Veterans need to learn how to communicate with their civilian peers, navigate a non-hierarchical organization, and discover what their next life role will be. Student affairs offices can contribute to veterans' successful transition by offering programming such as transition seminars and opportunities for veterans to foster relationships with their military peers on campus. Equally important are opportunities for student veterans to work with their civilian peers in an environment where they can express their interests and encounter new learning experiences outside of the classroom. Veterans should be sought out to organize and facilitate training programs to educate the larger population on their experiences and transition needs. Internships and shadowing opportunities that focus on veteran leadership and applicable skill set areas are examples of effective experiential learning. Finally, colleges and universities must evaluate how best to support their student veterans, depending on institutional mission and culture, by asking these students what their needs are and how we in student affairs can better serve them.

References

American Council on Education (2010). *Veterans success jam: Ensuring success for returning veterans*. Retrieved from http://www.acenet.edu/

Baker, D. G., Heppner, P., Afari, N., Nunnik, S., Kilmer, M., Simmons, A., Bosse, B. (2009). Trauma exposure, branch of service, and physical injury in relation to mental health among U.S. veterans retuning from Iraq and Afghanistan. *Military Medicine, 174*(8), 773–778.

Chapman, S., McPhee, P., & Proudman, B. (1995). What is experiential education? In K. Warren, (Ed.), *The theory of experiential education* (pp. 235–248). Dubuque: Kendall/Hunt Publishing Company.

DiRamio, D., Ackerman, R., & Mitchell, R. L. (2008). From combat to campus: Voices of student-veterans. *NASPA Journal, 45*(1), 73–102.

Donahue, W. T., & Tibbitts, C. (1946). College and university procedures in the reorientation of veterans. *Journal of Clinical Psychology, 2*(2), 131–139.

Healey, M. & Jenkins, A. (2000). Kolb's experiential learning theory and its application in geography in higher education. *Journal of Geography, 99*(5), 185–195.

Onestak, J. (2009). *For veterans returning from war*. Retrieved from http://www.jmu.edu/counselingctr/Resources/veterans.html

Rumann, C. & Hamrick, F. (2009). Supporting student veterans in transition. *New Directions for Student Services*, (No. 126, pp. 25–34). San Francisco, CA: Jossey-Bass.

Starr-Glass, D. (2011). Military learners: Experience in the design and management of online learning environments. *Journal of Online Learning and Teaching, 7*(1), 147–158.

Thompson, J. (2011). Our student soldiers: Lessons from the north and left. *Journal of College & Character, 12*(3), 1–5.

Toven, J. R. (1945). College counseling for the war veteran. *Journal of Educational Sociology, 18*(6), 331–339.

Washton, N. S. (1945). A veteran goes to college. *Journal of Higher Education, 16*(4), 195–196.

SECTION IV

Learning Processes and Student Affairs Pedagogy

14

USING POPULAR CULTURE TO ENHANCE STUDENT LEARNING

Margaret Miller and Ruth Harper

Introduction

Student affairs professionals in a wide variety of instructional roles draw on many resources to enhance student learning. This chapter highlights the effective use of popular culture as a way of engaging student interest, building critical thinking skills, increasing diverse perspectives, and approaching difficult, controversial topics in "relatable" ways. We swim in a sea of popular culture, yet rarely critically consider the tremendous impact it has on our (and our students') thinking. Leib (2006) noted that more people voted to determine the winner of *American Idol* than the presidency of the United States.

We all are aware that college students (and most of the rest of us in higher education) constantly use smartphones, iPads, laptops, gaming systems, and other devices to not only keep in touch with friends and family but also to take the pulse of the issues and individuals we follow via social media and favorite websites. Students in 2009 spent "$6.5 billion on technology items" and devoted "an average of 12 hours per day engaged with some type of media" (MarketingCharts, 2009). They use their devices to watch videos, television shows, and films, as well as play video games.

An example that provides context for college students' extensive engagement with popular culture is their use of the online media streaming provider Netflix. At Texas Tech University (Solis, 2014), a study revealed that nine out of ten students watch Netflix on a regular basis, including "binge-watching" TV shows; the article defines binge-watching as viewing three or more episodes in a row at a time (para 8). Another source also points out that Netflix has come to play a significant role in students' daily lives (Kline, 2013). While there are many options available to students for engaging with media (e.g., Hulu, Amazon Prime, etc.), the high (and perhaps extreme) use of Netflix underscores the prevalence and rapid consumption of popular culture in the lives of college students. Educators, including student affairs professionals, can do a better job of accessing the learning possibilities that exist right in our students' hands.

Transformative learning is a concept introduced by Mezirow (2000), and has to do with encountering ideas that present what he calls disorienting dilemmas. As students experience ideas or situations that challenge their existing assumptions about life, they may experience difficult emotions (that may include resistance). However, given the right amounts of challenge and support (Sanford, 1967), many students can begin to explore not only new ideas, but also implications of those notions in their own lives. Whether or not they are familiar with the term "transformative learning," student affairs professionals both witness and engineer encounters that are transformative on a regular basis. When a student comes to the residence hall director or academic advisor with a personal concern (e.g., my parents are divorcing and my dad is gay; my teammates are using illegal drugs and I don't know what to do; my roommate is Lakota and wants to "smudge" in our room and I do not understand, etc.), there is an opportunity to initiate the process of transformative learning.

King and Kitchener (1994) drew on the concept of transformative learning in their reflective judgment model, familiar to most student affairs practitioners as a way students cope with changes in knowing what they know and go about inspecting and evaluating alternative possibilities. As new experiences, both sought and unsought, impact and challenge students' perceptions and beliefs, they (students) can "transform" the meaning of the event and gain a more mature or inclusive perspective (e.g., my dad may be gay, and he is still my dad, etc.). Supporting this type of learning is a crucial element of student affairs work. (Note: for a more complete explication of transformative learning, see the article by Kitchenham [2008] on the development of this theory.)

Tisdell (2008) claims that media today both reflect the culture and impact beliefs about self and others. Using popular cultural reference points in teaching, she states, "is the point of critical media literacy, as well as of transformative learning—to raise questions and awareness, and to help people think about issues and assumptions in new and creative ways" (p. 52). This transformative learning Tisdell refers to is achieved by helping students become judicious consumers of the media that surrounds them, as well as teaching them to question assertions, sources, and dominant ideologies.

Films and Television

Films are very popular among college students and student affairs professionals, and have long been used in a variety of teaching and learning contexts. Over many years, I (Harper) have attended and presented conference sessions on how feature films can serve to illustrate student development theories (Harper & Rogers, 1999). "Films can be used by students, professional staff, or even faculty in meetings to make abstract concepts tangible" (Kelly & Porter, 2014). Social activist scholar bell hooks states it unequivocally:

> Whether we like it or not, cinema assumes a pedagogical role in the lives of many people. It may not be the intent of the filmmaker to teach audiences anything, but that does not mean that lessons are not learned. . . . Movies not only provide a narrative for specific discourses of race, sex, and class, they provide a shared experience, a common starting point from which diverse audiences can dialogue about these charged issues. (2013, p. 101)

We would argue that today many television shows serve this purpose as well. Most of us can name a film (or several—or television shows) that changed the way we see the world. For us, those influential sources include Spike Lee's *Do the Right Thing* (1989) and the Showtime dramatic series, *Homeland* (Gensa & Gordon 2011–2017).

As a filmmaker, Spike Lee's creative choices not only invite, but truly require, viewers to interpret and make meaning of their viewing experience. *Do the Right Thing* (1989) is a film that does just that, bringing a powerful emotional and social impact. The film is set in Brooklyn, New York, in the scorching summer of 1989. Lee utilizes a range of elements including a potent soundtrack, vibrant colors, unusual camera angles, and cultural references to the civil rights era to draw viewers into a complex, racially charged set of relationships in a neighborhood that is under stress. Both implied and actual conflict among characters prompts a visceral audience response. Reynolds (2011) proposes the approach of reception criticism to make meaning of this film; reception theory is used to "understand how social identities such as gender or race may influence interpretations" (p. 29). Lee's *Do the Right Thing*, as Reynolds describes, "requires his audience to interpret images actively so they will think critically about issues of race in their everyday lives" (p. 30).

This film can be used in a variety of settings with college students to engage difficult social issues, question previously-held assumptions, and unpack how meaning is constructed. A central conflict that plays out through the film is the running of Sal's pizzeria. Sal, an Italian American, is adamant in defending his business practices (e.g., his refusal to display portraits of African Americans of note in the store, etc.), while African-American character Buggin' Out confronts Sal's exclusionary practices and how they affect residents of the neighborhood. Lee highlights contrasting perspectives; his characters enact how racial identity influences perception and passion. Non-traditional camera techniques startle and engage viewers, zooming in on characters' exaggerated expressions/reactions and having characters speak directly to the audience, yelling racial slurs.

Although set in 1989, the film retains its ability to compel viewers to consider what "doing the right thing" really means alongside the characters in the film. The end of the movie features a Martin Luther King, Jr. quote emphasizing peaceful action, which is replaced by a quote in support of violence by Malcolm X.

For college students, this film can be a powerful tool to consider how multiple, competing viewpoints (that changed over time) frame crucial social issues and events. As Reynolds (2011) underscores, being a consumer of film is a "complex activity" that "has great potential to incite action and change minds" (p. 38).

The Showtime series *Homeland* is an example of a television show that induces critical thinking because (though obviously fictional) it is rooted in geopolitical realities; further, every character is complex. No one is completely good or completely bad. A Pakistani terrorist is also portrayed as a patriot as well as a devoted husband and father; but in the next scene, he stabs to death a Muslim woman who works for the CIA. (The word "terrorist" itself becomes problematic—who exactly is a terrorist?) The CIA staff characters are seen to struggle with logistical, personal, political, and moral dilemmas that are many layered. In a global studies course, an international living-learning community, an interdisciplinary honors colloquium, an international relations student organization, *Homeland* would be a riveting, absorbing, and ultimately discussable resource. Watching this show forces viewers to come to terms with what they think they know about many things: how mothers behave; how Americans make international decisions; how a brilliant person copes with a chronic mental illness; what costs people are willing to pay for victory (and how victory is defined)—even what is right and wrong. Since neat resolution is not an option in *Homeland*, anyone who follows it must learn to tolerate a high degree of ambiguity and moral uncertainty. One review of this show describes it as containing "stark visual metaphors" that constitute "cyborg poetry" as well as "art that reflects the way that screens and lenses have altered our perceptions" (Nussbaum, 2014, para. 11).

Watching and discussing *Homeland* can provide a vivid, timely milieu for dialogue about a real-life event, such as a major political presidential candidate allowing a Muslim woman to be mocked and escorted out of a public rally. The protagonist's mental illness can illuminate the deep challenges of bipolar disorder while also demonstrating her ability to not only manage her disability, but also out-perform others and live a life worthy of respect. Students in pre-professional majors in psychology or social work will find actress Claire Danes's skillful portrayal of Carrie Mathison to be well researched, believable, sympathetic, and informative. The use of drones in this drama raises excellent questions for all students involved in leadership or citizenship activities. What constitutes responsible application of drone technology, as drones are now widely available? The overall issue of surveillance, its morality and amorality, is present in every *Homeland* episode.

As Tisdell (2008) notes, "films such as *Crash* and *Brokeback Mountain* have generated important conversations on controversial topics about race, ethnicity, and sexual orientation, which can help us look at social relations in new ways" (p. 49). More recently, movies (e.g., *The Revenant, Carol, Spotlight, Hidden Figures*, etc.) have been used to frame discussions in classrooms, student center meeting rooms, residence halls, student/staff retreats, online chat rooms, and more. Films, a medium well accepted and often accessed by today's college students, offer a ready venue for critical reflection and transformative learning if supported by appropriate resources.

A Novel Idea

Studies show that reading quality fiction may enhance personal empathy (Kidd & Castano 2013) and improve overall executive functions of the brain as well (Goldman, 2012). Using MRI imaging, neuroscientists documented how close reading of Jane Austen engaged readers' emotions and improved multifaceted cognitive operations (Goldman, 2012). "Practitioners in fields other than the humanities seldom think of imaginative texts as occasions for emancipation or the gaining of critical consciousness" (Greene, 1990, p. 251), but reading fiction can be a very freeing and transformative learning experience.

Many years ago, colleges discovered the virtues of a common read: it builds community by giving first-year students something to talk about right away; it can provide a programming scaffolding for student affairs and academic affairs collaboration. In our hometown, the university's common read has forged new campus-community relationships by including high school (and sometimes middle school, depending on the specific selection) students in shared reading, discussion, and interaction with the book's visiting author. Using modern novels or biographies can creatively bridge serious cultural chasms with popular culture, dramatizing and personalizing the issues while contextualizing them within an accessible, humanizing, memorable format.

Student affairs interns in my (Harper) master's-level program are required to participate in three hours of group supervision every other week. Part of this time is used to check in on the work at each site, to share successes, and gather collective wisdom about demanding issues. Each semester, I used a solution-focused question at the outset regarding how the remainder of our group time is structured: "What can we do in our time together that will make you feel that it has been very well spent?" The interns always come up with good topics, such as how to conduct a national job search, or inviting in the vice president for student affairs for a question and answer session. They also typically identify a professionally oriented common read (e.g., *Contested Issues in Student Affairs* [Magolda & Baxter Magolda, 2011]; *Where You Work Matters* [Hirt, 2006], etc.). However, in the final year of my teaching career, I took the prerogative of asking students to read and discuss works of fiction set in academia, and it turned out to be both instructive and a lot of fun.

First, I created a list of relevant titles, mostly contemporary literary novels, but some historical. It was easy, because so many excellent books involve college students and/or faculty members. By the time students are interns, I know them quite well, so I suggested a specific book to each student, giving them the option of choosing an alternative from the list. I also tried to frame the assignment in a way that would intrigue students. As West (1957) once observed, "Fiction reveals truths that reality obscures" (p. 39). What truths might be imbedded in a terrific modern novel about college life? How might these books interject new and diverse perspectives to our fairly homogeneous Midwestern group? Students were asked to consider specific questions as they read, and to bring their observations to share during group meetings:

- How are the characters in this book (students, parents, faculty, or staff members) different from or similar to those you encounter in internship?
- Would you like to work at this institution and/or with the students, faculty, and staff described in the novel you read? Why or why not? If yes, in what capacity?
- What did you learn about student development and/or higher education from reading this novel that you had not learned from your textbooks and journals?
- Do you think that this kind of reading belongs in a student affairs internship group? Why or why not?

These interns read (and, for the most part enjoyed and learned from) such titles as *Americanah* (Adichie, 2013); *On Beauty* (Smith, 2005); *The Namesake* (Lahiri, 2003); *Caleb's Crossing* (Brooks, 2011); *The Marriage Plot* (Eugenides, 2011); *The Art of Fielding* (Harbach, 2011)—and more. Student comments included: "I learned a lot about the realities and challenges 'non-American' black students experience; this book (*Americanah*) took me a lot deeper than a case study or journal article" (D. Schmidt, personal communication, December 3, 2015). "I became personally invested in the students' relationships and thought about how I would deal with the issues presented in real life—Title IX offenses, mental health and addiction issues, pressures on student-athletes" (*The Art of Fielding*) (C. Sorensen, personal communication, December 3, 2015). "This book helped me really understand the difficulties that students from less privileged backgrounds might experience at an exclusive, wealthy institution" (*On Beauty*) (S. Damjanovic, personal communication, December 3, 2015). "I was surprised at the portrayal of bipolar disorder in one of the main characters. His manic, hypomanic, and depressive episodes were described in detail" (*The Marriage Plot*) (V. Kleinjan, personal communication, December 3, 2015). Many students said that they enjoyed saying they were "doing their homework" as they curled up with a good book, and most found it a highly enjoyable learning experience.

There are also many powerful ways to engage complex issues via fiction with undergraduate students; utilizing fiction, or "narrative," allows students to contextualize, personalize, and bring potentially abstract issues to life. An example of this was the first-year seminar course I (Miller) took based around learning about the Palestinian-Israeli conflict. This course had an extensive reading list that included one non-fiction book to provide necessary historical background; the remainder of the list was exclusively novels. A wealth of contrasting perspectives and experiences were represented among these fictional accounts, including: Arab life in the Israeli-occupied West Bank (*Wild Thorns* [Khalifeh, 2000]); an account of love and loss during the Yom Kippur War (*The Lover* [Yehoshua, 1977]); a semi-autobiographical account of an Israeli Arab (*Arabesques* [Shammas, 1988]); the story of a Jewish couple in Jerusalem (*My Michael* [Oz, 1968]); and several others. Employing novels at the heart of instruction brought to light the humanity of individuals whose stories were set amidst the ongoing political and social turmoil of the Palestinian-Israeli conflict far more intimately and memorably than reading solely historical pieces ever could. With the opportunity to study abroad in Israel and Jordan for a month-long January term following the on-campus course, students were prepared to offer informed inquiries and sensitively investigate the complexities of life in Israel.

There are many ways student affairs professionals can use novels to enhance learning in contexts beyond the classroom. These books are an excellent means of personal and professional development—constructing and working through a list of great books can be as or more enriching and enlightening than any other such endeavor. Books also spark discussion, whether it be with one other person (e.g., a mentor, peer, supervisor, supervisee, etc.), a group (e.g., as a staff development activity, a college/community collaboration, etc.), or for a specific, targeted purpose (e.g., preparing to study abroad, informing a campus climate study, etc.). Keeping a reading journal will help readers retain the most stimulating or meaningful ideas encountered in their perusals, and will reveal over time which authors or types of books led to transformative learning and thinking. Goodreads is a useful, free website that allows readers to track books completed, post personal reviews, and see how other people rate books that might be of interest. Many fruitful relationships have been built on the opening question, "What are you reading?"

Strategies and Approaches

Media can be engaged intelligently and intentionally in student affairs work through many cultural approaches. Obviously, simply asking students "What did you think of (that show, film, book, etc.) and leaving it at that is insufficient—it is a missed opportunity to engage, follow up, dispute, or push further into a provocative idea, character, or situation. "The emotional power of films (or books) can be a catalyst for thinking and learning. It is important to remember, however, that (they) are a starting point, not an end in themselves" (Harper & Rogers, 1999, p. 90).

Student affairs professionals are called to help prepare students for their lives after graduation, and to assist in creating global citizens, as many institutions reference in their mission statements. Critical examination of media offers a crucial way to engage in dialogue and support students in becoming informed consumers of information and contributing members of society. As Kellner (1995) notes, "Media images help shape our view of the world and our deepest values: what we consider good or bad, positive or negative, moral or evil" (p. 1). Further, "the media are forms of pedagogy which teach us how to be men and women . . . (and) how to conform to the dominant system of norms, values, practices, and institutions" (Kellner, 1995, p. 1). Given the degree of media involvement of most college students, these observations are likely to be even more true today than when they were written. While many academic disciplines deal directly with media studies (e.g., English, cultural studies, American studies, communications, etc.), these sorts of meaningful interactions around media can be built naturally in many arenas led by student affairs personnel—new student seminars, residence hall programs, one-on-one appointments, student success workshops, and many more.

Critical theory is an approach that seeks to examine the ways in which texts intersect with society and/or social issues (e.g., how a film depicts people of color; how a television show portrays transgendered individuals, etc.) and can be used to analyze any textual form (including art, literature, music, film, etc.). While there are many types of critical theory, such as feminist theory, queer theory, or historical criticism, the broader purpose is to "open your mind to new ways of thinking" (Reynolds, 2011, p. 8). Utilizing critical theory to frame discussion of media and popular culture with students can serve as a powerful tool. Initial questions might include:

- What does a particular text or film say about our culture at this moment in time?
- Why was an author/director drawn to this topic? Why now? (Or why then?)
- How are various identities represented (e.g., gender, race, class, sexual orientation, faith tradition, etc.)?
- What sort of social response did a text receive? Why did it receive that response? With whom is it popular? Which audiences have been particularly critical, and why?

Reynolds (2011) also suggests three specific approaches for using critical theory to frame understanding of media, including reception criticism, structuralism, and identity criticism.

Three Critical Lenses

Reception criticism emphasizes the role of the audience and the ways in which viewers contribute to the meaning of a work. This asserts that one cannot simply view a movie or read a book, but must interpret and make sense of the experience, a concept relevant to working with college students as (distinct and disparate) audience members. Students as "consumers" are highly diverse and present contrasting, conflicting viewpoints. Questions that arise through the use of reception criticism might include: Who is watching (i.e., identities/demographics)? How should the impact of this work be evaluated? Who is responsible for meaning derived from this work? Using and discussing *Homeland* as a common experience in an international living-learning community would immediately pose such questions.

Structuralism is concerned with breaking down parts of a work in order to analyze specific pieces individually. In contrast to reception criticism's emphasis on audience, structuralism focuses on the understanding of artistic design, examining how pieces are put together to build meaning. Questions offered through this lens might include: "How do the ways in which we see or hear about events affect our understanding of such events?" (Reynolds, 2011, p. 53). How do film and television images influence our interpretations of social or political happenings? In *Do the Right Thing*, Spike Lee presents a series of provocative vignettes that are stitched together to offer multifaceted perspectives on a specific neighborhood at a specific time. In ending the film by juxtaposing quotes from Martin Luther King and Malcolm X, the filmmaker intentionally alludes to unreconciled racial tensions that persist in the larger American society.

As Kellner (1995) references, a significant part of critical theory in relation to media is tied to identity. Identity criticism explores how identity is defined and/or constructed by media/popular culture. Identity theorists consider ways in which audience members may integrate what they view in media sources into their own identity. This can occur in both positive and potentially negative ways. At times, media can exert a strong influence on identity exploration and validation; in contrast, media can present limited snapshots of reality, stripping the complexity of significant issues. Twitter, for example, limits tweets to 140 characters. While it is a popular and useful medium, it is not built for depth or subtlety. Questions to be examined through this approach could include exploration of essentially any social identity, but might also include broader questions: How does a film's depiction of a character or social issue affect viewers' understanding of their own identities? How does a text aid in increasing empathy or understanding across a particular issue? How might reading *Americanah*, for instance, spark discussion of the importance of a woman's hair to her identity—especially if the discussion group includes African-American women, African women, women of differing ages, roles, sexual identities, European-American women, Native-American women, or men? How might this book introduce awareness of the African diaspora and the great diversity within as well as between groups?

Conclusion: Student Affairs can Lead Transformative Learning

This chapter has highlighted some of the ways in which student affairs professionals can and should employ elements of popular culture to challenge the assumptions and enrich the learning of the students with whom they work in settings that go beyond traditional classroom-based courses. Drawing on elements of cultural media in which students are already immersed, as illustrated here, can bring new and diverse perspectives to complicated issues; it can even be fun.

But another important motivation student affairs professionals recognize in being intentional and strategic by using films, novels, and other popular cultural artifacts in learning is that we understand that media serve as filters to powerfully impact the way students make meaning of their own identities (Abes, Jones, & McEwen, 2007). Self-perceptions of aspects of personal identity, such as gender, race, class, sexual orientation, and more can be greatly influenced by how these characteristics are represented in the media and culture (both campus and at large). In updating and refining Abes and Jones's Model of Multiple Dimensions of Identity (MMDI) (Abes & Jones, 2004), Abes et al. (2007) developed the concept of a meaning-making filter. Contextual influences, such as attending a predominantly white campus, or having the opportunity for leadership in an LGBTQ student organization, make student identities more or less salient in certain circumstances. Student affairs practitioners strive to create residence halls, classrooms, student unions, advising centers, and off-campus learning experiences that are inclusive spaces that help to construct and affirm student identities. One way to do this is by accessing the rich resources of popular culture. Reading and discussing *On Beauty* (Smith, 2005), for example, can allow students and staff to talk about privilege in higher education (as well as race, gender, and sexuality) in a manner that can lead to productive insights about their own campus climate. Encountering and unpacking intricate and layered films, television shows, and literary novels can support students in building more effective meaning-making filters that allow them (students) to better determine for themselves how cultural references will enhance or diminish respective aspects of their identities. Films and novels can help us "provoke unease that leads to wonder and to inquiries—that awakens passion" (Greene, 1990, p. 266). In a media-driven society that often appears to enforce formidable standards of conformity, student affairs professionals can use media itself to work for more inclusive and transformative ends.

References

Abes, E. A. & Jones, S. R. (2004). Meaning-making capacity and the dynamics of lesbian college students' multiple dimensions of identity. *Journal of College Student Development, 45,* 612–632.

Abes, E. A., Jones, S. R., & McEwen, M. K. (2007). Reconceptualizing the model of multiple dimensions of identity: The role of meaning-making capacity in the construction of multiple identities. *Journal of College Student Development, 48,* 1–22.

Adichie, C. N. (2013). *Americanah.* New York, NY: Alfred A. Knopf.

Brooks, G. (2011). *Caleb's crossing.* New York, NY: Viking.

Eugenides, J. (2011). *The marriage plot.* New York, NY: Picador.

Gensa, A. & Gordon, H. (Creators & Writers), (2011–2017). In A. Gensa & H. Gordon (Executive Producers), *Homeland.* New York, NY: Showtime Networks.

Goldman, C. (2012). This is your brain on Jane Austen, and Stanford researchers are taking notes. *Stanford Report,* September 7, 2012.

Greene, M. (1990). Realizing literature's emancipatory potential. In J. Mezirow & Associates (Eds.), *Fostering critical reflection in adulthood* (pp. 251–268). San Francisco, CA: Jossey-Bass.

Harbach, C. (2011). *The art of fielding.* New York, NY: Little, Brown and Company.

Harper, R. & Rogers, L. E. (1999). Using feature films to teach human development concepts. *Journal of Humanistic Counseling, Education and Development, 38*(2), 89–97.

Hirt, J. B. (2006). *Where you work matters: Student affairs administration at different types of institutions.* Lanham, MD: University Press of America.

hooks, b. (2013). *Writing beyond race: Living theory and practice.* New York, NY: Routledge.

Khalifeh, S. (2000). *Wild thorns.* Brooklyn, NY: Interlink Books.

Kellner, D. (1995). Cultural studies, multiculturalism, and media culture. Retrieved from https://pages.gseis.ucla.edu/faculty/kellner/papers/SAGEcs.htm.

Kelly, B. T. & Porter, K. B. (2014). Using film to critically engage student development theory. *On Campus* (pp 24–28). doi:10.1002/abc.21165.

Kidd, D. C. & Castano, E. (2013). Reading literary fiction improves theory of mind. *Science, 342*(6156), 377–380. Published online October 3, 2013.

King, P. M. & Kitchener, K. S. (1994). *Developing reflective judgment: Understanding and promoting intellectual growth and critical thinking in adolescents and adults.* San Francisco, CA: Jossey-Bass.

Kitchenham, A. (2008). The evolution of John Mezirow's transformative learning theory. *Journal of Transformative Education, 2*(104), 104–123.

Kline, J. (2013). College students, Netflix and the common practice of password sharing. *USA Today.* http://college.usatoday.com/2013/07/12/college-students-netflix-and-the-common-practice-of-password-sharing/.

Lahiri, J. (2003). *The namesake.* New York, NY: Houghton Mifflin.

Lee, S. (Producer, Director). (1989). *Do the right thing* [Motion picture]. United States: Universal Studios.

Leib, E. (2006). Why not dial in democracy, too? *Washington Post*, p. B2. Retrieved from http://www.washingtonpost.com/wp-dyn/content/article/2006/05/26/AR2006052601711.html.

Magolda, P. & Baxtery Magolda, M. B. (2011). *Contested issues in student affairs: Diverse perspectives and respectful dialogue.* Sterling, VA: Stylus.

MarketingCharts. (2009, November 30). *College students spend 12 hours/day with media, gadgets.* Retrieved from MarketingCharts.com.

Mezirow, J. & Associates. (2000). *Learning as transformation: Critical perspectives on a theory in progress.* San Francisco, CA: Jossey-Bass.

Nussbaum, E. (2014). On television: Small differences. *The New Yorker.* Retrieved from http://www.newyorker.com/magazine/2014/12/15/small-differences.

Oz, A. (1968). *My Michael.* Israel: Am Oved.

Reynolds, M. L. (2011). *Analyzing the films of Spike Lee.* Edina, MN: ABDO Publishing Company.

Sanford, N. (1967). *Where colleges fail: A study of the student as a person.* San Francisco, CA: Jossey-Bass.

Shammas, A. (1988). *Arabesques.* Berkeley, CA: University of California Press.

Smith, Z. (2005). *On beauty.* New York, NY: Penguin Press.

Solis, L. (2014). Expert analyzes students' Netflix usage. *Daily Toreador.* Retrieved from http://www.dailytoreador.com/lavida/expert-analyzes-students-netflix-usage/article_0dfc194a-5412-11e4-9415-001a4bcf6878.html

Tisdell, E. J. (2008). Critical media literacy and transformative learning: Drawing on pop culture and entertainment media in teaching for diversity in adult higher education. *Journal of Transformative Education* (6)1, 33–58. doi:10.1177/1541344608318970

West, J. (1957). *To see the dream.* New York, NY: Avon Books.

Yehoshua, A. B. (1977). *The lover.* Wilmington, MA: Mariner Books.

15

RELATIONSHIPS AS PEDAGOGY

Using Dialogue and Group Work for Learning

Jane Fried

Pedagogy is not a term often used in student affairs. Historically, the word *pedagogue* refers to a person who possesses knowledge and communicates this knowledge by lecturing or writing. Ironically, this is typically a one-way process. Pedagogues tell the students what they know and the students inform pedagogues of what they have learned by repeating it. This is generally not an exciting process. Its use dates back to the founding of Oxford College in approximately 1100 CE, and its value is based on the absence of other sources of information beyond that which the pedagogue knows. In an era when good students can instantly find information about almost anything on the Internet, one must question the value of the traditional pedagogy of lecturing.

This traditional approach to pedagogy, which is still in wide use among academic faculty, is based on positivist epistemology, including the subject/object split between the knower and the known. In this epistemology, knowledge is présuméd to exist empirically in a sphere that is unconnected to the people who know. Knowers acquire knowledge in some mysterious process and the evidence that the process has occurred is that knowers can repeat what they know. This description of learning has limited utility. It can be called "fact-recall," one aspect of learning that is fundamental but simplistic when considering the full complexity of learning.

Student affairs professionals do not often discuss pedagogy and even less often use this word to describe their work with students. However, they teach every day in a wide variety of settings. The teaching that most student affairs professionals engage in is called advising, counseling, training, and supervision. A number of issues prevent the educational activities that student affairs staff members engage in from being seen as teaching. The two basic issues are pedagogy and epistemology. Student affairs professionals typically use dialogic, interactive, non-judgmental teaching practices that are based on conversations with students. Friere (1990) called this approach nothing less than "Liberation (which is), a praxis, the action and reflection of men (*sic)* upon their world in order to transform it" (p. 66). He also described this sort of education as "problem posing education . . . (which) consists of acts of cognition, not transferrals of information" (p. 67). Friere said that education should be "the practice of freedom—as opposed to the practice of domination" (p. 69).

In dialogues between student affairs professionals and students, knowledge is constructed as an activity that helps all participants understand what is happening in a particular situation and find ways to agree on the description so that they can transform it as they see the need. The epistemology is *constructivist.* This means that all participants engage in conversation to achieve a consensus about what needs to be known in that situation. Students are considered experts on their own experience, even though they may not be experts about group dynamics, résumé writing, conflict resolution, or similar kinds of problems. In these learning situations, there is generally little consensus about "the facts," bits of information that are consistent and used to describe the circumstances under discussion. Facts are understood to be embedded in perspective, context, and interpretation. Finding the "truth" is not the goal. Coming to a consensual understanding of the problem, its description, and its resolution is the goal. Can this be considered teaching or pedagogy?

One of my favorite questions is, "If teaching occurs but no learning occurs, how do we name that phenomenon?" My favorite answer came from a student: "A lot of hot air." More specificity would be helpful in attempting to understand the question and the answer. In constructivist pedagogy, coming to a useful understanding of a problem and its possible solutions might be considered learning. The person who has the problem learns a process to use in her inquiry so that the outcome helps her address whatever issue is pressing. Friere calls this naming the problem, a *praxis,* a combination of action and reflection whose purpose is to transform the world. One could scarcely deny that learning has occurred. It is my personal belief that teaching is a meaningless concept without learning, a remaining element of the Cartesian split that is no longer functional. One can lecture with or without the presence of listeners, but one cannot teach in a vacuum, because teaching implies learning. Otherwise it is a meaningless term. In constructivist epistemology and pedagogy, learning occurs in the presence of various kinds of support, including teaching and reflection. People who ask questions, stimulate reflection, demonstrate inquiry methods, and support dialogue are all engaged in helping people learn. Teaching, when defined as lecturing, may or may not be beneficial, but it is not necessary.

Pedagogical Methods

Most of the pedagogical methods of constructivist pedagogy are dialogic and experiential. Students may be asked to read new information, observe something they have not seen before, or interview a person who might have useful information for them. However, none of this information acquisition can become part of the student's metacognitive process until the student reflects on it and applies it to the issue under examination. Reflection can occur in dialogue, in journaling, or in any of the expressive arts, such as poetry. Evidence of this reflection should be accessible to the advisor/counselor, either through conversation or access to written or artistic products. The vignettes that follow are examples of dialogic pedagogy in several different student affairs settings. A comment on the specific methods used follows each situation.

Résumé Writing as Confidence Building

Adriana Thomas

Clark College, Career Advisor

As a career coach, I have assisted many students with the job search process, including writing résumés and cover letters. Students often view a résumé as simply a requirement to get an interview, but it can serve a much greater purpose. When I work with students, I focus on providing a learning experience, and writing a résumé can be a crucial one.

One particular student comes to mind who had been applying to jobs for several months. Luz was looking for work in health care as a certified nursing assistant. She had obtained her certification at the college and had previous work experience in the health care field. Luz was in a life transition, leaving the educational environment to be part of the work environment—a process that can be anxiety producing. She was overwhelmed with the job search and unsure about her next steps.

When I first looked over her résumé, Luz had listed her certification and related employment, but not the skills specific to the position. We worked together and discussed her strengths and skill sets. As she reflected on her experience and education, Luz started to realize the positive attributes she could offer a potential employer. She began to articulate what she could contribute to the workplace and the value that she could offer in the position. In assessing her background, Luz began to make meaning of her experiences and was then able to translate this onto her résumé, allowing her to tailor her résumé for the position.

Luz submitted a revised résumé to several employers and she received a call for an in-person interview the following week. She was enthusiastic about this opportunity and about the support she received in revising her résumé. After receiving a call for an interview, Luz felt more confident in doing the job and had less anxiety about putting her education into practice. Writing her résumé served as a learning experience that ultimately got her employed, but it also boosted her overall confidence in herself as an employee. This visible increase in confidence in her ability to successfully perform the job changed Luz's frame of reference about the job search and raised her self-esteem.

Reflecting on one's accomplishments not only helps hone a résumé; it also helps a student make the transition from school to career. It also acts as practice for an interview, as students speak about their résumés and about themselves in a positive light. In gaining self-confidence, students increase their independence as they embark on a new adventure in the world of work.

Dialogue, not Debate or Discussion

What is dialogue? "Mutual understanding" is one term that can be used. This process can be contrasted with debate, whose purpose is to establish one point of view as superior to another. Our typical debate-style approach to conversation is to establish the speaker's point of view as one description of truth (perhaps the best or only description) and then test it against other perspectives until the most valid approach dominates. Elements of the dialogue process are "understanding others, suspending judgment, walking in another person's shoes and uncovering and examining assumptions" (Flick, 1998, p. 5). The desired outcome of dialogue is a deeper understanding of the situation and the avoidance of the polarization that typically accompanies the search for truth or accuracy. Student affairs professionals are particularly adept at realizing the value of this process because of our constant conversations with students. Students often want to know "what really happened," or "whose fault is this?" These kinds of questions are typical of a fairly low level of cognitive development, an either/or approach to thinking. Student affairs professionals, even those with only a few years of experience beyond the typical undergraduate, generally realize that situations are complicated, that circumstances lead to outcomes, and that in most cases a problem is not likely to be anybody's "fault." The Buddhist phrase to describe this type of circumstance is "causes and conditions." If this hadn't happened, that probably wouldn't have happened, either. If one person had done a specific thing, the outcome of the problem situation probably would have been different. People who are prone to the "causes and conditions" mode of thought are generally advanced in cognitive development and understand interacting frames of reference as interpretive systems when attempting to disentangle conflicting points of view (Kegan, 2000).

Advising a Student Group

Hannah Pancak

Assistant Director of Student Activities

Springfield College

As students navigate the world of higher education, they come across new freedoms and ways of expression. Many take advantage of the one freedom they may not have had the opportunity to exercise during their high school education, freedom of speech. Student affairs professionals encounter situations where this freedom is used to overpower others' voices. As advisors, we mediate and facilitate these situations so that the student learns to look through other lenses and see multiple perspectives. I have run into this while advising clubs and organizations. These organizations already create a hierarchy of responsibility—for example, executive board positions. Often, I come across students in those roles utilizing their position and freedom of speech to persuade the general members that their way is the right way.

A recent example of this occurred as I worked with my Concert Executive Board. My students take their role very seriously. They are in charge of providing their peers with a concert that appeals to a broad audience. During meetings, we discuss potential genres and artists. I quickly realized that everyone in the group had opinions regarding who we should book, and they were advocating only their idea rather than hearing out others. I knew that if this continued our meetings would potentially turn into heated arguments rather than discussions.

At a recent meeting, the students started off by talking over one another and raising their voices. One student was speaking very strongly about a rap artist and repeatedly said, "I have a bias because I am a rap fan, but I believe the majority of our students would want a rap artist." Every time that student spoke, another student interjected the comment, "Well, my friends and other classmates want a country concert, and I believe this would be a success." Neither student shared detailed explanations of why their favored genre would do well besides the fact that their friends preferred it. Therefore, they did not give other students the opportunity to understand their reasoning and to develop well-constructed responses to it. These requests became assertions. Soon there was a battle between the two individuals and their own personal preferences in music. They were both embedded in their own viewpoints and, at that moment, incapable of imagining why another person might have a different point of view. I sensed hostility growing, so I had to step in because the conversation wasn't going anywhere productive.

I did not dominate the conversation or take over; instead, I suggested that we needed to listen to, respect, and try to understand each other's opinions. I also encouraged the use of reasoning to support our decision to move forward. I then asked the students to decide how they would like to proceed. They suggested taking turns speaking and having someone take notes to reference to help construct a pros and cons list.

I would describe my interjection at the meeting as providing insight into process, giving students time to collect themselves and be more productive. They did not know how to compare and contrast (Perry, 1968). This approach is often referred to as a "plus one" response that encourages students to think at one cognitive level higher than where they usually operate. In this case, I encouraged them to move from "Do it because I want to do it," to "Here's why I want to do it. Can we discuss this?" (Kegan, 2000). It's important to provide learning opportunities for students rather than telling them directly what to do. During these opportunities, student affairs professionals can stimulate increasing cognitive complexity, empathy, and perspective sharing. Learning these modes of thinking and feeling not only contributes to their effectiveness as group members in student activities. It also helps them understand the complexities of academic situations in which there is no "right" answer, and that multiple perspectives must be compared and understood (Perry, 1968).

Flick (1998) describes this approach to learning as an Understanding Process (UP) (p. 5) that involves "deepening self-awareness, positively transforming relationships and organizations, discovering shared meaning while honoring differences and collaborating insightfully" (p. 6). What makes this learning process different from our standard ideas about teaching is that "understanding someone from their point of view does not necessarily mean agreeing with them. Nor does deeply understanding another perspective require that we surrender our own beliefs and values" (p. 7). The elements of the UP emphasize connection, not separation. These techniques allow people to find commonalities that allow for collaboration. Participants learn new information and new processing skills.

In another type of situation, advising an individual student, similar skills are apparent. The student also needs to learn compare and contrast by searching out additional options and reflecting on them.

Advising Mark

Michelle Nickerson, Academic Advisor

Central Connecticut State University

The atmosphere was pre-set when Mark, a young African-American student, walked into my office. As an advisor, I not only inform my students regarding which courses to take the following semester, but I also work with them to succeed in their courses. Mark had been struggling in his classes and was below the GPA requirement for the school of business. He felt defeated because he had tried everything he was aware of to succeed and nothing worked for him. As a white female, I could tell he was reluctant to speak to me, but I was determined to help him.

Mark sat down in the chair next to my desk and avoided eye contact completely. I showed him his transcript and gently asked him how he got to this point. He hesitated, but he began telling me his story after I reminded him that my office was a safe space where he would not be judged. I assured Mark that he was not alone, and there were more than 100 students in the same situation in the school of business. I could tell his comfort level was increasing and he was slowly letting his guard down. Once I learned more about him, I began to ask questions about the courses in which he was currently enrolled. I asked him questions like: "What made you take this course?" "What is it you're struggling with, specifically?" "If you were the instructor, how would you teach this class?" I was trying to pinpoint the source of the academic difficulties—skill development or motivation.

I also asked whether Mark worked and, if so, how many hours a week. Time management is almost always a component of academic struggle. When students move from a very structured environment like high school and family to college, they often have trouble managing their time. Mark informed me that he had a job on campus that he enjoyed, and he was surrounded by people he liked. He also told me he was struggling in a history course that was difficult to get through, because he found the topic boring and irrelevant to his life. We discussed different ways he could earn a better grade in the class, such as recording the lecture and playing it back later or making the history lesson into a song, since he expressed an interest in music. Reluctantly, he agreed to try them.

Then, I asked why he was majoring in business, and Mark said that he wanted to manage a hotel one day. At that moment, I realized why he was unhappy in business. I asked him if he knew about the hospitality and tourism program, which he did not. We explored it together on the website and I left him with a decision to make: Which major did he really want? Prior to these conversations, Mark did not know his options, and he did not believe in himself. After learning that he could do what he was passionate about and that he could take courses relevant to that passion, he began to relax with me and he opened up more freely. I noticed that he began speak to me and not to my wall. He would tell me stories about the previous week, especially in that history class, with a smile. Anyone could sense that his demeanor changed. Mark came back a week later very excited to tell me he had decided to change his major to hospitality and tourism. He finally felt like he was working toward his goal.

****

There were several issues in Mark's situation that needed to be untangled so that he could make progress toward his goal. Initially, he didn't know or trust his advisor. He was also unaware that there were people at the college who were employed to support him in achieving success. There is an element of race in this conversation, although the author does not describe how that worked. Mark needed to trust his advisor before he was willing to take any advice from her. The advisor was sensitive to the issues. It is reasonable that a student who wasn't familiar with the range of options available to him might choose business as a major if he wanted to manage a hotel. Hotels are businesses. He didn't know he had other options that might be more engaging. The advisor's creativity was obvious when she suggested that he set some of the history content to music. Most young people are interested in music and music is a very large part of African-American culture. Only after the advisor had done a thorough review of the key issues that Mark was facing: time, motivation, finances, and probably whether he was a first-generation student, could she make suggestions that would be helpful and acceptable to Mark. Her process involved building trust, searching for appropriate information, expressing empathy, offering possibilities, and supporting Mark's transition. She was also quite attentive to body language, which is critical in these kinds of conversations. What did Mark learn? That he could trust this advisor, that he could make things more interesting and relevant for himself, that when he was struggling he could ask for help, and that there were options available. Once again, we must ask ourselves: if learning occurs, what do we call the activity that produces learning? It is clearly an interactive process and the skill level of the facilitator is very important.

The Hardest Lesson of All: Personal Hygiene

Shedia Christopher

Central Connecticut State University

This mediation resulted from an ongoing roommate dispute about personal hygiene. The conflict occurred in a residence hall for first-year students. The students in this situation were living in a triple room, an arrangement which is typically likely to produce "two on one" conflicts. Two of the women were not first-generation students and had family support, both economic and emotional. The third student was a first-generation student and was paying her own way through school with a financial aid package.

The two students who had the better level of support from their families were complaining about their third roommate, saying she was "nasty, dirty, stinky, and didn't change her underwear." They complained to the residence hall staff, who informed the third student and asked her what was going on. In this conversation with the staff member, the third roommate was made aware of the things her roommates thought of her and was hurt. The third roommate shared that she knew that she smelled but there wasn't much she could do about it. As a younger adolescent, she had been molested by her stepfather. As a result, she moved out and started living on her own. She had no money for body soap, detergent, or deodorant, and was waiting for her refund check to come in so she could purchase toiletries and her books. She also shared that living on a coed floor made her anxious. She didn't feel comfortable in the hallway in a towel or bathrobe. The idea of being in a bathroom while other people were in there was nerve-wracking for her. Bathrooms had been her safe space and having to share that space now with other people was extremely difficult.

The mediation was very positive. My first goal was to gain and retain the confidence and respect of the parties and help them learn to respect each other. I met with both parties separately and listened to their perspectives. I encouraged them to think about how the actions of the other party were impacting them. I also asked them to focus on any emotions they might have, name them, and then attempt to identify why they felt that way. For example: "I feel frustrated, I feel disrespected because, I feel betrayed when . . . "

I also challenged both parties' perspective by asking them to consider reasons why the other party was doing what they were doing.

When we met, I set ground rules, defining the space as safe. My primary role was to facilitate conversation. I asked questions, and reflected statements as needed.

The two young women who were from Long Island, New York, were floored by the stories shared by the third roommate. They had never heard of a situation where another student had been so abused and so deprived by her circumstances. The two more affluent students went shopping for their roommate and bought her the personal hygiene items she needed and that benefitted all of them. No further interventions were necessary.

Development and Delivery of Training Programs: Process, Content, and Skill

Training programs are essentially self-contained teaching sessions. Good training programs typically have pre-established learning outcomes and the trainer creates a method for assessing learning based on the outcomes. The assessment may be self-report or behavioral observation. Learning outcomes and assessment methodologies are a fundamental part of the training design, which should always begin with one question: "What do you want the participants to learn?" The second question is "How will you know they have learned it?" and, in sequence, "How will you describe the learning and share it with stakeholders?"

For example, there are currently many efforts to address the issue of racism on campuses throughout the United States. Some of these efforts involve training, some focus on changes in policy and procedure, and some begin with an assessment process to give greater clarity to the issue as it exists at a particular institution. How do we use training methods to address a subject as deeply embedded in our worldview and culture as racism in our society? In this case, training involves experiential education, analysis of campus problems, and the beginnings of dialogue among the affected groups. If a campus has had incidents of defacement of public space with racist symbols, demonstrations and counter demonstrations with no dialogue, distribution of hate literature or other forms of extreme behavior, what would be an effective way to begin training?

- Building trust among the trainees is always a precondition for effective work. Choice of the trainee group is related to the source of the problem or the identification of people who are willing to address the problem. Since this training involves behavioral change and subsequent changes in worldview, it is inevitably disorienting and threatening for all participants.
- The trainer should begin with a presentation of the total process and explain what changes in thinking might be expected, e.g., "You have probably thought about this problem in one way, but please consider a second way to interpret these issues."
- Early training activities should involve asking participants to identify and describe their own personal experiences with the issue at the least threatening level, e.g., "What were some of the early teachings you received at home about your family, ethnic, or religious group?" Invite participants

to think of ideas and activities that made them proud or happy: "In this family we work hard and always keep our promises;" "Nana does all the Passover baking;" "We go to church at least once a week;" "We always go to grandma's house for dinner on Sunday;" "We always buy our Easter breads at a particular bakery;" "When we go to church we always get happy and stay for at least three hours on Sunday;" "My mama's bammy/chicken soup/sauce/ribs are the best." At this point, appropriate use of self-disclosure by the trainer, i.e., sharing personal experiences about the topic, is often helpful. Such disclosures should always support the purpose of advancing group understanding, not just give the trainer the opportunity to talk about him/herself.

- The second phase of trust building is to share experiences that feel comfortable and realize that everybody is comfortable with different experiences. Participants should be instructed to focus on their reactions and try to remain open to new information. This is a compare and contrast process. Dialogue about meaning should follow.
- The next phase should involve reflection, body awareness, and probably self-disclosure. "How does knowing that something that makes another person uncomfortable also make you uncomfortable?"
- The training process involves iterations of dialogue on the subject that require increased risk taking by participants. The cycle is action/reflection/implications/new action.
- The final element might involve a conversation about what individual and collective action should occur as a result of this program. One of my favorite prompts for this segment is, "I am a _____ (fill in the identifier under discussion); I am or do (something typical of my group) _____; but I am not or do not (engage in a negative stereotypic behavior). Here are a few examples: I am a white person and I do not put mayonnaise on everything; I am a black person and I do not have any musical talent; I am a cheerleader and I don't sleep with the whole team; I am Jamaican and I don't smoke dope; I am a Jew and I am not greedy; I am Chinese, speak proper English, and have many white friends."

This outline is simply one approach to designing training on the topic of racism. The principles for designing training are derived from experiential or brain-based learning (Caine, Caine, McClintic, & Klimek, 2005).

- Create a state of relaxed alertness (icebreakers). This opens the entire learning system of the brain to receive new information accompanied by willingness to experience some discomfort;
- Build a sense of trust in the group. This process supports active attention, engagement, and curiosity;

- Create activities that are complex, engaging, and allow students to learn new skills and support each other;
- Engage participants' ability to process the experience verbally, including descriptions of emotional and physical reactions as well as meaning-making. This process involves the total learning system and allows learning to be integrated across the brain;
- Help participants identify both conscious and unconscious elements of their learning as well as both the details of what they have learned and the context in which they expect to use it.

The general outline for the process of training design is:

- Identify what the potential group of trainees needs to learn;
- Assess their current level of competence;
- Build trust—this is an iterative process throughout;
- Generate activities that relate to the subject of the training, e.g., write and critique résumés, practice writing meeting agendas, practice active listening, practice conflict resolution;
- At the end of each activity, give participants the opportunity to write or express in some visual form what they have learned, what it means to them, and how they plan to use the new knowledge. Committing learning to a public form of expression fixes the learning in memory.
- Assess the level of learning using the methods you have chosen before the training began. Give participants the opportunity to add their own information about what they have learned in a less structured format.

Training is a very specific, multifaceted form of teaching. It is cyclic and involves emotional engagement, acquisition of new information, practice in new skills, and integration of the new competency and awareness into the learner's metacognitive framework. The principles that govern experiential education govern training. In general, nobody learns anything unless they have a reason to learn, know, and use the information and skills. I will end this chapter with one story I will never forget. I was horrified.

Interview for Graduate School

As part of the admissions process for the master's degree program in student development in higher education, all qualified applicants were required to participate in a group interview of six or seven applicants. One group I interviewed included three women of color, at least one white male and a few other people. The final interview question asked the prospective students to explain their understanding of differential rates of graduation among various ethnic groups (e.g., why do white and Asian students tend to graduate from college at much higher rates than African-American and Latino students?). The white male applicant informed the group of the information he had learned in an undergraduate diversity course. His narrative was filled with stereotypes that were insulting and denigrated the intelligence of the two less successful groups. I asked a probing question about his perspective and his comments became even stronger. He had taken a course and he thought he knew about these groups and he was quite sure that they weren't as bright and didn't work as hard as members of the more successful groups. I looked at the three women of color and could see how much trouble they were having keeping their composure. Everybody wanted to interview well and they didn't want to tell him what they thought about his ideas. I finally asked him how he had developed these opinions and he told me more about the course he had taken. I told him that I thought he was probably misinterpreting the information he "knew," and he might want to reconsider. The relief in the room was palpable.

My point is that simply "knowing" information about complex and controversial topics without experiencing conversation about those topics and listening to other perspectives can be very dangerous, especially in the area of cultural differences. This insight illustrates the damage that simply knowing about a topic and being able to repeat what you know can do in real-life conversations, particularly if the knower is a member of a dominant group. In our program, we do a lot of talking about culture and race and a lot of talking to each other across groups. This process trains everybody in listening when it is difficult and speaking when it is even more difficult—guilt, shame, and anger being the predominant emotions. Training engages the total being of the learner. Teaching often does not.

Teaching and Learning in Student Affairs

When teaching looks like conversation, do people realize that they are learning? Pedagogy in student affairs looks like conversation. Advising, counseling, and training do not often rely on advance readings, explanations of the ideas of authors, or test taking. All of these elements make the teaching that is conducted by student affairs professionals frequently invisible in the academy. Perhaps we need a new framework for this process. We should ask: Did anybody learn anything? Did anybody help with the learning process? What was that person's designated role in the conversation? Do we have evidence of learning? Does this kind of information need to be presented in the aggregate? How do we document the learning we facilitate? How can we make evidence of our impact on student learning clearer to all higher education constituencies—including ourselves? Would such a presentation improve the credibility of the educational work done by student affairs professionals? As Einstein is rumored to have remarked, "Everybody is a genius but if you judge a fish on its ability to climb a tree it will spend its whole life thinking it is stupid."

References

Caine, N., Caine, G., McClintic, C., & Klimek, K. (2005). *Twelve brain-mind learning principles in action*. Thousand Oaks, CA: Sage.

Flick, D. (1998). *From debate to dialogue*. Boulder, CO: Orchid.

Friere, P. (1990). *Pedagogy of the oppressed*. New York, NY: Continuum.

Mezirow, J. (2000). *Learning as transformation: Critical perspectives on a theory in progress*. San Francisco, CA: Jossey-Bass.

Perry, W. (1968). *Forms of ethical and intellectual development in the college years: A scheme*. New York, NY: Holt, Rinehart, and Winston.

16

GROWTH MINDSET IN STUDENT AFFAIRS

Applications of a Study of First-Year Students' Mindsets and Goal-Setting

Chelsea Sorensen and Ruth Harper

Introduction

As student affairs professionals, we share a common goal in each of our interactions with students: to help students achieve lasting success while encouraging growth and supporting development. Dweck's (1986) theory of motivation, which stated that achievement behavior is a function of learners' implicit views of intelligence and goal orientation, paved the way for a significant body of research surrounding learning and interventions to improve student achievement over time. Mindset and goal-setting interventions have direct implications for students in higher education and student affairs professionals concerned with increasing student motivation, goal setting, and success. Specifically, professional academic advisors may find growth mindset an effective framework from which to work with students, ranging from high-achieving honors students to those who may be struggling academically. Other student affairs professionals, in settings as varied as residence life, student activities, multicultural affairs, career counseling, and more, will also find these concepts intriguing and useful.

This chapter introduces the concepts of growth mindset and mastery-based goal orientation in higher education, and presents the results of a study that explored these concepts, conducted at South Dakota State University by one of the authors (Sorensen, 2016). Implications and applications of growth mindset for student affairs professionals are presented as well.

Background

What happens when students are seriously challenged by their first difficult college course? And ultimately, how is their transition to college influenced by their existing mindset and its far-reaching outcomes? To explore these questions, we must first understand the key concept of growth mindset and its relation to motivation and goal-setting.

Several key studies provide the foundation of growth mindset and mastery goal orientation that lead us to the discussion of applications in higher education and student affairs. The concept of implicit theories of intelligence, or the beliefs individuals hold about intelligence, which are shaped by their own experiences, has been explored for several decades (Dupeyrat & Marine, 2005; Dweck, 1986; Ying-Yi, Chi-yue, Dweck, & Wan, 1999). This concept has developed into what is more commonly referred to today as mindset (Dweck, 2009). Implicit theories of intelligence may be categorized as either fixed or growth mindsets. A fixed mindset is the belief that one's intelligence is a set, static trait, that each person possesses a finite amount of intelligence that cannot be changed (Dweck, 2000). In contrast, an incremental theory of intelligence, or growth mindset, is the belief that intelligence is more fluid, and can be strengthened through learning and effort. Each of these implicit theories greatly impacts the way people encounter the world, and the repercussions of these beliefs, as seen in Figure 16.1, have been studied a great deal.

In addition to implicit theories of intelligence, a closely related concept, goal orientation, has been identified as a predictor of achievement. In general, two frameworks have been used to discuss goal orientation and motivation in academia. The first, called performance-based, is characterized by the construction of goals that rely heavily on a demonstration of ability, such as skill or intelligence, to be satisfactorily achieved (Dweck, 2000). Students who focus on grades, test scores, and the like, exemplify performance-based goals. Examples of performance-based goals created by student participants in my (Sorensen's) study are, "To get at least a 70 percent on the next exam," and "Don't fail." The alternative, called learning-based or mastery-based, is characterized by the improvement of skill and/or the ability to overcome a challenge. In this orientation, the process of trying hard and putting in concentrated effort is often seen as achieving the goal in itself. Students who say, "I got a B in that class—or even a C—but it completely changed the way I look at research!" have learning-based goals. One such goal created by another participant in my study stated, "I hope to correct previous mistakes to avoid future mistakes."

In an early study of these concepts, researchers examined motivational patterns and goal orientations of academically advanced high school students who were randomly selected to answer a questionnaire on their use of effective learning strategies, task choices, attitudes, and causal attributions (Ames & Archer, 1988). The results showed that whether students held a mastery- or performance-goal orientation affected their task choice, attitudes, and beliefs about success and failure based on their perception of experiences in the classroom and use of particular learning strategies. Students with mastery goal orientations were more likely to seek challenging tasks, liked their class more, and viewed success and effort as interdependent.

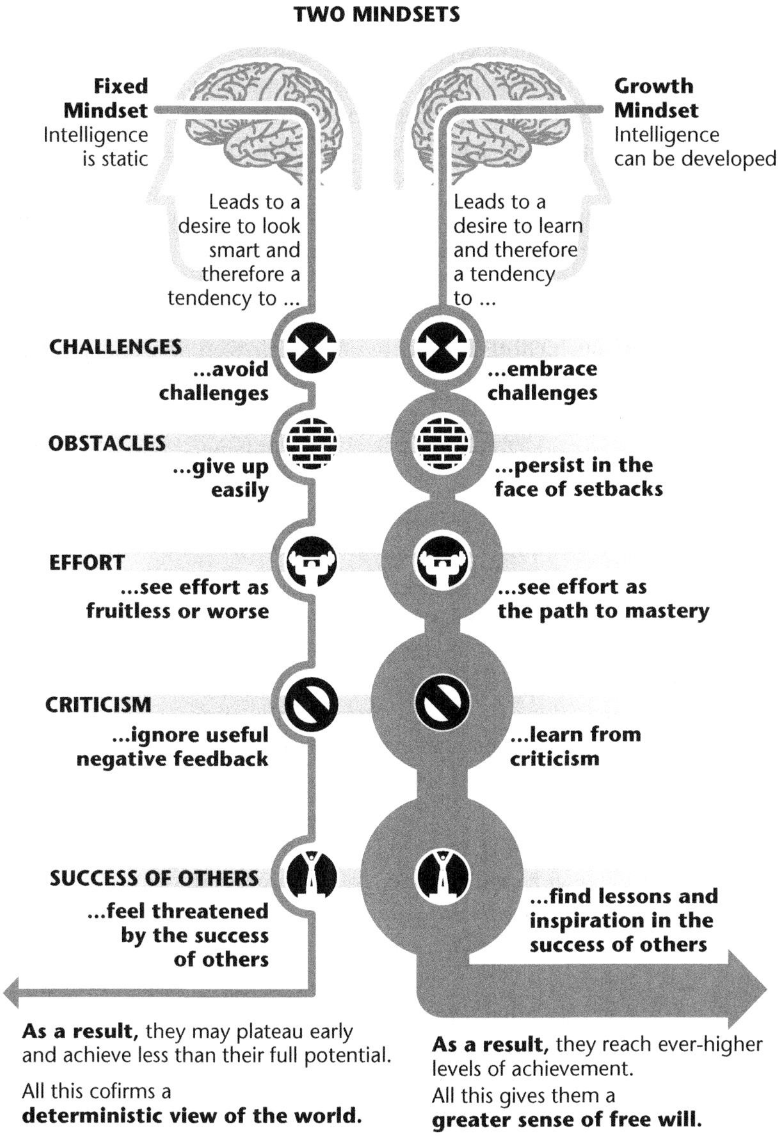

TWO MINDSETS

Fixed Mindset
Intelligence is static

Growth Mindset
Intelligence can be developed

Leads to a desire to look smart and therefore a tendency to ...

Leads to a desire to learn and therefore a tendency to ...

CHALLENGES
...avoid challenges

...embrace challenges

OBSTACLES
...give up easily

...persist in the face of setbacks

EFFORT
...see effort as fruitless or worse

...see effort as the path to mastery

CRITICISM
...ignore useful negative feedback

...learn from criticism

SUCCESS OF OTHERS
...feel threatened by the success of others

...find lessons and inspiration in the success of others

As a result, they may plateau early and achieve less than their full potential.
All this cofirms a **deterministic view of the world.**

As a result, they reach ever-higher levels of achievement.
All this gives them a **greater sense of free will.**

FIGURE 16.1 Diagram of Mindsets by Carol S. Dweck (2009). (Graphic by Nigel Holmes.)

Student affairs professionals may find this association to be directly applicable with college students, wherever learning takes place. For example, in encouraging a student from an under-represented population to take on a leadership role, growth mindset can offer unique support for challenging stereotype threat, which marginalizes certain groups and creates unwelcoming environments (Schwartz, 2016).

To combat this prevalent obstacle, researchers conclude, "Incremental theories . . . can create resiliency to the stereotype's debilitating message and enable stereotyped individuals to live up to their potential" (Good & Dweck, 2006, p. 48).

In addition, a more recent study found that mindset and goal orientation are intricately related in academic achievement, with significant implications for students in a variety of contexts. Dupeyrat and Marine (2005) applied Dweck's (1986) theory of motivation with adults who selected the challenging task of going back to college as nontraditional students. The researchers administered a questionnaire assessing motivation and academic engagement, and collected homework exercises completed by the adult students from participating teachers to determine how much effort students put into their work. Dweck's model was supported by the results, which showed a relationship among implicit theories of intelligence, goal orientation, and cognitive engagement in learning. Underscoring similar research, this study found that a mastery mindset positively impacted learning activities and outcomes.

Although mastery goals are recognized as a positive influence in education, in my (Sorensen's) experience as an academic advisor, I find that growth mindset and mastery-based goals do not come naturally to most students. It can be hard to not focus on grades when a student is on academic probation or when a final exam score will determine whether a student must retake a course that alters an entire plan of study. This is especially true in courses that may be prerequisites or non-major-specific. When students lack passion for a subject, how do you motivate them to really tackle the material or to take healthy risks by expanding their knowledge, or to learn something simply for the value of learning?

Reframing short- and long-term goals in relation to the specific course(s) that students are struggling with can be a useful tool to connect students with concrete applications of unfamiliar concepts. For example, students may not see how a difficult chemistry class will prepare them for a career as a livestock producer. By discussing how chemistry relates to animal nutrition and serves as a building block for senior capstone classes, which are the hands-on, experiential courses that many students *do* enjoy and have direct application to their long-term goals, students may be able to better appreciate how a short-term, mastery-based goal in chemistry class may pay off in a very practical way in the future.

In another study, researchers looked to determine the relationship between students' entity versus incremental views of intelligence and academic outcomes (Blackwell, Trzesniewski, & Dweck, 2007). Intelligence- and achievement-related beliefs of students in junior high school were assessed using a motivation-based questionnaire that addressed theory of intelligence, goals, students' beliefs relating to effort, and coping responses to failure. Then, students' academic achievement was measured over the course of two years. Participants with incremental views of intelligence had an upward trajectory in grades, were more likely to believe that effort leads to positive outcomes, and were also more likely to use effort-based learning strategies to cope with failure than those with entity views. An incremental theory intervention also created a positive academic trajectory for students who started with fixed views of intelligence. This demonstrates that students' views of intelligence can be impacted via intervention, which supports the utilization of this theory by college educators.

Intervention strategies that encourage growth mindset can be used in everyday conversations with students regarding study habits and time management. As students experience difficulty in college courses, they may question their method of preparing for exams and its impact on their academic performance. This is an opportunity to discuss how they are studying, to explore whether students are strictly memorizing material, or more broadly understanding key concepts and drawing independent connections. If it seems that the student is merely memorizing answers to questions that might be on the test, suggest studying with a classmate. By explaining material to someone else, students synthesize and apply course content, making them more likely to master the material.

Ask students how often they review their notes and how they schedule their study time before tests. Rather than cramming the night before an exam, encourage students to set a goal to reread their notes regularly for at least a week leading up to the test. Last-minute cramming sets up the kind of "fact regurgitation" characteristic of meeting performance-based goals. By budgeting time for repeated exposure to notes and course material, and spending that time summarizing overarching concepts, students may more deeply process the content, which will serve them well beyond an individual exam.

In a study of motivation and goal-setting, college students in a pre-med course completed a learning and performance orientation scale that measured the types of goals they set (Grant & Dweck, 2003). Then, the participants completed indices of intrinsic motivation, mastery-oriented coping, and performance, based on a hypothetical setback or failure. Results found positive effects of learning goals on students' intrinsic motivation and performance in the difficult class. Approaching academic work in this way was also predictive of mastery-oriented coping, better processing, and higher grades. This study directly shows that learning goals may be a pivotal component of students' educational success in college, particularly in terms of resilience and coping with failure.

Growth Mindset in Action

Student affairs professionals who aim to bring a growth mindset to their work with students should consider modeling a growth-oriented lifestyle and visible commitment to their own learning. They must ask open-ended questions like: What do you really want to understand? What are your dreams for yourself? For your family? For this planet? In (absurd) contrast are questions like, "So, given your ACT scores, do you want to major in English or speech?" As mentioned, reframing is another powerful technique. Some students carrying the fixed mindset arrive at college thinking they just cannot do math or completely lack talent in art. When a student says, "I have terrible math anxiety and will do anything to avoid another math class," we can carefully hear that anxiety but respond with: "Many smart students struggle with math, especially in high school. We have found that even those students do well in the college algebra course that Dr. X teaches, especially if they also attend the peer-led supplemental instruction sessions." The idea is to help students replace the belief that "this is too hard for me" with the belief that "this is going to take time and effort—and I can do it." Also, we can notice and comment when we see a student take a risk, try something different, or stretch to reach a challenging goal. Finally, we can help students put things into perspective. Everyone makes mistakes. Sometimes failure is noble and comprises the very best learning experience imaginable if it is processed with support, compassion, and humor.

An additional word about helping students cope with and learn from their inevitable failures is important here. A growth mindset and a learning orientation are enormous assets when it comes to navigating mistakes and missteps, trivial or serious, as they motivate students to regroup, rethink, and try again rather than give up. Persistence represents a huge part of success, as Dweck (2010) noted, but many students operate under the misconception that success does not require hard work.

As reported by Schwartz (2016), Catherine Good experienced a strong sense of not fitting into the math major she initially sought. The "pervasive cultural stereotype" (p. 1) against women in math was so palpable that Good became a psychologist and studied brain plasticity as one way to protect students from the constrictions of non-welcoming academic settings. In her work with Dweck, Good found that "students' perceptions of what's going on in their learning environments are often more important than their own beliefs" (as quoted in Schwartz, 2016, p. 1). In other words, although Good knew she had demonstrably strong skills in math, she still questioned her ability to succeed in that field because of her negative experiences in the classroom. This research suggests that if educators can examine and challenge intrinsically fixed mindsets in the academy (consider majors that are "not for" any given segment of the population) and start to apply a growth mindset to the situation, positive change can occur.

Although the results of these studies demonstrate a convincing connection between incremental theories of intelligence and learning-based goals with academic success, most of the research found this correlation via survey, without intervention. Previous intervention studies have focused on manipulating participants' implicit theories of intelligence, not the types of goals they set (Blackwell, Trzesniewski, & Dweck, 2007). Because of this, my (Sorensen's) study explored the effects of assigning goal categories to students in relation to an upcoming chemistry exam. Previous findings of high exam scores but poor processing by those who set performance goals identify a common flaw in educational assessment, particularly at the college level (Elliot, McGregor, & Gable, 1999). Just as performance goals predict selection of a task that will protect one's ego by not threatening one's display of superior competence and ability, research has found that success in school does *not* foster mastery-oriented qualities; rather, students with high ability are often the most worried about failure, most likely to question their ability, and less likely to persevere in the face of obstacles (Dweck, 2000; Jagacinski & Duda, 2001).

Perhaps surprisingly, Dweck's theory of motivation does not rely on a strict measurement of learners' intelligence, but rather their mindset, or *how they think about learning*, to predict achievement. This suggests that students for whom school work comes easily, while very bright, may be relying on the performance aspect of education that is constantly reinforced by a system focused on testing. When examined in terms of cognitive engagement or deep processing, these students may not fare so well (Dupeyrat & Marine, 2005). In this way, these capable students may be inadvertently taught to select easy tasks that do not threaten their view of their own intelligence, and may subsequently miss out on valuable learning experiences. Additionally, when these students encounter failure for the first time, they are more likely to demonstrate helpless or defeatist behavior, rather than to believe that they may become more successful in the future by taking remedial action or putting in greater effort (Grant & Dweck, 2003).

So where does that leave first-year college students, particularly in advanced courses and/or honors programs? Did they get to that point in their education because of their desire for a learning experience and their belief in growth, or have they sheltered their high-performing ability by engaging in a series of low-effort successes? And how is their transition to college affected by the types of goals they set? To explore these questions further, I (Sorensen, 2016) designed a small pilot study conducted at South Dakota State University.

Study Design

The participants in this study were 35 students enrolled in Chemistry 115, Atom and Molecular Structure – Honors. When this group of participants first met as a class, a stack of worksheet packets was passed around the room. The first three pages of the packets were identical, but the final page differed between the two conditions, learning or performance goal. The stack was arranged ahead of time so that the packets alternated between the two conditions. These packets were distributed randomly, so there was no predetermined path, and students took packets off both the top and bottom of the stack. All participants completed a demographic information form, followed by a theory of intelligence scale and goal choice questionnaire, taken from Dweck (2000). These two measures gave a baseline reading of participants' implicit theories of intelligence, and provided some insight regarding whether the mindset of each of the students was more growth or fixed in nature.

As mentioned, the final page of the packet differed between conditions. Those who received the learning goal packet read a description of the criteria necessary to create a learning goal, as well as relevant examples. Then, the instructions asked students to write down their own learning goal in relation to the first exam in the course. In this context an example might be, "I intend to fully understand the material covered in this class and feel prepared for the exam." The performance goal version was arranged in the same manner, with descriptions and examples, followed by an invitation to write down a performance goal in relation to the first exam in the course, such as "I want to get an A on this test." Then, five days before the first exam, participants were emailed individually with a reminder to keep their goal in mind as they prepared for the upcoming exam, and given a transcription of what they wrote in their packet.

On the final page of the exam, participants were asked how many hours they spent preparing and studying, as well as what actions they took toward achieving their goal. This question was asked with the intention of determining whether the participants remained cognizant of their goal after they made it and used it as a motivation tool, or forgot about and failed to utilize it.

After receiving exam grades, students were asked to complete a reflection form. This form asked about participants' satisfaction with the outcome of their exam, whether or not their goal was achieved, and how much they believed it influenced their performance. It also asked participants if they planned to change their goal, giving them the option to write a new one uninhibited by the constraints provided in their randomly assigned goal condition. This was done with the intent of monitoring which participants changed their goal, and specifically their *type* of goal, based on their existing mindset. Again, five days before the second exam, participants were emailed individually with a reminder to keep their goal in mind as they prepared for the upcoming exam, as well as a transcription of what they wrote in either their initial packet or post-test form, depending on their decision to change goals or not.

The same questions were asked on the final page of the second exam as on the first. Then, after participants received feedback on their second exam, they were asked to complete the same reflection form, allowing for the comparison of students' satisfaction in their exam performance when assigned to a goal condition or given freedom to create their own type of goal.

Results

Perhaps the most noteworthy result from this study (Sorensen, 2016) was the statistically significant finding ($p < 0.05$) that participants who chose to set learning goals in relation to the second exam scored significantly higher than those who chose to set performance goals. Although more students chose to set performance goals when freed from the constraints of their assigned condition, those who voluntarily set learning or mastery goals scored an average of eight points higher than their counterparts. This outcome speaks to the power of this particular type of goal setting and academic achievement. The tendency for students to set performance rather than learning goals when given the freedom to choose may indicate that students have been conditioned to think about their education as performance-based. Instructors and administrators at all levels of education may consider if the design of their class or program is truly mastery-based, or if it relies heavily on performance and memorization. Perhaps with years of experience in mastery-based classrooms, growth mindset and learning goals would come more naturally to students.

In addition, this study found through an odds ratio estimate that for every one unit increase in reported growth mindset, students were 28.6 percent more likely to set learning goals (Sorensen, 2016). The higher students scored on the measure of growth mindset, the more likely they were to choose to set learning goals. Because of this, the importance of teaching students about mindset and learning as subjects that deserve their effort and attention is underscored. As shown in this study, growth mindset and incremental theories of intelligence led to the tendency to set learning goals, which resulted in significantly higher test scores and better academic performance.

Implications for Higher Education and Student Affairs Professionals

Professional advisors may be familiar with the academic coaching terminology at some institutions; interestingly, growth mindset is also very popular among athletic coaches (Dweck, 2009). The parallels between advising and coaching are the same reasons growth mindset is so applicable in these groups. Growth mindset acknowledges the natural ability of students, but emphasizes the cultivation of hard work and effort through setting short- and long-term goals. Similarly, academic coaching uses a framework of self-assessment, reflection, and goal setting to promote student success (Robinson & Gahagan, 2010). Additionally, academic coaching provides students with a one-on-one relationship tailored to their unique needs and interests. This relationship allows students to continually reconnect with their academic coach throughout college as they engage in integrative learning and progress toward their educational and life aims (Robinson & Gahagan, 2010). By encouraging students to think about intelligence as a muscle that must be strengthened and improved through a course of difficult tasks, growth mindset is inherently instilled. When students experience a setback or failure, they can learn to not attribute the cause to their lack of innate ability, but rather to examine their inadequate or ineffective effort leading up to that point. The "muscle" exists; it just may need more time and training before it is strong enough to master a particular task. This frame of reference will encourage students to persist in the face of failure and is ultimately psychologically healthier for students who may not be used to being challenged. Students who rely on high performance as a key part of their identity, holding a fixed mindset, may feel threatened and even frightened if they struggle during the transition to college. Experiencing a first failure or even true challenge can cause some students to completely rethink their majors and career plans. Even more drastically, this dynamic could result in capable students questioning whether they belong in college in all, and may impact the retention and transfer of those students.

Extending the strategies of growth mindset and learning vs. performance goals beyond the realm of academic advising, and beyond a classroom setting, where they are clearly relevant and supported by evidence, consider the following scenarios:

- As student affairs practitioners, we often urge students to study abroad. That experience in itself presents a challenging learning goal that takes most students outside their realms of comfort and mastery. How much more might students learn and develop if their study abroad experience is somewhere other than Western Europe? How often do we encourage students to test their mettle by locating their learning experience in a place where few people speak English, where they will encounter widespread poverty, or within a community in which their faith tradition is not represented at all? How might we suggest learning goals or present the opportunities for tremendous growth within a wider range of the study abroad alternatives?
- In assisting students in program development, be it in Greek life, student engagement, multicultural affairs, residence hall programs, or any area of student activities, how might we introduce ideas of growth vs. fixed mindset or learning vs. performance goals in order to expand the scope and range of options to be considered? For instance, given a successful annual event, how could an orientation toward learning goals push students to ask "What if?" rather than rely on "but we always . . ."?
- In career counseling, how many students truly examine all of their options? How many choose a "safe" vocation, rather than stretching to see whether they might, in fact, be admitted to medical school or thrive in a two-year stint in the Peace Corps? Even those who pursue ambitious goals may look at graduate schools only within the confines of their state or region and not apply to a program in a community culturally different from their own.
- In all areas of student affairs, professionals seek to reinforce student learning. In assisting students with general study skills, through a success center, writing lab, supplemental instruction in math or science, how often do we emphasize learning over performance, understanding important concepts over passing a quiz, experimenting with different ways to "work the muscle" of our minds to develop strength in an area previously perceived as a weakness?

These scenarios are familiar to anyone who works with college students. What kinds of questions or strategies emerge from an effort to integrate a growth mindset into student affairs work? How do we model this mindset in our own lives? Do students see us work hard to achieve a goal? Do they observe us struggling with certain ideas (e.g., Black Lives Matter vs. All Lives Matter, gender-neutral bathrooms, newly restrictive immigration policies, etc.), digging into traditional and nontraditional resources (e.g., checking the institution's library and professional websites, but perhaps also consulting an elder, etc.), coming to the table with alternative perspectives? Do we let students know all of the gifts we see in them? Do we unconsciously reinforce certain values or personal assumptions over others (e.g., "You are a pharmacy major, and that's terrific—but have you ever considered teaching science?" Or, "As one of the few women in your required physics class, you're setting the curve on every exam. Have you thought about taking the next higher sequence next semester?").

Because growth mindset has become increasingly popular in discussions about educational theory, a note of caution is in order. Popular psychology interpretations of growth mindset may misconstrue its meaning by implying that if students fail, they simply must not be trying hard enough. Although incremental theories of intelligence do emphasize effort in the creation of learning goals, educators must be vigilant and cognizant of barriers to success that are beyond students' control. For disadvantaged students, putting in increasing amounts of effort in repeated attempts at achieving their goals inherently and unfairly blames them for their own failure. As educators, we must identify the shortcomings of our education system and assist all students in their endeavors through reflection and changing strategies for success, not merely telling students to try harder next time. Sometimes the changes must be aimed at the system itself, as no amount of harder work will bring success to students who are impacted by certain socioeconomic or other (e.g., racial, gender-based, etc.) barriers.

Engaging college students in conversations about mindset and learning can be very empowering for the students, and invigorating for those who work with them. Many students as well as practitioners may be unfamiliar with concepts regarding implicit theories of intelligence and metacognition. By challenging students to move beyond the performance aspect of education and fixed mindset, student affairs professionals can encourage and support learning and successful student development in many contexts throughout the college experience.

Conclusion

The range of implications of growth mindset in higher education is critical for student success. Student affairs professionals are often responsible for helping new college students negotiate the transition from high school to college through orientation programs, first-year seminars, and various advising roles, all with the ultimate goal of facilitating student development and success. Given the abundance of research supporting growth mindset/incremental theory of intelligence and its relationship to motivation, task selection, resiliency, and effort-based mastery, mindset seems a natural topic for universities, if not K-12 schools as well, to address with students.

As demonstrated by the results of Sorensen's (2016) study, specifically the finding that participants who voluntarily set learning-based goals earned higher scores on their exams than those who set performance-based goals, the way students frame academic goals can greatly impact their success in a challenging college course. With this result in mind, the other noteworthy finding that for every increase on the measure of growth mindset, students' likelihood of setting a learning-based goal increased 28.6 percent, demonstrates the importance of talking with students about the way they think about intelligence and encouraging a growth mindset.

Higher education provides students with tremendous opportunities for personal and career development. The primary concern of many student affairs professionals is helping students achieve their potential by facilitating this development and success through a variety of means. The application of growth mindset and learning/mastery goals in student affairs professional practice, whether in academic advising, multicultural affairs, career counseling, co-curricular advising, or residence life, holds great promise for the long-term success of students. In whatever context students experience challenge, there is the option to implement a growth mindset approach.

To combat the fixed mindset tendency of first-year college students, student affairs professionals must bring the topic of implicit theories of intelligence to the forefront in their work with students. Growth mindset and mastery goals directly coincide with this mission of student development, including the social justice aspects of our work. By empowering students to think about their own concepts of learning and intelligence, and challenging them to embrace a growth mindset, students will be more likely to set mastery goals associated with better academic performance, more willing to take healthy risks that result in more learning, resiliency, and long-term success. With this supportive framework, student affairs professionals may better facilitate student success and, through experiences within and beyond classrooms, help students catalyze the great potential they hold.

References

Ames, C. & Archer, J. (1988). Achievement goals in the classroom: Students' learning strategies and motivation processes. *Journal of Educational Psychology, 80*, 260–267.

Blackwell, L. S., Trzesniewski, K. H., & Dweck, C. S. (2007). Implicit theories of intelligence predict achievement across an adolescent transition: A longitudinal study and an intervention. *Child Development, 78*, 246–263.

Dupeyrat, C. & Marine, C. (2005). Implicit theories of intelligence, goal orientation, cognitive engagement, and achievement: A test of Dweck's model with returning to school adults. *Contemporary Educational Psychology, 30*, 43–59.

Dweck, C. S. (1986). Motivational processes affecting learning. *American Psychologist, 41*, 1040–1048.

Dweck, C. S. (2000). *Self-theories: Their role in motivation, personality, and development.* New York, NY: Psychology Press.

Dweck, C. S. (2009). Mindsets: Developing talent through a growth mindset. *Olympic Coach*, *21*(1), 4–7.

Dweck, C. S. (2010). Even geniuses work hard. *Educational Leadership*, *68*(1), 16–20.

Elliot, A. J., McGregor, H. A., & Gable, S. (1999). Achievement goals, study strategies, and exam performance: A mediational analysis. *Journal of Educational Psychology*, *91*(3), 549.

Good, C., & Dweck, C. S. (2006). A motivational approach to reasoning, resilience, and responsibility. In R. J. Sternberg & R. F. Subotnik (Eds.), Optimizing student success in school with the other three Rs: Reasoning, resiliency, and responsibility (pp. 39–56). Charlotte, NC: Information Age.

Grant, H., & Dweck, C. S. (2003). Clarifying achievement goals and their impact. *Journal of Personality and Social Psychology*, *85*, 541–553.

Jagacinski, C. M., & Duda, J. L. (2001). A comparative analysis of contemporary achievement goal orientation measures. *Educational and Psychological Measurement*, *61*, 1013–1039.

Robinson, C. & Gahagan, J. (2010). In practice: Coaching students to academic success and engagement on campus. *About Campus*, *15*(4), 26–29.

Schwartz, K. (2016). How to integrate growth mindset messages into every part of math class. *Mind/Shift*, KQED.org. Retrieved from https://ww2.kqed.org/mindshift/2016/12/05/how-to-integrate-growth-mindset-messages-into-every-part-of-math-class/?utm_source=twitter.com&utm_medium=social&utm_campaign=npr&utm_term=nprnews&utm_content=2038.

Sorensen, C. E. (2016). *The relationship of growth mindset and goal-setting in a first-year college course* (unpublished master's thesis). South Dakota State University, Brookings, South Dakota.

Ying-Yi, H., Chi-yue, C., Dweck, C. S., Lin, D. M., & Wan, W. (1999). Implicit theories, attributions, and coping: A meaning system approach. *Journal of Personality and Social Psychology*, *77*, 588–599.

17

CONTEMPLATIVE AND MINDFULNESS PEDAGOGIES TO DEEPEN LEARNING

Jane Fried

A lot of modern life involves mental chaos—too much information, too much stimulation, no time to process what is coming in or going out. The teaching methods we use in much of higher education exacerbate this problem. We identify learning as the ability to ingest new information and repeat it as requested. If the input/output model is assumed, traditional teaching methods, i.e., reading and lecturing, are rather inefficient ways to help students learn. Use of technologies in the learning process improves efficiency by making more information, at a faster pace, available asynchronously so that students can access it "on the go" or at their own convenience. The problem with this approach to learning is that students are often even less likely to pay careful attention to the information they are supposed to be learning than in a traditional classroom because they are often multitasking while they listen to lectures or watch videos. More mental chaos!

Meaningful learning involves four basic steps (Fried, 2016): 1) *information acquisition*; 2) *emotional engagement* or caring about the information; 3) *application* of the information via behavioral change or problem solving; and 4) placement of the information and its emotional substrate into the *metacognitive neural system* through which the student makes sense of the world. Traditional teaching often ignores the emotional component of learning and may or may not include practical applications or skill development. The student's metacognitive system typically has no role in this approach to learning because the personal implications of what is learned are not considered part of the teaching process. Functionally, this means that the professor isn't expected to ask whether or not the students care about why they need to know whatever they are expected to learn. Faculty members are also not expected to engage students emotionally in their learning, although the best professors realize that learning doesn't really occur if students are not emotionally engaged (Sylvester, 1994). Memorization occurs—and although that process is often considered synonymous with learning, it is a miniscule element of the process and certainly not a component of meaningful learning.

Contemplative Pedagogies

Contemplative processes are relatively new to secular education, but they are as old as the mystical traditions of East and West. During the Enlightenment, when religion was separated from most educational activities, contemplation disappeared from almost all of the traditional approaches to teaching. The essence of contemplative practice is to help students realize connections among ideas, experiences, and their own values. Contemplation emphasizes interiority while most positivist approaches emphasize exteriority or understanding external phenomena. Barbezat and Bush (2014) state that contemplative practices are often referred to as introspective or reflective approaches. These terms are roughly interchangeable.

Whether they are analytical exercises asking students to examine a concept deeply or opportunities to simply attend to what is arising, the practices all have an inward or first-person focus that creates opportunities for greater connection and insight . . . the practices focus on the present experience, either physical or mental (Barbezat & Bush, 2014, pp. 5–6).

The learning process that uses contemplative practice becomes "something personally meaningful yet connected to the world" (p. 6).

In *The Heart of Higher Education: A Call to Renewal* (Palmer & Zajonc, 2010), the authors present a deep and convincing discussion of the ways in which they believe that higher education has become fragmented and personally irrelevant to many college students. Essentially, the positivist pedagogy of the Enlightenment represented a huge leap in the "ways of knowing," or epistemologies generally used in higher education. Positivism made the scientific and industrial revolutions possible. Positivist pedagogy asserts that the learner is separate from that which is learned, as the subject is separate from the object (Fried, 2012, 2016). Positivism is a particularly beneficial pedagogy in the experimental and applied sciences and mathematics. The problem with this "subject observes object" approach is that while it is effective in some circumstances and misleading in others, it is almost always presented as the most universally accurate approach to teaching and learning.

Historically, the major purpose of colleges was to educate young people in their own history and culture by exposing them to the liberal arts. College graduates were expected to give serious consideration to a wide range of subjects in the general categories of the arts, physical science, mathematics, literature, philosophy, and more recently, social sciences. The overarching goal of college attendance was to permit graduates to understand their place in their own world, how the world developed the culture that produced them, and then to use that knowledge as citizens and leaders. At least that was the theory when the Westernized/

Christian narrative was used to explain the world and the place of humanity in it. This narrative gave meaning to learning, culture, and purpose for students. This Christian narrative dominated higher education until the nineteenth century. It was not necessary to engage students at the metacognitive or meaning-making level because meaning was generally inferred from the Christian worldview. The German model of scientific research, and the creation and transmission of new knowledge, was imported into the United States along with the Industrial Revolution and its incessant demand for new scientific knowledge. The belief system of American culture became increasingly materialistic. Discussions of personal meaning and purpose lost their place in the lecture halls of universities. New systems of meaning began to evolve. These systems present possibilities, not revealed truths. They are tentative and rely on the insight of the individual. The range of systems for making meaning in the modern world extended from nihilism to the more rigid forms of fundamentalism that exist in all religions and in secular belief systems as well.

The evolving worldviews are evoked rather than received. They direct our awareness to a range of possible interpretations of all events. Poetry and metaphor are often used to help students reflect slowly on the issues they are considering. Poetry slows things down and points the way to a deeper understanding of the world and our experience in it. Any information that a student wants to learn in the twenty-first century can be acquired through an Internet search. Such searches can be conducted quickly. Student "learning" can take the form of repeating what one has read or writing a paper without giving any consideration to context or meaning. Learning can be accomplished by "cut and paste," if that's the way the student wants to do it. Poetry forces a deeper reflection on the words used to discuss a phenomenon and the various ways in which the words themselves might be interpreted. I have found the poetry of Wallace Stevens, an American, and William Butler Yeats, an Irish writer, particularly helpful in this regard.

The purpose of incorporating contemplative practices into higher education is to slow down and deepen inquiry, and poetry is one of the vehicles often used to accomplish this purpose. Poetry causes people to examine ideas and experiences from several points of view at different levels of awareness. These practices help us evoke meaning and move beyond standard or facile interpretations. The time for using the Western Grand Narrative, based on the Christian worldview, to give meaning to our experiences and our learning processes is past. Our universities have become international institutions and our students use many narratives, based on their own cultural heritages, to explain their world and make sense of what is happening in it. Interestingly, it has been estimated that at least half of American college students have no acquired meaning-making system that is based in any faith or humanistic tradition. These students are often referred to as "nones," secular humanists, or spiritual seekers. Many have no metacognitive, organizing core belief system. People need to make sense of their life experience. They need meaning as a frame of reference. "The purpose of organisms is to organize and what human beings organize is meaning. Meaning making is an activity of composing a sense of the connections among things: a sense of pattern, form, and significance" (Parks, 2000, p. 19). Students, regardless of age, are in a developmental process that demands the creation of some kind of meaning-making system to frame development as it becomes more complex. Academic freedom and positivist epistemology demand that we do not try to impose meaning-making systems on students, but nevertheless, students are still searching for meaning. Why go to college in the first place if you are not dealing with questions of "why"? Why assume leadership roles in student organizations if you don't have a reason for putting up with the inevitable difficulties that accompany those roles? These questions go on forever and the college experience has very little opportunity for students to think deeply or address these questions in the context of their own lives. Contemplative methods can provide us with an approach that maximizes personal freedom while encouraging the development of insight.

Why Positivist Epistemology has Eclipsed the Pedagogies of Student Affairs

It is a very short leap from understanding a positivist worldview to understanding how positivism has made the various pedagogies used in student affairs very difficult to discuss in higher education. Student affairs pedagogies are largely constructivist. That is, the ways in which student affairs professionals teach or help people learn is based in a different epistemology. Positivist epistemology presumes that "the facts" are objectively existing, external phenomena that can be known or apprehended by observers. This position presumes that all observers, looking at or learning about the same set of facts, will "know" the same thing. Constructivist epistemology presumes that perspectives shape knowing and that awareness of one's personal perspective supports intelligent dialogue about any subject. Knowledge that is considered the most powerful is that upon which the largest numbers of "knowers" agree, based on a similar interpretation of these facts. Knowing, in constructivism, is a social phenomenon. Knowledge reflects the consensus of the knowers about the validity of information available in a particular discussion. In positivism, the purpose of knowing is to learn the truth about phenomena. In constructivism, the purpose of knowing is to develop an accurate understanding in a particular time and place with a particular group of people. Constructivist knowing is far more fluid than positivist knowing.

Student affairs professionals tend to teach in environments that demand a constructivist approach. In the situation of a roommate conflict, there is typically no way of knowing what "really" happened. Various perspectives on what participants think happened is the only knowledge that can be gleaned. If a student affairs professional wanted to teach fighting roommates how to resolve their conflicts equitably, she would have to use some formal framework for conflict resolution, help each roommate learn how to use it, and attempt to understand the different levels of cognitive development of the participants. She probably could not teach conflict resolution in the same way to two people who were three levels apart on Perry's scheme of cognitive development (1970). There would be no effective way to assess the students' learning except by the absence of new conflicts going forward. However, if the general relationship between the roommates improved, it would be reasonable to say that the students learned something about conflict resolution. This is not the same thing as solving a physics equation and discovering the correct answer. How would a student affairs professional explain the teaching/learning process used in helping students learn to solve conflicts? New language and a new understanding of learning is required (Fried, 2016).

Contemplative Practices are Both Positivist and Constructivist

Student affairs educational practices are often referred to as "soft" or "touchy-feely." These terms are derogatory and generally intended to insult the various educational processes used by student affairs professionals. What these terms really suggest is that learning that occurs because of student affairs interventions involves the emotions and is often ambiguous. Traditional academic teaching/learning is generally intended to be non-emotional, non-personal, and relatively unambiguous. Contemplative practices can provide a bridge between the two pedagogies if student affairs professionals are able to explain the pedagogies of their profession to the people who use other pedagogies.

Contemplative practices involve learning information on the cognitive level, but they push students to go beyond simply being able to explain what new information they have acquired. For example, the following vignette illustrates the process a professor uses to help students understand addiction and recovery.

Addictions and Cellphones: An Experiential Exercise
Peter V. Oliver
University of Hartford

How much time do we typically spend each day online—texting, emailing, and in social media venues, etc.? For many of us, such technologies have become an essential part of our daily lives. In fact, try to imagine what life today would be like without a cell phone. While the ability to connect with someone immediately or to find information instantly has distinct advantages, there are also downsides to such forms of immediate gratification: we have come to expect it! And when we don't get satisfied immediately, we can become frustrated. Imagine, for instance, that you have sent someone an important text and are awaiting a reply. How frustrating is it to wait for that person to get back to you, especially when you consider the message to be important! Furthermore, when you feel or hear the familiar buzz of your device, how quickly do you check it?

When teaching classes about stress management, I ask students to think about how reliant or perhaps even dependent they are on their cell phones and laptops. We discuss the amount of time people typically spend texting, exploring the web, or perhaps watching Netflix. Students share stories about a call that got "dropped" and how stressful it can be to be without a signal in a cell phone "dead" zone. Also, we talk about how some of us find it difficult to resist checking our phones even when it is inconvenient or ill-advised to do so, such as when we are driving a car. During class meetings, students are asked to refrain from using cell phones and are told that they may not use their laptops for any purpose other than taking notes. Such restrictions may be experienced by students as challenging, frustrating, and even difficult to follow. In an attempt to promote students' learning and increase their self-awareness, I lead an informal experiential class exercise designed to highlight students' possible dependency on electronic devices. I will now describe the exercise and suggest ways it might be used as a potential teaching tool.

The cell phone exercise includes the following steps, which can be modified depending on instructor preferences, instructional objectives, and classroom setup. It is important to remind students before beginning the exercise that their participation is voluntary and that they do not have to participate if they do not wish to do so. Students who choose to not participate can be asked to simply observe. The instructional steps include: (1) after moving chairs to create an open seating area in front of the room, students are invited to sit in a large circle together on the floor with the open space in the middle of the group. They are asked to take out their cell phones and to turn up the ringer volume as high as possible. Instructors should place their own cell phones in the middle of the open area and invite students to do the same. Also, students should be reminded that while they may retrieve their cell phones whenever they wish during the exercise, it is preferable that they wait until the exercise is complete so that everyone gets their phone back at the same time.

(2) Instructors can take several minutes to allow everyone to simply observe the phones in a scattered pile on the floor and students should be encouraged to simply "be" with their experience—that is, paying attention to their breath and to note any thoughts, physical sensations, or emotions they might be experiencing. After several minutes, student comments can be invited by asking the group something like this: "Does anyone have anything to say about what this experience is like for them?" This question and its responses may be followed by another period of sustained silence and self-observations. Invariably, a phone (or several phones) will ring and everyone's attention is immediately riveted on those phones. When that happens, the instructor might continue to process and explore the experience with questions such as these: "If that is your cell phone making noise, what are you noticing right now about your experience?" "Are you wishing that this exercise was already over?" "Do you want to reach in right now and grab your phone?" Again, students may be encouraged to pay attention to awareness of their internal experience(s). At this point, students who choose to not participate could potentially be invited into the exercise by being asked to note to themselves (or to the group if they feel comfortable doing so) what they are noticing about their own experience or what they are observing about the group. If the class is mostly silent and appears to be uncomfortable talking out loud to everyone, instructors could suggest that students converse in pairs or small groups (3–4 students) about their experience with the exercise.

When it seems like students have had enough of processing their experience, they can be invited to retrieve their phones. After returning to their seats, students may be given additional minutes to write down any additional thoughts they might have about their experience during the exercise, and particularly, what they have learned about themselves and others.

Following this activity, the concept of addictions, particularly signs of substance-related and addictive disorders can be introduced. Information from the 2013 Diagnostic and Statistical Manual of Mental Disorders (DSM-5) may be used to support and facilitate the discussion. Some potential signs that someone might be experiencing an addiction have been adapted from the DSM-5 and include:

- *Intense desire to use the substance*
- *Failing to meet one's responsibilities and duties because of using the substance*
- *Engaging less in social or other activities in order to use the substance*
- *Using the substance when it is dangerous to do so (e.g., driving a car)*
- *Experiencing signs of withdrawal (e.g., distress, frustration, etc.) when trying to stop using the substance*
- *Lying to others to hide one's use of the substance*

It is not difficult to move the discussion from addictions to seeing how similar language might be used to describe some people's relationship with technology. It is also important to keep in mind that having a discussion that addresses subject matter that may be personally relevant and potentially challenging might be difficult. Therefore, it is important to maintain an atmosphere of respectful compassion and sensitivity to students' well-being. Moreover, it is critical to be clear that the point of discussing addictions is not to be prescriptive or to render formal diagnoses. Instead, students should be reminded throughout the discussion that the point of the exercise is to provide an opportunity for everyone to learn more about themselves by reflecting on their relationship with using technology and, more specifically, whether someone might be more dependent on access to technology than he or she ever realized.

After all questions are addressed and the class is dismissed, the instructor might wish to remain available in case some students have questions (or concerns) that they may not have felt comfortable expressing during class. If so, it might be wise to have information available about addiction treatment resources and professional services available on campus if students raise issues that warrant further attention.

In closing, cell phones are a marvelous invention and they have their rightful place in learning, although perhaps not the classroom. Nonetheless, the popular expression, "A strength overused becomes a weakness" might be applicable for some. So while cell phones and related technologies offer us ways to stay informed and connected with each other in unprecedented ways, there are potential unforeseen liabilities and consequences that deserve thoughtful consideration. What makes this classroom exercise a potentially transformative learning experience is that students are able to learn from their peers, in the relative safety of a college classroom, about how cells phones (and related technologies) are potentially affecting them negatively in ways they may have not have previously considered. It is hoped that a major take-away from this exercise is that when students "tune in" to devices, they may unwittingly be doing so at the expense of fully connecting with themselves (and each other) in the only place where learning and growth occurs: in the here and now.

Professor Oliver preceded this exercise with some information about addiction. He then conducted the exercise and followed it with more information about addiction. The information is as valid as anything available about the process and related physiology. However, as a part of the learning, the students experienced some very strong feelings about their connections to their cell phones and then could connect themselves and their experiences to other people and to the new information. The term for this form of awareness activity is mindfulness. It is widely used in contemplative practice to help students become aware of their physical and emotional reactions to learning challenging information. I use mindfulness processes frequently when helping students learn about race, oppression, and the structures of white supremacy. These subjects tend to generate fear and the attending physical reactions. If students are not aware that fear is part of the learning mix, they will create infinite numbers of "intellectualizations" about the subjects that keep them blocked from meaningful understanding of the content. Students with a significant level of privilege, usually white, will also be prone to voicing micro-aggressions like, "Everybody has hard times sometimes. How do you know that problem had to do with your race?" Or "You're overreacting, I was joking," etc.

Contemplative Processes and How to Use Them

Contemplative processes are intended to guide students' inquiry into the deeper significance of information they learn. These processes can unleash emotions in students that are atypical in classrooms, but not atypical in student affairs activities or programs. For example, if an activities advisor conducts leadership training with a student group, it might involve asking one student to confront another about behavior that the second student found offensive or disturbing. Ethically, the facilitator is obligated to have enough skill in group process and emotional support to help any student who becomes upset by some activity so that there is minimal damage, increased awareness, and few if any negative long-term consequences. The use of contemplative processes requires the same skill set.

Contemplative processes have been represented graphically as a tree with roots and branches, which can be accessed here http://www.contemplativemind.org/practices/tree (Center for Contemplative Mind in Society, 2014). The roots of the tree encompass and transcend differences in religious traditions from which many of the practices originated and allow for the inclusion of new practices that are being created in secular contexts. The branches represent different groupings of practices, including stillness, moving meditations, relational dialogues, creative activities, and activist actions. The purpose of all these practices is to help students take time to reflect on the context of learning and living, integrate new information, or to understand previously known information in new ways (Barbezat & Bush, 2014). For example, I was very upset by the flood tide of refugees pouring through Europe in the summer of 2015. The scenes reminded me of post-World War II Europe displaced persons camps. I have revisited what I know about the end of that war, the camps as they were described to me by my parents (I was about four years old at the time). I couldn't stop thinking about the people pouring out of Africa and the Middle East into worlds that were unfamiliar in so many ways. They had lost their homes, their livelihoods, and were without the basic elements that support life. Children and old people were dying. Other than an abstract awareness, why was I so upset? Historically, this kind of refugee situation happens all the time. Then, in a dialogue at a Quaker retreat, I suddenly heard myself saying, "They are my family." I realized that the WWII refugees indeed were my family and I was experiencing that trauma as I had while listening to my family's stories and meeting my refugee relatives in the 1940s. They had numbers on their arms. Today's refugees have scars at least as deep. I still don't know what to do with this insight, but it took a dialogue of "deep listening" for me even to become aware of this personal resonance.

Student affairs professionals may be uncomfortable learning how to use practices that can be characterized as spiritual, particularly in secular or public institutions. Spiritual may or may not signify religion. There are ritual practices used in and developed for contemplative experiences. However, in this context, spiritual signifies transcendent meaning, not participating in a particular faith tradition. Student affairs professionals are more familiar with the phrase "meaning-making," and the questions used to stimulate discussions about meaning, such as "Why does this matter?" Or, "Why do you care about this?" "How do you think about this, given your values or beliefs?" Use of these open-ended questions leaves students free to include their own ideas about spirituality, divinity, or humanity.

Examples of Contemplative Practices

Barbezat and Bush wrote an entire book called *Contemplative Practices in Higher Education* (2014). Their emphasis is on use of these activities in the academic classroom. Some of their work can be used to apply contemplative practices to student affairs pedagogy.

Mindfulness has become a huge trend in education and psychotherapy in recent years. The concept of mindfulness is derived from the basic Buddhist meditation practice, but it has largely become separated from this or any other faith tradition when used in secular settings. Mindfulness begins as the process of paying attention to whatever is happening in the immediate moment. This is quite a challenge in the era of devices that never seem to go away and contribute to distraction. Mindfulness begins with the practice of the facilitator and her comfort with silence. Mindfulness must be a personal practice before one attempts to teach it to others. Functionally, mindfulness can be used before any meeting to focus attention on the meeting itself, and not the dozens of other issues meeting participants have on their minds. Small gongs are often used to silence a group at the beginning of a mindfulness practice. Basic mindfulness focuses on breathing, which has the effect of settling the mind and lowering the adrenaline levels of participants.

Sample Instructions

Instruct students to put down their writing implements and close their screens. Invite people to put their feet flat on the floor and close their eyes. Some people do not feel comfortable closing their eyes. The alternative is to simply lower their eyes to the floor. Strike the gong two or three times and wait for a moment. Suggest that they listen for the sounds of their breathing, sounds in or outside the room, and then focus on their breathing as an experience. Some people use the ends of their nostrils, some focus on their diaphragms moving in and out. Continue this experience for as long as you are comfortable. Then suggest some appropriate thoughts for reflection: "What do you hope this meeting will accomplish?" "How will you listen to the ideas of others?" "Do you have any issues with others in this room that might interfere with good work? Can you put them aside for the moment?" "What could you do during this meeting that would help this group achieve its goal?" Use only one or two questions and then leave space for silence. Finally, strike the gong again and suggest that people open their eyes. If you have time, ask the students for their reaction to the exercise before beginning the agenda.

Listening Practices

Hearing is a natural process. Listening must be cultivated. Students are used to listening to music, answering their phones in the middle of a conversation with a person who is present, or engaging in other distractions that interfere with their listening attentively. When one learns to listen, one becomes aware of what the other person is saying but also of one's own reactions, physical, emotional, and intellectual. Barbezat and Bush (2014) suggest beginning a class with quiet music to reinforce listening. I have also begun classes by reading a short poem aloud and asking students to write a couple of sentences in reaction. Probably the most important element of listening in student affairs practice is helping students learn to listen to each other. This practice is the first thing we teach in introductory counseling classes, but most of us are not teaching those classes. If students really listened to each other in working groups, the groups would probably be a lot more productive.

Sample Listening Practice

Place students in dyads. Have one person speak for at least a minute while the other listens. Then ask the listener to repeat as much as he can remember. Then ask the listener to summarize briefly, not repeat every detail. The speaker then describes his or her feelings at being listened to so carefully. Finally, ask the listener to describe what he believes the speaker was feeling while talking. This is the most difficult part. Reverse roles. I have used this exercise for years in counseling classes. The results are remarkable. We do not realize how distracted we are as listeners until we try listening in a more focused way, not rehearsing what we will say in response to the speaker. If you really want to help your students listen carefully, extend the time the speaker has to talk. In groups, when things are getting a bit chaotic, stop the conversation and ask one or more people to repeat what they think is being discussed. Participants will be amazed at the different ideas that each person hears and reacts to. This kind of practice can be inserted into any inattentive conversation with relative ease and very productive results.

Variations on this practice can be done while standing and walking. For example, place students in two concentric circles, with the inner circle facing the outer circle. Give the students a prompt for speaking, e.g., "Today has been . . .;" "I really wish . . .;" "My most difficult task is . . ." and the like. Inner circle speaks; outer circle summarizes and adds feelings. Move to the right and repeat. Then ask the outer circle to speak and the inner circle to summarize with feelings. If this is a group in the midst of conflict or disagreement, suggest prompts related to the subject causing the differences of opinion.

Observing and Attending

It is also helpful to show students how to pay attention carefully to events in which they are not participants, such as observing a floor meeting, a club meeting, a campus program. Students should attend the event, note what was happening. including dynamics among participants, and then record their own reactions. This type of observation helps students connect the outer and the inner experience.

Contemplative Pedagogy

Contemplative practices help students become more fully engaged in any activity. Contemplative pedagogy is the intentional effort to help students learn by using these practices. Whenever you use contemplative practices, begin planning the activity by asking yourself what you want students to learn and how this exercise will help them learn. A second reflective question might be "What do I have to learn in order to facilitate this exercise effectively?" A third would be "Why do I believe that this particular learning outcome is important to me, to the students, to the context of their lives?" Spend some time in mindfulness regarding your own motives, values, and self-awareness. If you want to suggest that contemplative practices be used in other educational settings, it is important to be clear about all of this. Contemplative pedagogy can be used in any academic discipline (Palmer & Zajonc, 2010). It is one of the bridges between what Esther Lloyd-Jones called arid German intellectualism (1939) and the English tradition of educating the whole student. Lloyd-Jones suggested that student personnel professionals "consider all aspects of the student" (1939, p. 9), and take into account all elements of their present and future lives so that they may function as productive members of society, being able to work, make friends, create families, and understand and contribute to their own culture. The current model of pedagogy that most academic faculty members use is one that is more closely related to the German intellectual model than the English model of character development as well as intellectual development. Contemplative pedagogies fall within the domain of contributions that the student affairs staff can and do bring to student learning (Fried, 2016). When these contributions are described as learning activities, our profession will make one more contribution to the education of the whole student and the placement of student affairs activities within the pedagogical mission of institutions of higher education.

References

American Psychiatric Association. (2013). *Diagnostic and statistical manual of mental disorders* (5th Ed.). Arlington, VA: American Psychiatric Publishing.

Barbezat, D. & Bush, M. (2014). *Contemplative practices in higher education.* San Francisco, CA: Jossey-Bass.

Fried, J. (2012). *Transformative learning through engagement: Student affairs practice as experiential pedagogy.* Sterling, VA: Stylus.

Fried, J. (2016). *Of education, fishbowls, and rabbit holes: Rethinking teaching and liberal education for an interconnected world.* Sterling, VA: Stylus Press.

Lloyd-Jones, E. & Smith, R. (1938). *A student personnel program for higher education.* New York, NY: McGraw-Hill.

Palmer. P. & Zajonc, A. (2010). *The heart of higher education: A call to renewal.* San Francisco, CA: Jossey-Bass.

Parks, S. (2000). *Big questions, worthy dreams.* San Francisco, CA: Jossey-Bass.

Perry, W. G. (1970). *Forms of intellectual and ethical development in the college years: A scheme.* New York, NY: Holt, Rinehart, & Winston.

Sylvester, R. (1994). How emotions affect learning. *Educational Leadership, 52*(2), 60–65. Retrieved from www.ascd.org/publications/educational leadership/Oct.94.

The Center for Contemplative Mind in Society. (2014). *Tree of Contemplative Practices.*, Amherst, MA. Retrieved from www.contemplativemind.org.

18

ENHANCING LEARNING THROUGH THE SUPERVISORY RELATIONSHIP

Ruth Harper and Katelyn Romsa

Student affairs professionals enhance student learning in many ways, as this book amply demonstrates. One key teaching method that is constantly engaged but rarely critically examined is the supervisory relationship. Sometimes these relationships are superficial or even dysfunctional; but often, they develop into true, deep mentoring connections that are maintained for up to a lifetime. Although learning that occurs in a classroom is obviously important, researchers have found that the learning that comes about through supervised experience in combination with classroom instruction leads to greater learning outcomes and student development (Council for the Advancement of Standards in Higher Education [CAS], 2012). This chapter presents ways to intentionally facilitate learning through supervision.

Supervisors and supervisees are sometimes close in age, but often there is a generational difference. Many students and young professionals are Millennials, at times requiring a shift in learning styles and expectations on the part of older supervisors (Wilson, 2004). Millennial students are described as cooperative team players who prefer collaborative learning environments (Howe & Strauss, 2000). Given this generational cohort's group-oriented style, Kuh (2003) recommends incorporating more peer evaluation observations and group projects for effective teaching and learning.

Coming up right behind Millennials is Generation Z, which *The New York Times* notes as comprised of complete "digital natives" who "do not remember a time before social media" (Williams, 2015, para 19). Born beginning around 1996, these young people are more savvy about personal privacy, more concerned with personal well-being, and more focused on "safe" careers than their immediate predecessors. The point, simply, is to be alert to generational differences that might impact supervisory relationships and expectations—and also to be acutely aware of the characteristics of the individual you are supervising, as there are exceptions to every stereotype.

Student affairs professionals supervise undergraduates (and sometimes graduate students) in a multitude of contexts. From residence hall community assistants to peer mentors to service-learning project participants to student government and student organization members, we are involved with and frequently responsible for students on a number of levels. One of the most rewarding elements is that of relationship; in fact, these rich relationships with students are likely one of the primary, enduring motivations for our work. The irony in this is that, despite the centrality of this role, few of us were trained as supervisors.

Acquiring Supervision Skills

How did you learn about supervision? Who supervised and mentored you most effectively in the profession? Many of us can easily recall the director of the women's center who encouraged us to share a successful program idea at a conference, the administrator in student activities who tapped us for a leadership role, or the advisor who noticed an area of passion and helped us develop it into a major and maybe even a career. As you reflect, think about what made your mentor or supervisor important to you. How did that person approach and build your relationship? How were expectations communicated? What strategies do you now recognize as valuable in stretching your own undergraduate experience to include more interactions with people different from yourself, responsibilities that were new and perhaps daunting, opportunities to request or contribute assistance as needed? How are you like or unlike your past supervisors and mentors? What kind of supervisor do you most want to become? Finally, what is your definition of the supervisory relationship? How prepared do you feel to be an effective, strategic supervisor who can tailor interventions based on an individual student's strengths and needs for growth?

Supervision is a synergistic process; that is, all elements work together to create a relationship that is greater than the mere sum of its parts. Tull (2006) describes synergistic supervision as a holistic approach that "enhances the personal and professional development of new professionals" through strong, open communication, trust, and regular, fair feedback (p. 466). It also involves assessing possible career trajectories and offering support for achieving professional goals. This type of supervision both orients students or new employees to the work environment and helps socialize them toward success and job satisfaction. Synergistic supervision acknowledges the distinctive qualities of each individual and stresses that each person must be supervised uniquely.

A dissertation project that explored the acquisition of supervision skills among new post-master's degree student affairs professionals found that many who enter the field do so without any formal training in supervision (Holmes, 2014). Much like in parenting, these graduates learned about supervision when they were required to do it, and tended to supervise as they had been supervised. In this qualitative study, Holmes found that her eight participants had little to no training in supervision during their master's programs, and would have appreciated a case study approach that allowed them to practice supervision skills while still in graduate school. And although supervision has been identified as a key competency area (ACPA & NASPA, 2015), many (if not most) master's-level professional preparation programs neglect to include any courses on supervision skills (Holmes, 2014). In addition to not gaining such background in graduate school, participants in this study also revealed that they obtained minimal on-the-job training in supervision. Asking for feedback and accessing resources on their own (e.g., books, conference sessions, etc.) were this group's primary methods of developing their supervision skills (Holmes, 2014).

Some people believe that if you are good at your job, you will naturally be a good supervisor. Most of us are aware of notable exceptions to that assumption. And while there is no single theory or model of supervision that is recommended in student affairs work, frameworks exist that can help us become more intentional, confident, and helpful as supervisors—and thus maximize student learning. Coming from backgrounds in counseling, we draw here from one of the most widely-used supervision models for counselors in training (Bernard & Goodyear, 2014) and consider how aspects of this model might enrich supervisory relationships in student affairs settings.

Bernard and Goodyear's Model

Bernard and Goodyear (2009, 2014) conceptualized supervision as comprised of three roles and three contexts. The roles include teacher, counselor, and consultant. The contexts, or foci, as they are called, consist of interaction, conceptualization, and personalization (Bernard, 1997).

Each of these will be briefly described, and then expanded upon and illustrated with examples and vignettes drawn from the experiences of young professionals in student affairs. By offering this model, we do not seek to prescribe supervisory interactions. Rather, we hope to suggest a way, new to student affairs professionals, that acknowledges the fluid dynamics of most supervision situations, personnel, and higher education contexts.

Teacher Role

In supervision, we often function as teachers. We observe and evaluate student work, both inside the classroom (e.g., first-year seminars, leadership courses, etc.) and beyond (e.g., internships, practica, service-learning, etc.), often creating assignments, assessment rubrics, and timelines. We share information and demonstrate desired behaviors, techniques, or strategies. We offer rationales for why things are done a certain way. We identify relevant issues of class, gender, sexuality, culture, and more, and introduce resources for increasing student understanding of diverse and intersecting identities. In counseling, this role centers on the nature and progress of the therapeutic relationship, noting effective therapeutic interventions, and providing theory-based explanations. But in a student affairs setting, supervisors maintain a wider focus that encompasses regular feedback on a variety of behaviors, interpretation of institutional or programmatic mission, and modeling of (non-counseling) interventions that work.

Considering supervisors as teachers underscores the role of students as learners and our crucial function as more experienced professionals who take students where they are and help them set and achieve developmental goals. Teaching also incorporates the "evaluative role" incumbent upon supervisors (Bernard & Goodyear, 2014, p. 10). However, most explicit teaching roles involve use of an established curriculum, a resource typically unavailable to student affairs professionals, whose supervisory responsibilities can be ambiguous and complex. In teaching, as in all supervisory roles, the supervisor needs to offer interventions that are appropriate to the readiness of the supervisee. Here is an example from a young student affairs professional in Indiana (vignette #1):

> Calvin, my supervisee, was an energetic, first-time peer mentor. He had thorough understanding of topics that the peer mentors were expected to cover with new students, but I noticed that he struggled to recognize and respond to social cues and boundaries during training, practice mentoring sessions, and our 1:1 meetings. After an initial discussion with Calvin about my observations, he shared that he had received similar feedback in a high school leadership position but did not know how to successfully change his behavior. Using the teacher role, I provided him with further training on communication and social norms across various cultures. We did several role-plays so that he could practice his mentoring skills with the ability to pause for questions or restart a situation. For "homework," I assigned Calvin to view some online clips of a TV show and provide his observations of what we had discussed. As we continued to work on his awareness and response to social cues throughout the semester, I provided less direct feedback and Calvin took over in providing reflections on his own actions. By the end of the year, Calvin was more confident in his mentoring abilities and had made observable improvements in creating a comfortable environment (Katie DuFault, personal communication, 2/7/17).

Counselor Role

The second role, counselor, is obviously highly related to counselor education. In that milieu, the supervisor explores the supervisee's thoughts, feelings, and behaviors and offers opportunities for the supervisee to process personal reactions or defenses, as well as to discuss the impact that individual values and characteristics might have in relationship to their own personal counseling style and preferences (Bernard & Goodyear, 2014). In student affairs, site supervisors must guard against becoming therapists for the students they supervise (even or perhaps especially those who are counselors). And although site supervisors may be hesitant to engage in the counselor role because of a lack of skill, knowledge, or training in counseling, it is important to recognize the need for this role. Students and supervisees do come to us with intense feelings, fears, hopes, and anxieties. They share crises and triumphs, as well as the prosaic, humorous, or touching aspects of their daily lives. While maintaining healthy boundaries that exclude a professional therapeutic relationship, we regularly offer support and guidance and serve as caring, compassionate mentors.

Establishing and preserving healthy boundaries in student affairs work can be very challenging. This illustration is from a new professional in North Carolina (vignette #2):

> I have seen the importance of understanding of "like" versus "respect." As a supervisor, your job isn't to be liked, but to be respected and to create an understanding that you are going to provide the best experience for your employees and students, even if it means doing something that someone won't like. I have witnessed friendship get in the way of conversations with a supervisee about professionalism. There was "like" but no respect to accept feedback. Due to the "friendship," several serious behavioral concerns were never confronted (Stephanie Olson, personal communication, 1/15/17).

We often work very closely with students, and programs, events, or conferences may include evening and weekend activities, as well as travel. In many cases, new supervisors are not much older than the students they oversee. It is fascinating to observe entering professionals as they grapple with the transition to supervisor, particularly with students they know. Suddenly, individuals they may be attracted to are no longer potential dating prospects; they gain heightened awareness of underage drinking at parties they used to attend. Images in social media of undergraduates using a recreational drug in a residence hall room go from a mild concern to a mandatory reportable offense. The issues are myriad and daunting. Learning to think as a counselor at these times can be very useful.

Supervision in student affairs tends to be relationship based. Carl Rogers (cited in Overholser, 2007) believed that three core conditions are necessary for building a counseling relationship: (a) being genuinely engaged; (b) demonstrating unconditional positive regard; and (c) expressing empathy. These conditions enrich almost any relationship, including that between supervisor and supervisee. As Romsa and Romsa (2016) note, "a supervisory relationship will blossom while supervisors take the time to teach, actively listen, and genuinely care for their . . . students" (p. 9). Such interactions can be intensely educational and gratifying for all parties; they can also enter the hothouse world of what counselors call enmeshment. You can tell problems are starting when you begin to feel that you are the only person who can help a student; you are tempted to bend the rules and not inform your own supervisor; you are providing "atypical levels of support and contact;" or you feel overwhelmed or over-invested in the student (Harper & Wilson, 2010, p. 80). As professionals, supervisors are the ones who must monitor these dynamics in themselves and model healthy, respectful boundaries.

Many supervisors have preferred student development theoretical frameworks, methods, and techniques that they embrace, whether they be psychosocial, cognitive-structural, integrative, and/or social identity in emphasis (Meyers, 2014). Certainly, Sanford's well-known concept of challenge and support (1967) is extremely relevant in supervision. As Bernard and Goodyear (2014) note, "if the supervisor offers too little challenge, the supervisee might slip into stagnation . . .; with too much challenge and too little support, the supervisee may get discouraged or defensive" (p. 37). Discerning this critical balance in any given supervisory situation is obviously an essential skill.

Although student development theories and techniques have the potential for being useful in supervision, they will fail without a strong *working alliance*. A working alliance is a counseling term that can be applied to having a solid supervisory relationship in student affairs as well. One classic counseling text refers to the three tasks of supervision as: agreement on goals, agreement on duties/responsibilities, and positive relationship dynamics of trust and caring (Bordin, as cited in Bernard & Goodyear, 2014). These tasks also define quality supervisory relationships in higher education and lead to strong working alliances. Recalling a positive working alliance I (Romsa) had with a past supervisor while I was in graduate school, I remember the following aspects of her supervision that were especially effective in establishing our alliance (vignette #3):

> When I was a graduate student pursuing my master's degree in counseling and student affairs, I felt very fortunate when I discovered that my favorite professor would be my internship supervisor. At our first supervision meeting she shared with me her supervision philosophy, which highlighted the supervisory relationship as the vehicle for change, growth, and development (Loganbill, Hardy, & Delworth, 1982). My supervisor was a storyteller. Initially, I wondered why she would share stories about her life with me. Over time, I recognized that it was her storytelling that facilitated a bond between us. Looking back, I see that her *intentional* storytelling helped us to establish trust and a caring relationship. She was also an empathic listener and allowed me to similarly share stories, which included not only what was going on at my internship site but also what was happening in my life. I can remember applying for my first student affairs job and feeling very distressed. During that difficult time of uncertainty, she listened intently to my concerns and articulated that distress back to me, but also encouraged me to be hopeful. When I shared my future dream with her of pursuing a doctoral degree, she believed in, supported, and helped me to develop goals to make that dream a reality.

Consultant Role

The final role, that of consultant, is most readily apparent in student affairs. Within counseling, the supervisor as consultant offers alternative interpretations or conceptualizations, fosters discussion of client issues, and the like. Counselors seek consultation with supervisors when they are stuck, in need of expertise, and/or need to process complicated emotions (e.g., attraction to or disgust with a client, etc.). In student affairs, however, a supervisor as consultant performs frequent and ongoing strategic planning and training functions. Supervisors orient students to the particular work context; they introduce, explain, and reinforce the rules, regulations, policies, and procedures to be enacted. They share institutional, divisional, program, and service missions and goals. Also in the consultant role, the supervisor can generate creative problem-solving conversations and suggest alternatives when the student is feeling overwhelmed or performing at a less than satisfactory level. Supervisors are evaluators and guides who see that supervisees operate within ethical and legal restrictions, and help students navigate the higher education labyrinth. Supervision frequently develops into consultation (Bernard & Goodyear, 2014).

Self-efficacy is often an important component in the consultant role. Self-efficacy refers to supervisors' beliefs about their ability to perform certain behaviors. It can include having a comfort, confidence, and skill in each supervisory role (teacher, counselor, and consultant). This greater sense of perceived competency or self-efficacy determines how people behave, how they think, and how they react emotionally to stressful situations (Bandura, 1982). Supervisors with high self-efficacy are more likely to accept greater challenges, recover quickly from failures, and attribute failures to a lack of training (Bandura, 1994).

Resources that strengthen supervisor self-efficacy and confidence can be varied and discovered in unexpected venues. Bjornestad, Johnson, Hittner, and Paulson (2014) recommend that supervisors enhance their self-efficacy skills by participating in online educational modules and networking sessions as well as using assessments that measure skill development over a period of time, while simultaneously receiving supervision themselves. More creative approaches also have the potential to increase supervisor self-efficacy skills (Tierney & Farmer, 2002). The literature in this area is sparse, but in one study, both teachers and students took a five-day or a condensed one-day creativity course based on social cognitive theory. The course had a combination of lectures, practicing, brainstorming, and cognitive modeling (Tierney & Farmer, 2002). Self-efficacy levels increased significantly for both students and teachers. The cognitive modeling that was provided demonstrated thought patterns that parallel the guidelines for brainstorming, such as not criticizing ideas, building on each other's suggestions, and free association. Similar creativity sessions like this, designed for supervisors and/or graduate students, may be a fruitful approach for supervisors who aspire to increased self-efficacy levels for themselves as well as increased innovation and resourcefulness levels for their students. In this study, positive effects resulted from a one-day experience; therefore, it is possible that this type of creativity training could be effectively and feasibly applied in student affairs settings.

Literature and poetry have become sources of meaningful reflection for me (Harper) as a supervisor, an avenue I enjoy sharing with students. In working with a perfectionistic student who is feeling discouraged and isolated, I have offered Mary Oliver's poem "Wild Geese" (1986), which urges the reader to discover his or her singular place in the world and to know (in my interpretation, at any rate) that such a place does not have to be earned. In helping over-committed students drowning in the busy-ness of graduate school, internship, job search, and other challenges, the William Stafford poem "You Reading This, Be Ready" (1998) can help us all stay in the moment and feel comforted, even affirmed, by the work we have done and are doing. A supervisee struggling with multiple opportunities as well as complicated responsibilities appreciated a copy of David Whyte's "Sweet Darkness" (1997), which concludes with the assertion to invest only in what brings you alive.

Drawing on poetry in supervision allows the introduction of encouraging, diverse voices, such as American-Indian writer Joy Harjo (Muscogee), who beautifully writes about soul, inclusion, and powerful affirmation (2015). A gifted African-American poet is Nikki Giovanni, whose wordplay and insights on friendship, love, and growing up are extraordinary (1997). (Note that actual excerpts from these poems are not included due to permission rights to reprint, but books by these poets are included among the references to this chapter.) Many poems are available as read by the poet on YouTube; some are embedded in TED talks (another great resource to share and discuss with supervisees). There are many ways to incorporate poetry into supervision beyond literally handing a student a poem. Obviously, if a student does not respond favorably to the notion of reading and reflecting on a poem, do not force the issue. But I have found several students in my long career who were surprised, intrigued, and grateful for an unexpected insight gained through poetry. In fact, former students sometimes make contact to request an appropriate poem to bring to a challenging situation or a public speaking event.

Context or Situation

The three foci of intervention, conceptualization, and personalization can be added to the three roles of teacher, counselor, and consultant (Bernard, 1997; Bernard & Goodyear, 2009). Interventions are based on what a supervisor observes the supervisee doing (or actions of which the supervisor becomes aware). Most supervisors are likely to intervene when they observe a student employee, intern, or group member misquoting college policy, excluding certain other students from consideration for special roles on campus (e.g., admissions ambassador, residence hall community assistant, etc.), or performing basic missteps like arriving at work late, dressing inappropriately, posting confidential matters in social media venues, etc. Conceptualization refers to how the supervisee understands the world. This is an immensely educational factor to process on a recurrent basis with a student employee or intern, and is a complex but richly rewarding facet of student affairs supervision. Is the world a safe place? Is life fair? Why do others experience this campus differently than I do? And personalization has to do with development of the supervisee's work style. Is she the organizer? Is he the one who helps the group get along? Where might individual students' strengths take them, in the short term (e.g., leading the planning for a major campus event) or even in the long run (pursuing a career in student affairs, for instance)?

Finally, the Bernard and Goodyear framework (2009) asks supervisors to look at how the various roles and foci interact. With three roles and three foci, nine combinations are possible. A good supervisor, using this model, reflects upon both the specific circumstances and developmental levels/issues of the supervisee. Then, the supervisor carefully selects the appropriate supervisory role to best address the situation (echoing the theme of synergistic supervision). Because the response is always specific to the supervisee's needs, it changes within and across meetings. The supervisor first assesses the supervisee's ability within the focus area, and then selects the appropriate role from which to respond. Bernard and Goodyear (2009) caution supervisors to not repeatedly utilize the same focus or role out of personal preference, comfort, or habit, but instead to ensure that the chosen focus and role meet the most salient needs of the supervisee in that moment.

Consider a white, middle-class, female undergraduate student intern in the university wellness center who is observed to remark under her breath to a peer who is checking in for a workout, "You might not want to go into the weight room right now. I just saw three black guys go in there." The supervisor in this situation has the choice of responding as a teacher, a counselor, or a consultant. Where is this student developmentally? Is she hateful? Fearful? Ignorant? What is the best supervisory approach that will not merely extinguish the behavior (though that is not negotiable) but help the student grow and change her thinking? Here is another example. A non-Native academic advisor is heard to say with what he sees as respect and conviction, "American Indians are good at art. I always encourage the Native students I advise to take art classes." How does the director of advising most effectively deal with this stereotypical thinking in a new employee—as a teacher, a counselor, or a consultant?

Another young professional in Indiana dealing with supervisees at differing levels of development shared how he bears level of student development in mind in supervision (vignette #4):

> As a hall director with a background in college counseling, I see myself as a teacher and counselor in an educator role (providing non-clinical services/ interventions) by helping students reach their potential. The developmental level of the RA staff differs from year to year. Our returning RAs (juniors

and seniors) seem to have more confidence in fostering conversations regarding academic concerns among their peers than some of our younger student leaders. As a supervisor, I spend extra time working with my supervisees on starting the conversation, how to ask the right questions, and how to help the student determine what kind of assistance is needed (Alex Trout, personal communication, 1/19/17).

Conclusion

Most of us in student affairs would happily admit that much of our most cherished teaching and learning occurs through relationships. And many key relationships throughout our careers are supervisory. We might be less happy to concede that we often rely largely on our interpersonal skills and our own experiences in becoming supervisors. By examining our potential roles as teachers, counselors, and consultants in supervision, we can be aware of options that might increase our effectiveness in any given supervisory situation. Here is a final real-life example from a young professional in Michigan (vignette #5):

> When I first became director of a department, it was in a student activities office. I had supervisory experience, so anticipated no problems. But as a new director, I encountered some rocky relationships. I was lucky enough to have my own supervisor challenge me to reflect—on my methods, my approaches, and the feedback I received. This process underscored my stunning revelation about the importance of reflecting and asking good questions. Once I began viewing supervision and my team through this lens, I found myself asking far more open-ended questions during one-on-one meetings. My team was happier, I was happier, and we were all performing so much better. I can't even describe the level of trust and respect that thrived among us after that. We challenged each other, laughed together, and most importantly, served our students in the best possible ways.
>
> There is a significant portion of being a teacher, counselor, or consultant, that requires constant and deep reflection. Reflection is the piece I was missing as a supervisor. I am far from a perfect supervisor, and I recognize that it's a continuous journey of reflection. I don't know everything, but now I'm not afraid to admit this. I admire Dr. Brené Brown, and her quote is apt: "Vulnerability sounds like truth and feels like courage. Truth and courage aren't always comfortable, but they're never weakness" (2012, p. 37). Being vulnerable isn't easy, but I have found that it paves the way for self-reflection and strengthening a team. And I was honored to receive the outstanding supervisor award at my institution last year (Joe Cooper, personal communication, 1/20/17).

Supervision has been called more an art than a science. Quality supervisory experiences are less common than one might think. In any informal query among experienced student affairs professionals, horror stories emerge as often as examples of healthy, nurturing supervisory relationships. The interpersonal alchemy of supervision is tricky to decipher; success can be demonstrated in many (sometimes surprising) forms. The Bernard and Goodyear model (2014) offers perspectives new to most student affairs professionals that can enrich and enlighten the crucial student learning dynamic and potential always present in the supervisory relationship.

References

ACPA & NASPA. (2015). *Professional competency areas for student affairs practitioners.* Washington, DC: Author. Retrieved from http://www.naspa.org/images/uploads/main/ACPA_NASPA_Professional_Competencies_FINAL.pdf

Bandura, A. (1982). Self-efficacy mechanism in human agency. *American Psychologist, 37*(2), 122–147. doi:10.1037/0003-066X.37.2.122

Bandura, A. (1994). Self-efficacy. In V. S. Ramachaudran (Ed.), *Encyclopedia of human behavior* (Vol. 4, pp. 71–81). New York, NY: Academic Press.

Bernard, J. M. (1997). The discrimination model. In C. E. Watkins (Ed.), *Handbook of psychotherapy supervision* (pp. 310–327). New York, NY: Wiley.

Bernard, J. M. & Goodyear, R. K. (2009). *Fundamentals of clinical supervision* (4th ed.). Needham Heights, MA: Allyn & Bacon.

Bernard, J. M. & Goodyear, R. K. (2014). *Fundamentals of clinical supervision* (2nd ed.). Upper Saddle River, NJ: Pearson Education.

Bjornestad, A., Johnson, V., Hittner, J., & Paulson, K. (2014). Preparing site supervisors of counselor education students. *Counselor Education and Supervision, 53*(4), 242–254.

Brown, B. (2012). *Daring greatly: How the courage to be vulnerable transforms the way we live, love, parent, and lead.* New York, NY: Gotham Books.

Council for the Advancement of Standards in Higher Education (CAS). (2012). *CAS professional standards for higher education* (8th ed.). Washington, DC: Author.

Giovanni, N. (1997). *Love poems.* New York, NY: William Morrow.

Harjo, J. (2015). *Conflict resolution for holy beings.* New York, NY: Norton.

Harper, R. & Wilson, N. L. (2010). *More than listening: A casebook for using counseling skills in student affairs work.* Washington, DC: NASPA.

Holmes, A. C. (2014). *Experiences of supervision skill development among new professionals in student affairs.* Unpublished doctoral dissertation. Iowa State University. Ames, Iowa.

Howe, N. & Strauss, W. (2000). *Millennials rising: The next great generation.* New York, NY: Vintage Books.

Kuh, G. D. (2003). What we're learning about student engagement from NSSE. *Change, 35*(2), 24–32.

Loganbill, C., Hardy, E., & Delworth, U. (1982). Supervision, a conceptual model. *Counseling Psychologist, 10*(1), 3–42.

Meyers, L. (2014). Connecting with clients. *Counseling Today.* Retrieved from http://ct.counseling.org/2014/08/connecting-with-clients/

Oliver, M. (1986). *Dream work.* New York, NY: Atlantic Monthly Press.

Overholser, J. (2007). The central role of the therapeutic alliance: A simulated interview with Carl Rogers. *Journal of Contemporary Psychotherapy, 37*(2), 71–78.

Romsa, K. & Romsa, B. (October, 2016). Preparing new professionals in student affairs: A supervisory model to maximize graduate student success. *Developments*, *14*(3), 1–15.

Sanford, N. (1967). *Where colleges fail: A study of the student as a person.* San Francisco, CA: Jossey-Bass.

Stafford, W. (1998). *The way it is: New and selected poems.* Saint Paul, MN: Graywolf Press.

Tierney, P. & Farmer, S. M. (2002). Creative self-efficacy: Its potential antecedents and relationship to creative performance. *Academy of Management Journal*, *45*, 1137–1148.

Tull, A. (2006). Synergistic supervision, job satisfaction, and intention to turnover of new professionals in student affairs. *Journal of College Student Development*, *47*(4), 465–480.

Whyte, D. (1997). *The house of belonging.* Seattle, WA: Many Rivers Press.

Williams, A. (2015, September 18). Move over, millennials, here comes generation Z. *New York Times.* Retrieved from https://www.nytimes.com/2015/. . ./move-over-millennials-here-comes-generation-z.html

Wilson, M. E. (2004). Teaching, learning, and millennial students. In M. D. Coomes & R. DeBard (Eds.), *Serving the millennial generation. New directions for student services* (No. 106, pp. 59–71). San Francisco, CA: Jossey-Bass.

CONTRIBUTING AUTHORS

Kristine E. Barnett, EdD, is the Assistant Provost/Dean for the Division of Student Engagement and Liberal Studies at Bay Path University in Longmeadow, Massachusetts. A long-time advocate of women's education and women's colleges, she is experienced in program development, curriculum design, and leadership in higher education. She has held leadership roles at the University of Saint Joseph and Johnson & Wales University.

Constanza A. Cabello serves the Stonehill College community as its Director of Intercultural Affairs, providing senior-level leadership and decision making focused on diversity, equity, and inclusion. She is a speaker, trainer, and presenter, specializing in leadership, diversity, and social justice education. Connie's work allows her to contribute towards increasing multicultural competence among students, faculty, and staff while creating communities where areas such as student equity initiatives, staff development, and institutional diversity remain a priority.

Aynsley Diamond, EdD, is the Director of Faculty Development at the University of Connecticut and a faculty member teaching in the Graduate Certificate in College Instruction Program. As the author of the "Adaptive Military Transition Theory," Dr. Diamond seeks to support service members transitioning to academia following their military service.

Jane Fried has been a member of the student affairs profession for more than 40 years, beginning as an resident assistant in 1964. Her first publication, *Education for Student Development*, appeared in 1985. She has been thinking about the educational role of student affairs ever since and has published three additional books on the subject, *Shifting Paradigms in Student Affairs* (1993), *Transformative Learning Through Engagement* (2012), and *Of Education, Fishbowls, and Rabbit Holes: Rethinking Teaching and Liberal Education for an Interconnected World* (2016). She was also a primary author for *Learning Reconsidered 1* (2003) and *2* (2006).

Ruth Harper has worked as a college counselor, administrator, and faculty member and holds degrees from Cornell College, the University of Wisconsin-Oshkosh, and Kansas State University. Her research and consulting interests are in college student mental health and American Indian college student success. She is co-author of *More Than Listening: A Casebook for Using Counseling Skills in Student Affairs Work* (2010) *and Assisting Students with Disabilities: A Handbook for School Counselors* (1999; 2007).

Greg Heiberger, Undergraduate Program Manager and Lecturer in Biology and Microbiology at South Dakota State University, holds a PhD from Colorado State University and earned his BS in Mathematics and MS in Student Affairs Administration from SDSU. His research focuses on interventions that leverage new technology to impact student engagement and learning.

John M. Howe, EdD, was born in India, reared in Germany, and worked as an educator in Taiwan, the United Arab Emirates, India, and Afghanistan. He completed his doctoral studies in higher education administration with a minor in international comparative education at Indiana University. He serves as Associate Dean of Students at the University of South Dakota.

Barbara Jacoby is a higher education consultant. She was the founding director of service-learning at the University of Maryland. Her research interests include all aspects of higher education community engagement and the educational experience of commuter students.

Seán Carson Kinsella, MEd, is a nêhithaw/nêhiyaw (Woods/Plains Cree)/Nakawé (Saulteaux)/otipemisiwak (Métis)/Irish Two-Spirit/Queer urban Indigenous person in the territory traditionally known as Tkaronto, which is covered under the Dish With One Spoon Wampum treaty as well as other agreements that have covered this land. He has worked in student affairs since 2007 and is currently a part-time faculty member in Indigenous Studies at Centennial College in Toronto. He is Coordinator of Transition Programs in Student Housing and Residence Life at the University of Toronto Mississauga.

Michael R. Laliberte was born in Pawtucket, Rhode Island He holds degrees from the University of Rhode Island, Northeastern University, and Johnson & Wales University. Dr. Laliberte has been a student affairs professional for over

25 years, having held positions at The Pennsylvania State University, Springfield College, The University of Massachusetts Dartmouth, Boise State University, and the University of Wisconsin-Milwaukee.

George S. McClellan has served students as a student affairs professional/ educator for over 30 years at a variety of institutions including service as SSAO at Dickinson State University and Indiana University-Purdue University Fort Wayne. He has (co)authored or (co)edited a number of books, monographs, and articles; teaches regularly in graduate preparation programs; and is active as presenter and speaker. He has been named both a NASPA Foundation Pillar of the Profession and ACPA Annuit Coeptis Senior Scholar.

Margaret (Maggie) Miller is an area coordinator supervising residence hall directors at South Dakota State University. She is a graduate of Hamline University in St. Paul, Minnesota, and of the Student Affairs / Higher Education master's program at Iowa State University. Her interests include literature, spirituality, and college student development.

Melissa Morriss-Olson, PhD, is the Provost at Bay Path University in Longmeadow, Massachusetts. An experienced academic entrepreneur, she writes and speaks nationally on higher education disruption and innovation. Her research interests include small and single-gender college sustainability, women's leadership, and inclusive college campus practices. Prior to Bay Path, she held senior level roles at North Park University in Chicago.

Daniel Murphy currently works in residence life at Rhode Island School of Design in Providence, Rhode Island Hailing from Owego, New York. Daniel, a certified K-6 teacher, received a Bachelor of Science in Education from Bucknell University and a Master of Arts in College Student Personnel from Bowling Green State University. Through his relatively short career, Daniel has found innovative ways to utilize numerous K-12 best practices through a student affairs lens, as he does in this book.

Elsa M. Núñez has served as President of Eastern Connecticut State University since 2006, and has held other senior administrative positions at City University of New York (CUNY) and the University of Maine System. Dr. Núñez has been a tenured faculty member of English at Ramapo State College, the College of Staten Island (CUNY), Lehman College (CUNY), and now at Eastern. She received her BA from Montclair State College, her MA from Fairleigh Dickinson University and her EdD from Rutgers University.

Katelyn Romsa is an Assistant Professor at South Dakota State University specializing in College Counseling and Administration of Student Affairs.

Her research interests include the evolution of student-faculty interactions, what matters to millennial college students, initiatives to improve student retention and satisfaction, and supervisory models to maximize graduate student success.

Chelsea Sorensen is a professional academic advisor at South Dakota State University. She received a bachelor's degree in psychology from Northwestern University in 2014 and a master's degree in counseling and human development from South Dakota State University in 2016. Her research interests include theories of intelligence, achievement, and student development.

Stephanie J. Waterman, PhD, Onondaga, Turtle clan, is an Associate Professor at the Ontario Institute for Studies in Education/University of Toronto, in Leadership, Higher & Adult Education, and coordinates the Student Development/ Student Services in Higher Education program. Her research interests are Indigenous student college experiences, transition, First Nations/Native American Student Affairs units, Indigenous methodologies/pedagogy, and critical race theories. She is a co-editor of *Beyond the Asterisk: Understanding Native Students in Higher Education* (2013, Stylus).

INDEX